THE RICH GET RICHER AND THE POOR GET PRISON

A READER

THE RICH GET RICHER AND THE POOR GET PRISON

A READER

Jeffrey Reiman
American University

Paul Leighton
Eastern Michigan University

Allyn & Bacon

Boston   Columbus   Indianapolis   New York   San Francisco   Upper Saddle River
Amsterdam   Cape Town   Dubai   London   Madrid   Milan   Munich   Paris   Montreal   Toronto
Delhi   Mexico City   Sao Paulo   Sydney   Hong Kong   Seoul   Singapore   Taipei   Tokyo

Publisher: Karen Hanson
Editorial Assistant: Courtney Shea
Marketing Manager: Wendy Albert
Production Editor: Patrick Cash-Peterson
Manufacturing Buyer: Debbie Rossi
Editorial Production and Composition Service: Omegatype Typography, Inc.
Cover Administrator: Joel Gendron

Library of Congress Cataloging-in-Publication Data

Reiman, Jeffrey H.
  The rich get richer and the poor get prison : a reader / Jeffrey Reiman, Paul Leighton.—1st ed.
       p. cm.
  Includes bibliographical references.
  ISBN-13: 978-0-205-66179-4 (pbk.)
  ISBN-10: 0-205-66179-3 (pbk.)
   1. Criminal justice, Administration of—United States.   2. Social classes—United States.
  3. United States—Social policy.   I. Leighton, Paul.   II. Title.
  HV9950.R466 2010
  364.973—dc22

                                                                                2009023780

10 9 8 7 6 5 4 3 2   13 12 11 10

Allyn & Bacon
is an imprint of

www.pearsonhighered.com

ISBN 10: 0-205-66179-3
ISBN 13: 978-0-205-66179-4

For Sue,
and
For Satoko, Sala, and Aiko

CONTENTS

PREFACE

As we were putting together this reader, *The Rich Get Richer and the Poor Get Prison* was going into its ninth edition, having been in print some thirty years. As it became an increasingly popular critique of the criminal justice system, professors who used the book and other fans called for coverage of existing issues in more depth as well as more examples of injustice to be included. We agree that there are an unfortunately large number of issues related to criminal justice that need extended critical discussion and detailed proposals for remediation; however, *The Rich Get Richer* is not meant to be a complete survey of injustices in the criminal justice system—and certainly not a complete survey of social problems in the United States—nor is it meant to be a complete recipe for fixing all the injustices and social problems. *The Rich Get Richer* has a more focused aim—to show students that much that goes on in the criminal justice system violates their own sense of basic fairness, to present evidence that the system does not function in the way it says it does or in the way that students believe it should, and then to sketch a whole theoretical perspective from which they might understand these failures and evaluate them morally—and to do it all in a short and relatively inexpensive book, written in plain language.

The preface to *The Rich Get Richer* notes many of the suggestions from professors who have used the book that have resulted in changes to that book, and the publication of this reader represents an effort to provide supplemental materials addressing some of the suggestions that reviewers and instructors have offered, while at the same time leaving *The Rich Get Richer* intact in a form that has proven successful for classroom use. In selecting articles for the reader, we have been guided by the spirit of *The Rich Get Richer*, focusing on readings that should be of high interest, written in plain language, and presenting sophisticated arguments or important evidence. Because *The Rich Get Richer* is usually assigned for courses along with other books, the reader has been kept to a modest size by limiting the number of articles and carefully selecting readings to highlight their relevance to *The Rich Get Richer*. The chapters in this reader parallel the structure of *The Rich Get Richer*, as the chapter titles indicate. The readings in this anthology usually raise multiple issues discussed in *The Rich Get Richer*, and our introductions to the chapters of this reader try to make those connections explicit while still leaving room for classroom discussion and exploration. The following overview indicates what to expect in the chapters of the reader.

Chapter 1, "Readings on Crime Control in America," presents articles that support the thesis of Chapter 1 of *The Rich Get Richer*, namely, that the war on crime is a failure and an avoidable failure. These articles examine critically the claim that recent decreases in crime rates are due to the massive growth in the use of imprisonment that has occurred since the 1980s, report on the collateral damage to communities—including increased crime—that result from the policy of massive imprisonment, give an inside and personal view of the counterproductive—even crime-producing—features of the imprisonment regime from someone who survived it, and reveal an unexpected harmful dimension of the so-called "war on drugs."

Chapter 2, "Readings on A Crime by Any Other Name . . . ," presents articles that support the thesis of Chapter 2 of *The Rich Get Richer,* namely, that the criminal justice system and the government in general do not protect us against the gravest threats to our lives, limbs, and possessions, because the acts that cause these threats are generally not even treated as crimes. These articles explore in detail such diverse processes as how government watchdogs fail to use their powers to protect workers from occupational hazards, how British legislators are trying to make corporations criminally responsible for occupational deaths resulting from corporate executives' neglect of occupational safety, how lives can be saved in hospitals by means of a simple checklist that doctors nevertheless resist using, how the Federal Drug Administration and other agencies fail to protect consumers from known harmful consequences of chemicals in consumer goods, and how—for comparison—harsh is the approach taken in the People's Republic of China against those responsible for selling dangerous consumer products.

Chapter 3, "Readings on . . . And the Poor Get Prison," presents articles that support the thesis of Chapter 3 of *The Rich Get Richer,* namely, that among those guilty of the dangerous acts that the criminal justice system does label "crimes," the system works to make it more likely that those who end up in jail or prison will be poor people. These articles consider whether a seemingly harsh sentence for white-collar crime is justifiable by comparing it to the much harsher sentences doled out to poor criminals, and report on how racial prejudice and bias against ex-convicts continues to function in employment decisions, thus making it all the more difficult for ex-offenders to go straight. There are also two articles on the recent U.S. financial meltdown, which triggered a worldwide financial meltdown and the gravest recession since the Great Depression. It's too early yet to know how far criminal acts are involved in this, but what the articles make clear is that while the criminal justice system was locking up more and more poor people it was doing nothing to protect people in the United States from the dangerous financial shenanigans that have cost many their homes and investments.

Chapter 4, "Readings on To the Vanquished Belong the Spoils," presents articles that support the thesis of Chapter 4 of *The Rich Get Richer,* namely, that the failure of criminal justice in the United States continues because it produces ideological benefits for those who could change it. These articles place the high incidence of black imprisonment in the United States in the context of a long history of legal mechanisms to control and stigmatize African Americans, offer a look at the punishment of criminals from "the other side" by viewing it through the distinctive lens of African American "hip-hop" culture, darkly parody the way the criminal justice system functions as a spectacle to promote biases against poor and nonwhite people, and argue—against the prevailing criminal justice ideology—that social injustice weakens the moral obligations of its victims to obey the law and spreads responsibility for lawbreaking to those who profit from social injustice and fail to work against it.

The Conclusion, "Readings on Criminal *Justice* or *Criminal* Justice," includes articles that take the next step required by the thesis of the Conclusion of *The Rich Get Richer,* namely, recognition that there are policies that can and should be adopted by the criminal justice system to make it genuinely a system of *justice* rather than a *criminal* system. These articles discuss promising ways to improve the criminal justice system, by basing sentencing on social science findings rather than on political pandering, by aiming to heal the breach between criminal and victim that crime causes rather than by focusing on exclusively punitive responses, by devoting greater resources to rehabilitation programs that are shown to work to reduce recidivism, and by supporting early social interventions to help children at risk from sliding into a life of crime.

As a reminder, other supplemental material for *The Rich Get Richer* includes the two appendices to that book and the websites for *The Rich Get Richer* and this reader. The first appendix is a short essay by Jeffrey Reiman entitled "The Marxian Critique of Criminal Justice," which covers the ground from a general statement of Marxian theories of capitalism, ideology, and law, to a Marxian theory of criminal justice—and the ethical judgments to which that theory leads. The argument of *The Rich Get Richer* is compatible with a number of different progressive theoretical perspectives, from liberal to Marxian. To make it accessible to a wide spectrum of students and instructors, it has intentionally not been tied to any particular one of these perspectives. This appendix, then, shows how the argument of *The Rich Get Richer* could be integrated into a Marxian theoretical framework. Thus it offers additional food for thought for those who are sympathetic to Marxian theory and to those who are critical of it.

A second appendix, also authored by Jeffrey Reiman, is entitled "Between Philosophy and Criminology." Unlike the first appendix, however, "Between Philosophy and Criminology" is a very personal statement. It aims to stitch together the disparate parts of Reiman's intellectual life as a professional philosopher interested in criminal justice. He argues that criminology has a special need for philosophical reflection that other social sciences may not have, because accepting the legal definition of crime as the boundaries of criminology would mean the state dictating the research agenda of criminology.

The websites for the *Rich Get Richer* continue to evolve. They are available at www.MySocKit.com or www.paulsjusticepage.com, "Rich Get Richer." The second website is managed by Paul Leighton, who has posted concise chapter outlines and summaries with links to additional related resources, as well as Internet-based exercises for students. Several articles that we have written about corporate crime are also available there. With the current edition of *The Rich Get Richer,* we have discontinued the practice of putting lists of additional readings at the end of each chapter and now list them on the website so they can be easily revised as noteworthy books are published. Book titles are linked to online bookstores to make it easier for students stimulated by the material in a chapter to read further on particular topics. This arrangement should also help instructors when they assign outside reading or research on the topics touched upon in the book. Paul Leighton will also keep readers abreast of new developments through his blog (http://paulsjusticeblog.com), which has a category for *The Rich Get Richer.*

ACKNOWLEDGMENTS

As with the latest edition of *The Rich Get Richer and the Poor Get Prison,* Jeffrey Reiman dedicates this reader to his wife Sue, and Paul Leighton dedicates it to his wife Satoko and his twin girls, Sala and Aiko.

We are grateful to Carrie Buist, who did a large number of literature reviews to get this project off the ground; Rachel Songer, who did research for the ninth edition of *The Rich Get Richer* that was also very useful for this reader; Devah Pager, who graciously provided updated information for, and edits to, her "Race at Work" piece; Dana Radatz, Paul's graduate assistant, who helped with the final push on this project; and H. Bennett Wilcox, who provided dependable and helpful support during the final stage of manuscript preparation.

Readings on Crime Control in America

EDITORS' INTRODUCTION

Chapter 1 of *The Rich Get Richer and the Poor Get Prison* has four main objectives: (1) examining the exclusive use of police and prison as the response to high crime rates in the United States, (2) reviewing the "excuses" that are made for the failure to significantly reduce our high crime rate, (3) discussing the known sources of crime and thus the kinds of policies that stand a good chance of reducing crime significantly, and (4) introducing the Pyrrhic defeat theory to explain the continued existence of policies that fail to reduce crime. The subtitle of Chapter 1, in our original text, *The Rich Get Richer,* is "Nothing Succeeds Like Failure," which highlights an important aspect of the larger argument: The criminal justice system is allowed to continue to fail to reduce crime because this failure benefits those with power to change the system. Crime in the streets draws people's attention away from crimes in the suites and, even more so, from the noncriminal harms that result from the actions of the well-off.

Crime rates have fallen noticeably since the early 1990s, and many believe this is because of the success of criminal justice policies, especially the increasing imposition of harsh prison sentences. *The Rich Get Richer* reviews some of the research showing that changes in criminal justice policy had little to do with the drop in crime rates, and Chapter 1 of this reader provides additional evidence so that criminology students can have a more sophisticated understanding of the dynamics behind the falling crime rates. This chapter also has several readings that highlight the important *sources* of crime, such as the availability of guns (which increase the temptation to crime and the harm that results from it), the illegality of drugs (which makes a criminal occupation more appealing to people with few alternative opportunities), the extent of poverty (which makes crime more tempting and staying straight less attractive), and the overuse of prison as well as prison's harsh conditions (which harden inmates and make it harder for them to succeed legally once released). They all provide intervention points that could be used to reduce crime instead of exclusive reliance on police and prisons.

"Why Is Crime Falling—Or Is It?" by Alfred Blumstein is quoted in Chapter 1 of *The Rich Get Richer* in support of the assertion that increases in incarceration had little to do with the decrease in crime rates. Blumstein notes that attempts to show that increased incarceration leads to reduced crime mistakenly focus only on the period from 1991 on, which yields a "simplistic" understanding that creates "misleading" results. Crime rates started falling in 1991, so the increasing incarceration rates seem to be strongly related to a falling crime rate. Looking at a longer time period illustrates the weak relationship that Blumstein and others have found. This point is illustrated with updated data in Figure 1.1.

Blumstein presents a range of data and analysis based on a book he co-edited with Joel Wallman, *The Crime Drop in America*. Blumstein argues that "multiple factors" contributed to the crime drop, "including the waning of crack markets, the strong economy, efforts to control guns, intensified policing (particularly in efforts to control guns in the community), and increased incarceration." Poverty lures many people into the drug trade but a strong economy supports the declining crime rate. His analysis implies that a great deal of drug violence could have been reduced if the drug trade were not illegal and drug dealers had legitimate means to resolve their disputes. Thus his analysis supports *The Rich Get Richer*'s contention that the illegality

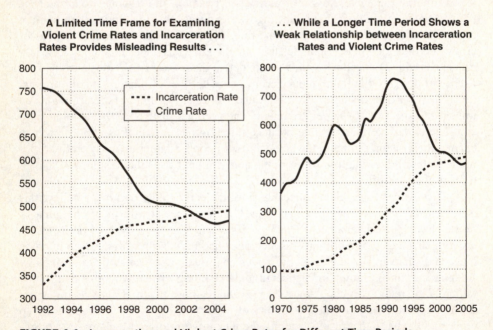

FIGURE 1.1   Incarceration and Violent Crime Rates for Different Time Periods

Source: Sourcebook of Criminal Justice Statistics Online, Table 6.29.2006 and Table 3.106.2006. For an extended discussion of these charts, see Donna Selman and Paul Leighton, *Punishment for Sale* (Rowman and Littlefield, 2010).

of drugs is a source of crime. Blumstein also notes that the proliferation of high-powered fast-action guns were a major cause of the increasing number of homicides and that successful efforts to control guns deserve some of the credit for the declining crime rate. Consequently, his argument is consistent with the notion that the availability of guns in the United States is a source of crime. Finally, some of the positive effects of incarceration on reducing the crime rate were "at least partially negated by violence committed by the replacements," those individuals who are quickly recruited to take the place of imprisoned drug dealers. Indeed, because many replacements were young people, who have a greater propensity to settle disputes with violence, the net effect of imprisoning so many drug dealers may have been an increase in violent crime.

The question mark in the title of Blumstein's piece reflects caution based on the flattening out of crime rates in the preliminary data from 2000, the latest available when he did the presentation. Crimes rates did flatten out in 2000 and 2001, although violent crime rates finally bottomed out in 2004; property crimes increased from 2000 to 2001, then started declining again.

In "High Incarceration Rate May Fuel Community Crime," Michael Fletcher of the *Washington Post* reports on a study suggesting that when many people from the same small community are taken out of that community and put in prison for crimes, the community itself is weakened in ways that may lead to crime. This early study making this link is supported by a growing body of evidence that under certain conditions high incarceration rates can have the unintended consequence of undermining the informal social processes that keep crime and other antisocial behavior in check. When many of the adults in a community are in prison, families are broken up, and because the vast majority of prisoners in the United States are men, there are fewer male role models for young people and fewer husbands for young women (some of whom are supporting children). Children are traumatized by the loss of a father, and more children grow up without ever having a man in the house. Criminology has well-developed theories about how social disorganization contributes to crime by eroding families and communities. Theories that link high incarceration to crime suggest that social disorganization arises from people being pulled out of the community into prison and dumped back into the community after a brutalizing prison experience.

Further, when many adults from a community are in prison, there is less money in the community, more poverty, and thus less trade to attract potential stores and businesses. Also, for purposes of the census, prison inmates are counted as residents of the county in which their prison is located, not where they lived before prison and will likely return. This practice inflates population counts in rural areas, where most prisons are sited, and causes changes in who gets elected and how federal aid grants are distributed and in other processes based on population. Cities then find themselves with more disorganization but less aid money and fewer elected representatives to advocate for help.

But perhaps the psychological effects are worst. With many adults from a community in prison, crime and imprisonment come to seem normal rather than exceptional. Youngsters growing up in such a setting come to think there is little they can do to avoid crime, little reason to try to avoid it, and little point to staying straight. This article should make readers wonder about the rationality of basing criminal justice policy exclusively on the idea of deterring crime by threatening lengthy prison sentences. Blumstein pointed out an unintended consequence of high incarceration rates was the increased violence from replacing older drug dealers with younger ones whose lack of maturity made them more prone to use lethal violence. Similarly, this article suggests the high incarceration rates in some communities have contributed to increased crime by undermining the ability of communities to raise and nurture law-abiding youngsters in the long run.

"From C-Block to Academia: You Can't Get There from Here" is written by Charles Terry, one of a new breed of criminologists called "convict criminologists." After spending much of his youth in prison because of drugs, Terry managed to get himself together, go to school, and get a Ph.D in criminology. He speaks about crime and punishment with a special kind of authority. He's been there, on the other side. Terry tells here about his experiences with the criminal justice system. He makes it clear that convicts, even those who want to go straight, must fight an uphill battle that in most cases they will lose. Terry makes no excuses for his early criminality, but he describes as well how very little was done for him besides locking him up. He tells of the lack of support and encouragement, the absence of treatment programs for poor drug addicts, and of how the prison experience alienated him from the "straight" world. He tells of the difficulty of reentry and the ex-convict stigma. Terry's struggle would be even more difficult today because the student loan programs he used to get an education and change his perspective are no longer available. About 700,000 people a year are released from prisons in the United States. With a prison record, and usually no job training, they face incredible obstacles to going straight. Is this intelligent social policy? Terry tells us it is not, and makes a number of suggestions to change prison, reentry, and even criminology itself. If we lock people up to prevent crime, shouldn't we help them avoid crime when they are released?

In "A New Suit by Farmers against the DEA Illustrates Why the War on Drugs Should Not Include a War on Hemp," Jamison Colburn introduces readers to a cost of the so-called "war on drugs" that they probably have not imagined. We know that the war on drugs costs billions of dollars, that it has largely failed to stem the drug trade, that it has led to the arrest and imprisonment of thousands of people who did nothing more than sell other people something that they wanted. But here is a cost of the war on drugs that you probably didn't expect: Marijuana is made from the same plant from which we obtain hemp. Hemp is a very useful material, grown from time immemorial to make paper, canvas, rope, and seed oil with numerous uses. Moreover, hemp can be produced in a manner that is ecologically sound. Hemp cultivation is far less dependent on pesticides and herbicides than crops like cotton. But because hemp comes from the same plant that produces marijuana, U.S. farmers have been legally prevented from cultivating and marketing this valuable material even though industrial hemp has just a trace of the chemical THC that gives marijuana users a "high." This article, written by a former lawyer for the United States Environmental

Protection Agency, gives a useful history of the attempts to outlaw marijuana. Interestingly, lawmakers tried to exempt hemp production from the legal prohibition but were thwarted by government agencies such as the Drug Enforcement Administration (DEA) that appear in retrospect to have been uncritically opposed to anything even remotely related to marijuana, no matter how harmless, no matter how useful. The suit discussed in the article ends up being another unfortunate example of the negative consequences of criminal justice policy.

Currently, hemp products like fiber and oil are legal in the United States. However, cultivating them requires growing cannabis plants that have trace amounts of THC, which makes them a controlled substance under federal law. Thus, the United States imports hemp from countries such as Canada and China, which are among the thirty industrialized nations where it is legal to grow cannabis for hemp. To help their own farmers, North Dakota passed a law allowing for the cultivation of industrial hemp so local farmers could supply the hemp products we currently import, but federal drug law was still a potential barrier. The federal court decision in this case explains the controversy over the law:

> The state regulatory regime provides for the licensing of farmers to culti-vate industrial hemp; imposes strict THC limits precluding any possible use of the hemp as the street drug marijuana; and attempts to ensure that no part of the hemp plant will leave the farmer's property other than those parts already exempt under federal law. The plaintiffs are two North Dakota farmers who have received state licenses, have an economic need to begin cultivation of industrial hemp, and apparently stand ready to do so but are unwilling to risk federal prosecution of possession for manufac-ture or sale of a controlled substance.[1]

The court dismissed the suit, thus not allowing the farmers to grow hemp. The court refers to the language of the Controlled Substances Act and prior cases interpreting the language to rule that the Act's "definition of 'marijuana' unambiguously includes the *Cannabis sativa L.* plant and does not in any manner differentiate between Cannabis plants based on their THC concentrations."

The court's opinion states that "there may be countless numbers of beneficial products which utilize hemp in some fashion" and there is "little dispute that the retail hemp market is significant, growing, and has real economic potential for North Dakota," but "the policy arguments raised by the plaintiffs are best suited for Congress rather than a federal courtroom in North Dakota." Unfortunately, a bill that would have amended the Controlled Substances Act to allow for hemp farming, the Industrial Hemp Farming Act of 2007 (H.R. 1009), died in Congress without even a subcommittee hearing on its merits.

Note

1. *Monson and Hauge v Drug Enforcement Administration and U.S. Dept of Justice*, 522 F. Supp 2d 1188 (2007)

WHY IS CRIME FALLING—OR IS IT?

Alfred Blumstein

THE RECENT CRIME DROP

To those who worry about crime in the United States, the period from 1993 through 1999 was a welcome relief. We witnessed a steady drop in crime rates to a level lower than we have seen for more than 30 years. My presentation focuses on violent crime, primarily homicide, because it is so serious. It also is the most reliable and consistently measured crime and is highly correlated with many other aspects of crime. Between 1993 and 1999, the U.S. homicide rate dropped by an impressive 40 percent to a level of 5.7 per 100,000 population, a rate not seen since 1966. This almost brings the United States into the range of some of the countries in Western Europe. . . .

These current favorable trends, however, cannot continue indefinitely. We should try to identify the factors that contribute to the downward trend and, as those effects are saturated, determine whether the downward trend will flatten or, because of other factors, reverse.

Whenever crime rates decrease, there are usually claims of both credit (e.g., "it's a result of my administration's policy of . . .") and explanation (e.g., "demographic shift"). Television newscasters always look for a single explanation and are particularly troubled when more than two mutually supportive factors come together. I recently co-edited with Joel Wallman *The Crime Drop in America*,[1] which addresses the multiple factors that together contributed to the crime drop, including the waning of crack markets, the strong economy, efforts to control guns, intensified policing (particularly in efforts to control guns in the community), and increased incarceration. . . .

[T]he increase in the level of homicide in the United States during the growth period of the late 1980s and early 1990s was due entirely to the trends in the younger age groups; homicide rates for those age 25 and older did not increase. However, the decrease since 1993 is due to both the recent sharp drop in offending among young people and the continuing decline in offending among older persons. . . . Explanations of the homicide decline must differentiate between the factors that are responsible for the long-term fall in homicide rates among the older adults and the ones causing the post-1985 rise and the more recent drop in homicide offending by the younger groups. Those two explanations are likely to be different.

THE ROLE OF WEAPONS

Young people experienced a major growth in the use of handguns in homicide after 1985. Figure 1 displays the number of homicides—relative to the number of handgun homicides in 1985, which is set to an index of 100—in each year with three types of weapons: handguns, other guns, and weapons other than guns. The figure focuses on

Source: Perspectives on Crime and Justice: 2000–2001 Lecture Series. Washington, DC: National Institute of Justice, 2002. This is an edited version.

FIGURE 1   Trends in Weapons Used by Youths in Homicide (18–24)

*Relative to handgun homicides in 1985, set at an index of 100.

Source: Estimates based on data from the Federal Bureau of Investigation, Supplemental Homicide Reports, 1975–2000, Washington, D.C.: U.S. Department of Justice, Federal Bureau of Investigation.

the weaponry used in homicides by youths between the ages of 18 and 24, using data from the Supplementary Homicide Reports (SHR), compiled by the FBI, of factors associated with individual homicide events. Before 1985, there was some oscillation, but no clear trend. But between 1985 and 1993, there was an increase of more than 130 percent in homicides committed with handguns, with no marked change in the number of homicides committed with long guns and about a 50-percent decrease with nonguns. This suggests that handguns were partly a substitute for nongun weapons (e.g., knives) and caused more homicides that, if handguns had not been used, may have been merely assaults. The decline started in 1994 and, by 1997, had decreased to about only a 50-percent increase over 1985.

Handgun homicides committed by juveniles younger than 18 *quadrupled* between 1985 and 1993, with a doubling in the number of long-gun homicides and about a 20-percent decrease in the number of nongun homicides. . . . There was no such increase in the number of handgun homicides committed by 25- to 45-year-old adults; that age group displays a downward trend that accelerates after 1991 and reaches a level about 60 percent of the 1985 level in 1997.

A major change occurred after 1985; young people were acquiring handguns in alarming numbers. Older people may have had more handguns during this period, but they appear to have exercised greater restraint in their use.

It is widely recognized that teenage males are poor dispute resolvers; they have always fought to settle their disputes. When they fight with fists, the conflict evolves relatively slowly; the loser will eventually find a way to withdraw or a third party, observing the incident, has time to intervene. The dynamics are extremely different when a handgun is present; the conflict escalates well before anyone can retreat or intervene. Once handguns become prevalent in a neighborhood, each person who carries one has an incentive to make a preemptive strike before his adversary does.

Between 1985 and 1993, the weapons involved in settling young people's disputes changed from fists and knives to handguns—and more recently, to semiautomatic pistols, which have much greater firepower and lethality. The growth in lethal weaponry is reflected in the changes in the weapons used in homicides committed by different race and age groups. Beginning in 1985, there was a sharp growth in the firearm homicide death rate among young people (those in their early 20s and younger; youths [ages 18–24], especially juveniles [under 18 years old]; but not among adults [ages 25–45]) that changed a flat trend to a sharply rising one, with the rise sharpest for young ages. At the same time, the shift was much smaller for the number of homicide deaths due to means other than handguns. . . .

The increase in suicide weapons-specific death rates before 1993 was similar to that of homicide death rates. Following a period of generally flat rates, the rate of suicide by firearms increased sharply after 1985, but the rate of suicide by other means did not change. This shift was especially marked in suicides of black youth and juveniles, whose suicide rate had previously been markedly lower than that of whites.[2]

These observations suggest that the growth in homicide committed by young people was more attributable to the weapons they used than to the emergence of inadequately socialized cohorts of "superpredators," as some observers claimed during the period that saw such an increase in the number of homicides. If the cohorts were indeed more vicious, then one would expect to see a growth in homicides by all forms of weaponry rather than by only handguns. The findings strongly suggest that teenagers had disputes as they always had, but that the availability and lethality of handguns, and later semiautomatic pistols, resulted in an increase in homicides. . . .

Changes in the rates of weapon arrests result from a combination of changes in the illegal carrying of weapons and changes in police aggressiveness in pursuing illegal weapons. . . . Police . . . became more concerned about weapons, especially in the hands of young people. That combination is reflected in the rise in weapon arrests, which peaked in 1993. There is no indication of any diminution in police aggressiveness in pursuing young people with guns after 1993, so the decline after 1993 is likely due more to a reduction in the carrying of guns than to a slackening of police efforts to capture the guns. This reduction in carrying seems to have been an important factor contributing to the decrease in homicides after 1993.

Thus, we have clear indications from [Supplementary Homicide Report] data on weapons used in homicides and weapon arrests that there was a significant decline in the use of handguns by young people after 1993. It is difficult to sort out all the factors that contributed to that. One important contributor was the aggressive stop-and-frisk tactics used by local police, especially in many large cities. Community groups in many cities also took an active role in negotiating truces among gangs and seeking to establish norms that precluded the carrying of guns.

Important Federal initiatives also are likely to have contributed to the decline. The Brady Handgun Violence Prevention Act (P.L. 103-159), which requires a 5-day waiting period for a background check for any person who wants to buy a gun from a licensed dealer, became effective in 1994, the first year of the decline. The denial rate under the Brady Act has been reported at 2.4 percent of those who apply to purchase a gun.[3] Uncertain is the degree to which these individuals simply accepted the denials or resorted to one of the many loopholes left open by the Brady Act: purchasing a gun at a gun show, buying one from a private individual, hiring a straw purchaser to buy it, stealing it, or using any of the other means left open to a determined illegal purchaser. . . .

All these efforts have a mutually reinforcing effect. A reduction in the carrying of handguns, because of either the threat of confiscation or the difficulty in acquiring them, would lead to a reduced incentive for others to carry, thereby reducing the likelihood of handgun homicides, especially among the young people for whom it was so deadly.

THE ROLE OF DRUG MARKETS

One important factor that has affected criminality throughout the 1980s and 1990s has been the problem of drug abuse and drug markets. In a survey conducted in 1991, 32 percent of prisoners reported using cocaine or crack regularly and 15 percent used heroin or opiates regularly. At the time of the offense that led to their imprisonment, 14 percent were using cocaine or crack. These numbers were appreciably higher than those reported in a similar survey conducted 5 years earlier.[4] These are much higher rates than one finds in general population samples (e.g., the National Institute on Drug Abuse household surveys), which strengthens the importance of a connection between drug use and crime rates.

Paul Goldstein developed a useful taxonomy of the drug–crime connection composed of three components other than the sale or possession of the drugs themselves:

- Pharmacological/psychological consequences. The drug itself causes criminal activity (most notably, the connection between alcohol and violence).
- Economic/compulsive crimes. Drug users commit crimes to get money to support their habit.
- Systemic crime. Crimes are committed as part of the regular means of doing business in the drug industry (including violence as the accepted way to solve disputes between competing sellers or as retribution between a seller and a buyer as a result of reneging on a drug deal).[5]

There is a fourth, more broad connection that should be considered: the community disorganization caused by the drug industry and its operations, including the manner by which the norms and behaviors in the drug industry, which can pervade some communities, influences the behavior of others who have no direct connection to that industry. For example, the widespread prevalence of guns among drug sellers can impel others in the community to arm themselves to similarly defend themselves, to settle their own disputes even if they do not involve drugs, or to gain respect.

The problem of crack cocaine emerged in the early 1980s and accelerated significantly in the late 1980s. One indication of this growth lies in the rate of arrests of adults for drug offenses, which, especially for nonwhites (primarily blacks) started to increase in the early 1980s and accelerated appreciably after 1985 with the wide distribution of crack, especially in low-income urban neighborhoods. The steady growth in drug arrests of nonwhite adults compared with those of white adults is reflected in Figure 2, which depicts the ratio of nonwhite-to-white drug arrests for both juveniles and adults.

The trend for juveniles is strikingly different. Throughout the 1970s, the arrest rate for nonwhite juveniles was below that of whites (the ratio is less than 1:1).

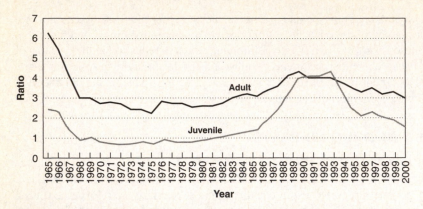

FIGURE 2   **Trends in the Ratio of Nonwhite Juvenile and Adult Drug Arrests to White Juvenile and Adult Drug Arrests**

Note: The values are the ratio of nonwhite arrest rate to white arrest rate for drug offenses. A ratio above 1:1 indicates that nonwhites have a higher arrest rate than whites, and a value less than 1 indicates that whites have the higher arrest rate.

Starting in 1986, however, their rate grew rapidly, reaching a rate four times that of whites during 1989–92, then began a steep decline to about 50 percent above the white juvenile rate in 1999. This pattern shows that the major recruitment of nonwhite juveniles into the drug markets did not begin until the distribution of crack became widespread in about 1985.

Figure 2 provides important information linking some earlier observations about the rise in homicides committed by young people and the role of guns in that rise. Three major increases—more than a doubling—occurred in the short period between 1985 (the beginning of the involvement of young people in drug markets) and 1993 (the peak year of youth violence):

- Rates of homicides committed by youths age 20 and younger, with no growth for adults 25 and older. . . .
- The number of homicides those younger than 25 commit with guns, with no growth in nongun homicides [Figure 1].
- The quadrupling of the arrest rate of nonwhite juveniles on drug charges compared with white juveniles [Figure 2].

One explanation for this dramatic combination of changes involves a process that is driven by illegal drug markets, which appear to operate in conjunction with the demand for drugs despite massive efforts during the [1980s and 1990s] to attack the supply side. In the late 1980s, the illegal drug trade recruited juveniles because they were willing to work more cheaply than adults, were less vulnerable to the punishments imposed by the increasingly punitive adult criminal justice system, and were willing to take more risks than adults. The rapid growth in the demand for crack required more sellers—many new users used crack because they could buy one hit at a time, unlike powder cocaine, which was not sold in small quantities—and encouraged the market to find its labor supply wherever it could. Furthermore, recruiting juveniles was the market's means of replacing the large number of adult drug sellers who were being incarcerated during the 1980s. The economic plight of young urban black juveniles, many of whom saw no other comparable route to economic sustenance at the time, made them particularly responsive to the lure of employment in the crack markets.

Because crack markets were run as street markets, especially those operating in inner-city areas, the participants were especially vulnerable to attack by robbers who targeted their sizable assets, either the drugs or the money from the sale of drugs. Calling the police for protection was not an option, so participants in those markets, including recruited juveniles, were likely to carry guns to protect themselves and solve disputes. Once these juveniles started carrying guns, other teenagers who were not involved in the drug markets but went to the same schools or walked the same streets also were more likely to arm themselves. These teenagers felt they needed guns for their own protection, but they also may have believed that weapon possession was a status symbol in the community. This initiated an escalating arms race: As more guns appeared in the street, there was an increased incentive for individuals to arm themselves. In light of the much tighter networking of teenagers than of older people, that diffusion process could proceed quickly. The emergence of teenage gangs—some involved in drug markets—in many cities at about this time contributed to that diffusion.

In view of the recklessness and bravado that often characterize male teenagers and their low skill level in settling disputes other than through the use of physical force, many of the fistfights that would otherwise have taken place escalated into shootings as a result of the presence of guns. This escalation in violence can be exacerbated by the problems of socialization associated with high levels of poverty, high rates of single-parent households, educational failures, and a widespread sense of economic hopelessness. Not until they reach their mid-20s do they develop some prudence, become more cautious even if they are armed, and display greater restraint.

This hypothesized diffusion process[6] has been tested further with city-level data on juvenile arrests for drugs and homicides, taking advantage of the fact that drug markets flourished at different times in different cities, such as in the mid-1980s in New York and Los Angeles and later in smaller cities. Daniel Cork[7] has shown the connection between the rise in handgun homicides and the recruitment of juveniles into crack markets. Using an epidemic model originally developed for marketing literature, Cork identified—in individual cities—the time when juvenile arrests for drugs began to accelerate and the corresponding time when juvenile homicide arrests increased. He found most typically a 1- to 3-year lag between the two, with homicides following involvement in drug markets. These results are consistent with the hypothesis that the rise in juvenile homicides was attributable to the diffusion of guns from young people recruited into drug markets to their friends and beyond. His analysis of individual cities also showed that crack markets generally emerged first in the largest coastal cities, especially in New York and Los Angeles, and then appeared in Middle America and smaller cities. Thus, the observed patterns in the rise of homicide committed by young people with handguns are highly consistent with explanations that assign central importance to the rise and decline of crack markets in the United States.

The fall-off in the nonwhite/white drug-arrest ratio (Figure 2) in the 1990s is a reflection of the changing tastes for crack, especially in urban neighborhoods.

As recognition of its deleterious effects became widespread, word spread through the streets that crack was an undesirable drug, and this wisdom had a major effect on diminishing the number of new users.[8] This contributed to a major reduction in the need for street sellers. As a result, the nonwhite juvenile sellers, who had been important participants in those street markets, were no longer needed. Older users continued to be major crack consumers, but their demand could be served more readily by individual delivery, thereby diminishing the need for street markets. All these changes contributed to a decline in street markets, the recruitment of juveniles, and handgun possession by young people following the 1993 peak.

One important contributing factor to the decline in violence as crack demand ebbed has been the strength of the U.S. economy during the [1990s]. If there were no legitimate jobs for young people, it is reasonable to anticipate that they would have found other criminal activity to provide economic sustenance. But the abundance of job opportunities, including those not requiring high skill levels, provided legitimate alternatives. Individuals in legitimate jobs have a strong incentive to conform and avoid criminal activity. This should indicate the desirability of finding approaches that bring young people into the legitimate economy through appropriate training to develop legitimate employment opportunities.

INCARCERATION

The United States has gone through a dramatic transformation in its sentencing policies and practices [since the mid-1970s]. . . . [T]he United States maintained an impressively stable incarceration rate (prisoners per capita) of about 110 per 100,000 population during the 50-year period from the early 1920s to the mid-1970s,[9] when it suddenly grew exponentially at a rate of about 6 to 7 percent per year.

Various attempts have been made to correlate the rising incarceration rate with the crime rate. The most aggressive of those analyses use the period after 1991—they argue that the crime rate has been steadily decreasing because the incarceration rate is increasing. But such simplistic attempts to estimate the incarceration effects on crime are likely to be misleading. For example, the analysis must also account for the period in the late 1980s when crime was increasing at the same time the prison population was growing.

Attributing the decline to incarceration is far more tenable if one focuses on older offenders, whose homicide rates have declined steadily since the mid-1970s. This group is the appropriate focus for estimating the incapacitative effect of incarceration (i.e., crime is reduced because offenders are removed from the streets). One can appreciate that the incapacitation effects were an important contributor to the continuing decline of violent crime rates among older people, especially for those over 30, who displayed about a 40- to 60-percent drop in homicide rates between 1985 and 1999. This connection is particularly appropriate because 32 is about the median age of State prisoners.

One of the contributors to the growth in incapacitation is the large number of drug sellers who have been sentenced to prison in the past two decades. Figure 3 shows the growth in incarceration from 1980 through 1996 by crime type. The greatest growth—by a factor of more than 10—was among drug offenders. Ironically, their

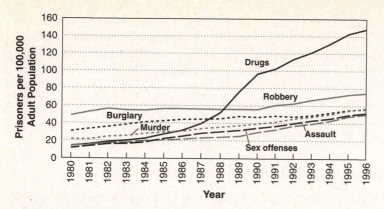

FIGURE 3   **Recent Trends in the U.S. Incarceration Rate for Six Crime Types**

Source: Blumstein, A., and A. J. Beck, "Population Growth in U.S. Prisons, 1980–1996," ed. M. Tonry and J. Petersilia, *Prisons,* vol. 26 of *Crime and Justice,* Chicago: University of Chicago Press, 1999: 17–61. Reprinted by permission of the publisher. Copyright © 1999 University of Chicago Press.

incarceration did not have a major impact on the drug trade because others, particularly younger sellers, replaced them. But if they would have engaged in violence on the outside, their incarceration could have contributed to the decline in violent crime rates. The incapacitation effect, however, is at least partially negated by violence committed by the replacements. Indeed, because many replacements were young people, who have a greater propensity for violence, the net effect may have been an increase in violent crime, undoubtedly a factor that must be considered when discussing the rise in violence of the late 1980s.

Even if drug offenders' incarceration contributed to the reduction in homicide, it is not clear whether imprisoning them was an efficient use of fiscal or prison resources. As the prison population grows, marginal offenders are likely to have a lower offending frequency . . . than those who were already incarcerated.[10] A sizable but unknown fraction of drug offenders who are incarcerated (comprising more than 20 percent of State prisoners and more than 60 percent of Federal prisoners) are predominantly entrepreneurs rather than generic criminals, and they are not likely to be violent.

Incarceration effects are far less likely to have been a significant factor in the more recent decline in violent crime rates among teenagers and youths, and most likely were limited to older youths, whose risk of incarceration is greatest. In addition, levels of violence have fallen in the younger age groups in recent years even as their risk of incarceration has increased. The decline might have been less steep in the absence of the "get tough on juveniles" sentencing policies enacted in recent years. But it seems more likely that the other factors considered in this paper—the reduction in the use of guns, changes in the drug markets, and the growing number of legitimate job opportunities—have had more dominant effects.

In *The Crime Drop in America,* William Spelman and Richard Rosenfeld derived estimates of the contribution of incarceration to the crime drop of the 1990s.

Spelman[11] used general elasticity estimates (percentage reduction of crime resulting from a 1-percent increase in the prison population) from the literature and estimated that the crime reduction is associated with steady growth in the prison population. Rosenfeld[12] used estimates of prisoners' offending frequency . . . based on homicide rates in the most disadvantaged neighborhoods of St. Louis and Chicago. . . . Both were crude estimates, and they used very different approaches, but both estimated that incarceration contributed about 25 percent of the crime drop, leaving 75 percent to other explanations.

CHANGING DEMOGRAPHIC COMPOSITION

Much of the speculation about the recent decline in homicide rates attributes it to changing demographics. This may be a holdover from the realization that much of the decline that began in 1980 was attributable to a demographic shift as the baby-boom generation outgrew the high-crime ages.[13] Those same demographic effects were not at work in the early 1990s, since demographic effects do not always move in the same direction.

The decline after 1980 was significantly affected by the shrinking size of the cohorts in the high-crime ages—late teens and early 20s. In the late 1990s and currently in the United States, those cohort sizes are growing. . . . Thus, if age-specific crime rates are to remain constant for teenagers, the aggregate crime rate should be increasing as a result of the larger cohort sizes.

These age-composition changes are relatively small, with cohort sizes growing at a rate of about 1 percent per year. . . . These demographic trends are small compared with the much larger annual swings in the age-specific crime rates, as much as 10 to 20 percent per year growth in the 1980s (16 percent per year for 18-year-olds from 1985 to 1991) as well as decreases in the 1990s (6 percent per year for 18-year-olds from 1991 to 1998).

SOME OBSERVATIONS

The sharp rise in violence by young people during the late 1980s and the correspondingly sharp decline in the 1990s are striking. The increase in the aggregate homicide rate was due to escalating rates among juveniles and youths, predominantly (although not exclusively) by and against black males, particularly in larger cities and exclusively involving handguns. By 1999, the rate of homicide perpetrated by youths finally returned to the stable rate that prevailed from 1970 through 1985.

Although the causes of the rise in violent crime are reasonably clear—homicides by young people with handguns, mostly as a result of diffusion out of drug markets—the factors contributing to the decline are more complex. Various forces are involved, some more salient in certain places. They include efforts by local police, communities, and Federal agencies to separate young people from their guns. Those efforts have been helped considerably by the waning of crack markets, especially the diminished participation of young people in those markets. As an alternative, the robust economy has provided legitimate job opportunities for them, which has created incentives to avoid illegal activities. . . .

One final observation is somewhat provocative. The UCR reports for the first half of 2000 were released by the FBI in mid-December 2000. They are strikingly different from the previous 6 years in which annual decreases in crime rates of 6 to 8 percent were common. The new report estimates both crime and homicide drops of merely 0.3 percent. This could be an indication that the decrease in crime, which could not continue indefinitely, has finally flattened out. We cannot be certain whether this flattening is an indication of one small disruption to a continuing decline, the start of a next increase, or a plateau from which changes will require particularly innovative approaches that are quite different from the actions that have taken us to this point. Regardless, we should take advantage of the current opportunity to better understand these processes and to pursue criminal justice and community-based policies to forestall the next increase as long as possible. As we look to the future, we should be concerned both about the possibility of a resurgence of active drug markets and any violence they may bring with them and about a downturn in the economy and the impact it would have in communities in which violence is most likely to reignite.

QUESTION-AND-ANSWER SESSION

DEVON BROWN, OFFICE OF THE CORRECTIONS TRUSTEE: . . . I was delighted recently to learn that . . . John DiIulio has recently . . . changed his view on the prediction that so-called "superpredators" would take over our cities. Could you share with us your view on that?

A.B.: When we saw this rise in juvenile violence, rhetoric started to flow. The "super-predator" theory argued that we are now seeing a breed of kids that is far worse in socialization, conceivably in genetics, than previously seen. A major thrust of everything I said about that rise in violent crime was that it was not different kids, it was the same kids doing what they had always done, with more lethal weaponry. The handgun became the major source of the problem when it got into the hands of irresponsible people. Violent crime was reduced not because we had changes in socialization after 1993, but because the nucleating role of the drug markets diminished. It declined because kids no longer had to carry guns and we saw a general disarmament. Another reason for disarmament was that the police were posing larger threats—taking the guns away and imposing other punishment. As we saw fewer guns in the street, the incentive to carry them was diminished. So we saw this gradual dropping away. John DiIulio has acknowledged that "superpredator" was really an inappropriate characterization. I think the essence of the data I presented today shows that it wasn't different kids; it was the weapons those kids were carrying. These factors should stimulate everybody to work to prevent handguns from getting into the hands of irresponsible people. There are many ways we can do that without significantly inconveniencing the large number of responsible people who have every right to have handguns legally. These include tracing guns, as ATF does to see where those guns are coming from; identifying dealers who are major sources of guns used in crimes; and restricting gun purchases to one gun per month to inhibit aggressive marketers. Federal laws will be necessary to ensure that one State is not vulnerable to neighboring States that do not enforce gun laws. As long as we see a clearly interstate commerce in guns, Federal intervention will be needed to identify the source of the problem and identify minimally intrusive methods to ensure that guns don't get in the hands of statutorily defined irresponsible people (youth, felons, and individuals who have been involuntarily committed to mental institutions). . . .

STEPHEN RICKMAN, EXECUTIVE OFFICE FOR WEED AND SEED, U.S. DEPARTMENT OF JUSTICE: . . . As a consequence of this increase in incarceration rate over the past 20 years, you have also had an increase in the number of people who are coming out of prison. . . . Given the fact that you have had this diminution in postrelease supervision and services with this population, how do you factor this into your trends and how it may affect crime in the future?

A.B.: That's a good question, because it really pulls together a number of important issues. Number one, we are keeping people incarcerated longer. We are keeping people longer partly because our sentences are increasing, partly because of mandatory minimums, and, most important, because of parole violations (increasingly for technical violations). We are increasing the probability that these people coming out are coming out well past their criminal careers—and we must think seriously about criminal careers. Research found that the duration of the residual criminal career goes up through the 20s, is fairly flat through the 30s, and then falls off in the 40s. So people in their 30s are the ones most likely to continue—if they are active in their 30s.

The issue of postrelease management is a complex one. It involves a mixture of providing services and exercising control by sending the person back to prison. The trends lately have emphasized the control aspect, often at the expense of services. Indeed, many States are finding that more of their admissions are now composed of parole violators than new court commitments. Service needs are complex, and perhaps the most essential is drug treatment, which everyone acknowledges is important. In addition, there has to be help in finding and keeping a job, treating mental illness, and various other forms of counseling.

The whole notion of parole has became politicized because parole officials rather than prison officials were the ones who made release decisions: "We will stop the release decisions by moving to [determinate] sentences" without attention to the guidance and the counseling needed and without attention to the rate of reincarceration. Parole officials took the political heat for being "soft on crime" at the time when everyone else was being "tough," so they began sending violators back to prison on the least provocation without dealing with the issue of the optimum policy for dealing with somebody who now is drug positive. The parole issue very much needs rethinking. Parole recommitments have been a major factor in the growing incarceration rate over the past 5 years or so. . . .

TED GEST, UNIVERSITY OF PENNSYLVANIA, CRIMINAL JUSTICE JOURNALISTS: . . . While your presentation related to government responses to crime, you concentrated almost totally on what you would call enforcement or incarceration remedies. Could you describe the field of so-called crime prevention in the past 10 years or so? . . . Does the absence of crime prevention from your comments indicate that either we don't know what any of these programs contributed or that you think they have had a marginal or insignificant effect on the phenomenon?

A.B.: I think that's an important question. There is so much I didn't talk about but I certainly didn't mean to slight prevention. I still think the efforts that governments, particularly the Federal Government, put into issues of prevention are quite minimal and the issue is compounded by the fact that we have [too] little research . . . to have any accurate assessment of what works best. The programs we get data on and that have been a major cornerstone of both Federal and State policies have been in the incarceration area. Prevention efforts are still strikingly minuscule in comparison to what is needed, particularly the need to combine those efforts with evaluations targeted at what looks like the most promising opportunities. OJJDP has been a major leader in, for example, the longitudinal research in tracking kids through emerging and eventually terminating criminal careers—and the factors associated with getting involved in crime—because that fundamental research helps to identify what kind of interventions are best for whom.

We went through this horrible period in the late 1970s and early 1980s when Bob Martinson's "nothing works" theme emerged out of a variety of evaluation studies that tried to find the "silver bullet" and tested individual technologies to estimate their effectiveness in reducing recidivism. Any such treatment cannot be universally applicable. Treatments have to link the individual offender or potential offender and his or her needs, the treatment provider and his or her skills in delivering various kinds of treatment, and the environment in terms of what kinds of crime that person might be getting involved in.

We have to experiment with many approaches and evaluate them, but budgets in the order of tens of millions of dollars are inadequate to deal with this problem. We continue to be impressively ignorant about the effects of any of our interventions within the justice system. And cutting that back would be the height of folly at a time when the establishment is ready to be open and interested in getting research findings. But we need much more research and evaluation to track the changes that are going on in this phenomenon—because they are changing. . . .

Notes

1. Blumstein, A., and J. Wallman, eds., *The Crime Drop in America,* New York: Cambridge University Press, 2000.
2. Blumstein, A., and D. Cork, "Linking Gun Availability to Youth Gun Violence," *Law and Contemporary Problems* 59 (1) (1996): 5–24.
3. Gifford, L., D. B. Adams, and G. Lauver, *Background Checks for Firearm Transfers, 1999,* Bulletin, Washington, D.C.: U.S. Department of Justice, Bureau of Justice Statistics, 2000, NCJ 180882.
4. Innes, C. A., *Drug Use and Crime: State Prison Inmate Survey, 1986,* Washington, D.C.: U.S. Department of Justice, Bureau of Justice Statistics, 1988, NCJ 111940, and Beck, A., et al., *Survey of State Prison Inmates, 1991,* Washington, D.C.: U.S. Department of Justice, Bureau of Justice Statistics, 1993, NCJ 136949.
5. Goldstein, P., "The Drug/Violence Nexus: A Tripartite Conceptual Framework," *Journal of Drug Issues* 15 (1985): 493–506.
6. Blumstein, A., "Youth Violence, Guns, and the Illicit-Drug Market," *Journal of Criminal Law and Criminology* 86 (1) (1995): 10–36.

7. Cork, D., "Examining Space-Time Interaction in City-Level Homicide Data: Crack Markets and the Diffusion of Guns among Youth," *Journal of Quantitative Criminology* 5 (4) (1999): 379–406.
8. Johnson, B., A. Golub, and E. Dunlap. "The Rise and Decline of Hard Drugs, Drug Markets, and Violence in Inner-City New York," in *The Crime Drop in America,* ed. A. Blumstein and J. Wallman, New York: Cambridge University Press, 2000: 164–206.
9. Blumstein, A., and J. Cohen, "A Theory of the Stability of Punishment," *Journal of Criminal Law, Criminology, and Police Science* 63 (2) (1973): 198–207.
10. Canela-Cacho, J. A., A. Blumstein, and J. Cohen, "Relationship between the Offending Frequency (34) of Imprisoned and Free Offenders," *Criminology* 35 (1) (1997): 133–175.
11. Spelman, W., "The Limited Importance of Prison Expansion," in *The Crime Drop in America,* ed. A. Blumstein and J. Wallman, New York: Cambridge University Press, 2000: 97–129.
12. Rosenfeld, R., "Patterns in Adult Homicide: 1980–1995," in *The Crime Drop in America,* ed. A. Blumstein and J. Wallman, New York: Cambridge University Press, 2000: 130–163.
13. Blumstein, A., J. Cohen, and H. Miller, "Demographically Disaggregrated Projections of Prison Populations," *Journal of Criminal Justice* 8 (1) (1980): 1–25. See also Blumstein, A., J. Cohen, and H. Miller, "Crime, Punishment, and Demographics," *American Demographics* (October 1980): 32–37.

HIGH INCARCERATION RATE MAY FUEL COMMUNITY CRIME

Michael A. Fletcher

TALLAHASSEE—Things were looking up in Frenchtown. After years of spiraling out of control, crime had been declining sharply in this neighborhood of rickety frame houses and tumbledown carryouts that forms the historic hub of this city's African American community. Observers credited a variety of aggressive police tactics, including more and longer prison sentences for offenders.

But in 1997, the declining crime rate in Frenchtown began to level off, failing to keep pace with drops in similar Tallahassee neighborhoods. And researchers analyzing crime trends here have fingered an unlikely culprit: the high number of Frenchtown residents sitting in prison cells.

Research here supports a controversial theory being advanced by an increasing number of criminologists, who have concluded that although high incarceration rates generally have helped reduce crime, they eventually may reach a "tipping point," where so many people in a given neighborhood are going to prison that it begins to destabilize the community and becomes a factor that increases crime.

"Until recently, nobody has really thought about incarceration in the aggregate," said Dina R. Rose, one of the researchers studying the relationship between incarceration and crime in the Frenchtown area. "Many people assume that incarceration reduces crime. But when incarceration gets to a certain density, that is when you see the effects change."

Rose, a sociologist at New York's John Jay College of Criminal Justice, found that in high-crime Tallahassee neighborhoods that were otherwise comparable, crime reductions were lower in those with the greatest number of people moving in and out of prison. With high incarceration rates, she argues, prison can be transformed from a crime deterrent into a factor that fuels a cycle of crime and disorder by breaking up families, souring attitudes toward the criminal justice system and leaving communities populated with too many people hardened by the experience of going to prison.

Frenchtown provides abundant evidence for the thesis. There are few men available to volunteer in the youth programs at the Fourth Avenue Recreation Center. And every day, dozens of men line up in front of a soup kitchen run out of a small frame house in the heart of Frenchtown. Robert J. Roeh, who runs the soup kitchen, estimates that four out of five of those who show up for the free meals have some type of prison record. "Going to prison keeps you locked up without bars for the rest of your life," he said. "We need to look at some other sanctions for people."

Dale Landry, a former police officer and Marine who heads Tallahassee's Neighborhood Justice Center, an alternative corrections program, said the volume of people going to prison has reached the point where it hurts the very communities it is intended to help. "When a crime is committed, an offender should be held accountable," Landry said. "But the way we do it now, when a crime happens there is a damaged relationship between people who live in this community. We need to work on fixing these relationships. But when we send people away, those relationships remain broken, but we are left with a false sense of security that the prisons are working."

It is a problem recognized by local police, who have increasingly turned to community policing in an effort to mediate some of the social problems that often arise in conjunction with crime. "We are looking at a lot of these issues," said Maj. George Creamer, head of the Tallahassee police operations bureau. "But if you are trying to clean up these neighborhoods and you don't arrest people who are breaking the law, then what do you do with them?"

In examining the impact of high incarceration rates in Tallahassee, researchers collected 1996 statistics on prison releases and admissions as well as demographic data from 103 Tallahassee neighborhoods. They also collected crime statistics for 1996 and 1997. The data then were mapped in order to compare incarceration rates with crime while controlling for socioeconomic factors. While crime dropped in virtually all of the Tallahassee neighborhoods examined in the study, the rate of the decline in Frenchtown was one-third lower than in surrounding neighborhoods. The most telling difference between the neighborhoods, the researchers said, was that Frenchtown had a higher incarceration rate.

Other researchers caution that it is too early to come to definite conclusions. Bert Useem, a University of New Mexico sociologist who is embarking on a national study of incarceration rates and crime, said "it remains to be seen" whether taking a relatively large number of people out of a community has the effect of increasing crime. "On the one hand, you have to be concerned about the number of people going into prison," he said. "But on the other hand, communities can become ravaged by crime. And the recent experience nationally has been these increases in incarceration rates and decreases in crime."

In any case, notes William J. Sabol, a researcher at the Urban Institute, "now you are getting many more people who previously were unconcerned asking about the unintended consequences of incarceration." Those consequences are likely to grow with the surging incarceration rate. Swollen by increases in drug offenders and longer, mandatory prison sentences, the nation's prison population has risen every year since 1973 and has tripled since 1980.

This wave of incarceration has had a disproportionate effect on black neighborhoods. Justice Department statisticians project that more than one in four black males born this year will enter state or federal prison at some point during their lifetimes, compared with 16 percent of Hispanic males and 4.4 percent of white males. "When you say that [almost] 30 percent of black males are projected to go to prison, that is a fact that no person who believes in freedom can be comfortable with," said Todd R. Clear, a John Jay criminologist working with Rose on the Frenchtown study.

The effect of high incarceration rates is intensified by the fact that they are often concentrated in relatively compact communities. A study in Hudson County, N.J., found that in 1995, one in 15 children experienced the trauma of having a parent go to jail for at least six months. In sections of South Central Los Angeles, an estimated 70 percent of the young men are in the clutches of the criminal justice system.

Researchers have found that men who have been in prison are less likely to marry, get good jobs or develop productive relationships with family members once they are back on the street. "Areas that have low crime rates are that way because people who live there do the job of providing social control," Rose said. "But people typically come back from prison more damaged and with less ability to contribute to society." Clear said the social impact of high incarceration is most profound for the children and families of those sent to prison. "At some point, having some involvement with the prison system starts to look like part of their destiny," he said.

That's exactly what Frenchtown resident Laura Anderson is worried will happen to her 6-year-old son Xavier. His stepfather, John L. Anderson, is in prison for armed robbery; his biological father is in jail awaiting trial. After her husband's arrest, Anderson and her son tumbled into homelessness and were forced to move in with friends and double up with in-laws. Finally, they settled in a dingy garden apartment back in Chattahoochee, her sleepy hometown located 40 miles west of Tallahassee. Xavier transferred to three different schools within a matter of months. He was left back in first grade. His teachers said he wouldn't concentrate in class.

But mostly Anderson worries about how her son will come to view the specter of prison. Once, when Xavier got into an argument with some young friends while playing in the breezeway, he came inside sobbing, fearful that the police were going to get him, she said. His mother said it is more than a childish fear. "His biological father is incarcerated. His stepfather is incarcerated," she said. "If somebody does not come along as a mentor or something and show him a different way, he is going to think that jail is the place where he will ultimately be too."

FROM C-BLOCK TO ACADEMIA: YOU CAN'T GET THERE FROM HERE

Charles M. Terry

John Irwin, our "gang leader," was really "on" that day. Placing the American imprisonment binge within a historical context, he gave a brief overview of some of the major changes that have taken place in the past 30 years—the main one being the dramatic increase in the numbers of incarcerated bodies (Austin and Irwin, 2001: 1–5). He held up the ASC [American Society of Criminology] conference program, entitled "Explaining and Preventing Crime: The Globalization of Knowledge." As Irwin turned the pages, he commented that 20 or 30 years from now a historian like Douglas Hay or Robert Hughes[1] will come along and, looking back at us during this period, say, *"What the fuck were they doing?"* He pointed out how the majority of research being done by criminologists today does not even address the fact that there are now 2 million people behind bars in the United States; let alone the ravaging effect this is having on communities, families, and individuals, most of whom are poor, minority, uneducated, and unemployed and/or underemployed. With passion, he pleaded for help in getting people to recognize the tragic damage being done to hundreds of thousands of individuals, as we build more prisons and lock up more people.

As he has in the past, Irwin (1980: 240) conceded that there are times when prison sentences are necessary. Nevertheless, trips behind bars should be short, safe, and humane. Moreover, resources should be available for prisoners who wish to make an effort to better themselves. Finally, he suggested that perhaps the most disastrous effects of the prison experience are related to what happens after people are released from confinement.

The issue of making the transition from prison to the outside world is in dire need of attention by criminologists. Based on my own experiences, and those of others, I view "making it" (Maruna, 2001) . . . after being released as an almost insurmountable obstacle.[2] The general effects of spending time (especially long sentences) in prison can be overwhelming. This is especially true for those of us who developed and internalized a convict identity.

My "criminal career," which stemmed from an inability to successfully support a heroin habit without getting arrested, spanned a period of two decades (1970–1990). During that time, I survived four prison sentences and spent roughly 12 years behind bars, in prisons and county jails in California and Oregon. . . .

My teenage years were spent hanging around other white, working-class youngsters with similar interests in my southern California hometown by the beach. During high school, which most of us completed, we became involved in activities that were popular in the later 1960s. We grew our hair long, surfed, listened to rock music, went to concerts, had girlfriends, got high on the popular drugs of the time (e.g., marijuana,

Source: Ross, J., and Richards, S. (Eds.). *Convict Criminology* (Thompson, 2003). This is an edited version; endnotes have been renumbered accordingly. Reprinted by permission of the author.

LSD), and tried to keep our actions hidden from figures of authority. Though not always successful in this regard, few of us got into serious trouble with the law or had to spend any time behind bars. . . .

By the time I was 19 years old, I was shooting heroin daily. Explaining why is impossible. What I will say, however, is that it *made me feel good!* Suddenly I found myself doing nice things for little kids and saying hi to old ladies on the street. Heroin made me feel alive, like I was connected to the universe. I remember telling the person I was with, shortly after the first time I tried it, "I can't believe I have been wasting my life doing anything besides shooting this stuff." My love for heroin propelled me into social worlds and a lifestyle I never knew existed.

Going from a surfer/hippie kind of guy to a heroin addict did not take long. My associations and actions quickly changed. I avoided old friends and family and quit surfing completely. Before I knew it, I was interacting with street-level addicts, many of whom were desperate and struggling to survive. Images remain of aged hookers with scarred, sore-covered bodies; poor, ethnic neighborhoods; people "nodding," overdosing, being arrested, getting out of prison, and dying. As my social world changed, so too did my self-concept, which eventually led me to being arrested and locked up for burglary.

At first, jail was a frightening place to be. Strange things happen in those environments. The sight of pain and suffering is common. I remember winos going through DTs, guard and prisoner violence, screaming at all hours of the day and night, addicts suffering from withdrawals, people having epileptic seizures, and homosexual activity that was sometimes consensual, sometimes not. Over time, the daily routine became familiar: chow lines, court lines, shower lines, holding tanks, strip searches, thoughts about the outside, and a lot of time to play cards or dominoes, write letters to girlfriends, and tell war stories about the streets.

In the Los Angeles County jail, we washed our clothes in toilets because they contained the best source of running water. We made wine (pruno) out of water, fruit, sugar, and yeast. We drank hot chocolate brewed by mixing melted Hershey bars and water. Using matchlit, tightly rolled toilet paper as fuel, we cooked grilled cheese sandwiches on the steel slabs we slept on. We also gambled, bought and sold cigarettes and candy bars for profit, and did everything we could to obtain drugs whenever possible. As I became more comfortable in "jail," . . . my fear and anxiety about living among the "rabble" of society (Irwin, 1985) became almost nonexistent. Over time, what once seemed like the caverns of hell became more like home. . . .

County jail experiences and associations helped prepare me for my eventual journey into the California prison world of the 1970s. Still, the differences were dramatic. Jails are community facilities, close to family, where inmates serve short sentences. In comparison, prisons are places where people spend many years. The men, both prisoners and guards, are bigger and tougher, many with tattoos (Sanders, 1988; Richards, 1995b). Penitentiaries, maximum-security "big house" institutions, are huge complexes, filled with thousands of men, and known for high levels of violence, blatant racism, and hatred. I remember the pain I felt deep down in my guts when I observed the de facto segregation that existed in the chow halls and in the yard; blacks with blacks, whites with whites, browns with browns. I recall the fear I felt when we thought a race riot was about to start. . . .

The way I saw the world and myself continued to change during my early prison years. I became a lot like those I saw around me who seemed to be doing the easiest time. These were the guys who were respected; the ones with tattoos all over their bodies, lifting weights, drinking coffee with cream and sugar, smoking tailor-made cigarettes, getting high, and laughing all the time. . . .

Topics of conversation were often about groups and individuals who did not live up to our standards and expectations. We depicted them as weak, untrustworthy, subhuman, snitches, child molesters, "dings" (mental cases), and scared. We told stories about the outside world that reinforced and validated our convict self-concepts. We never talked, at least in public, about being lonely or afraid ourselves. To do so would be unacceptable. The more I saw myself as a convict, the more alienated I became, not only from nonconvicts inside the prison, but from people I would meet in the outside world. . . .

The things I did after being released from prison had a great deal to do with the meanings I developed while still inside. There were times when my plans to "make it" centered around staying away from heroin. If I just don't use, I thought, I will be able to stay out of prison. On other occasions I had no such plans at all. The only thing I wanted to do was get loaded and have sex as soon as possible. Whatever my plans, the beliefs and values I learned in prison continued to affect my judgments, decisions, and actions. . . .

My relationships with parole officers varied. Some were more understanding than others. Urinalysis tests were the center attraction of all our encounters, whether they took place at the parole office, home, or work. Immediately after I was paroled, I tested positive for heroin eight weeks in a row. Because I was working at the time, and my parole officer (PO) did not believe I was doing felonies to support my habit, she encouraged me to get on a methadone maintenance program. Once on methadone, I managed to quit using heroin every day, continued working, and completed the parole supervision.[3]

A few years later, upon finishing another stretch in prison, on my first day out, I was assigned a PO who told me he did not think I was fit to live in the free world. He wanted me to immediately enter a long-term, live-in drug program. I told him the idea of doing more time right then was not appealing; that I was clean, planned on doing good, and had no intentions of going into any program. He responded by saying, "Terry, you belong in San Quentin [maximum-security penitentiary], and I will do everything within my power to send you there." The guy hounded me to urinate in bottles three and four times a week to see if I was using heroin. Each time I reported to his office, he examined my arms with a magnifying glass in the hopes of finding needle marks.

That time, I stayed clean for about a month. Once I started using dope again, I did what many parolees do when they know they will be sent back: quit reporting to the parole office. Like Irwin (1970: 113) said, "Many parolees career and ricochet through their first weeks and finally, in desperation, jump parole, commit acts which will return them to prison, or retreat into their former deviant world." Within 90 days I was jailed again for another crime and on my way back to prison.

The more time I did inside prison, the more alienated I felt around non-convicts. It got to where I couldn't even relate to most of the heroin addicts I met in the outside world. . . . Only a minority had been to prison. It became increasingly difficult to relate to conventional people in any context. Even when I was doing everything I could to "do good" (e.g., stay clean, work, not commit crimes), I felt out of place and uncomfortable. The reason, of course is that my reference group had become the convicts. The movement from one meaning world to another, from prison to the outside, was simply overwhelming. . . .

In 1981, I left a California prison and moved to Oregon. It was my hope that a change in scenery would help me "stay out." My plan failed. As it happened, I made it nearly three years before receiving another prison sentence.

Using heroin was not a problem because I became involved with a woman who had access to enough money to support both our habits. Consequently, I lived a relatively normal life for about two years. I worked regularly, ate good, slept OK, did not lose weight (as many of us do when we get addicted), and, except for purchasing and using the narcotic, did not break any laws. In the eyes of the people I interacted with who did not use heroin, I was likely seen as a normal, law-abiding citizen.

Eventually, the money supply dried up, and the script for another return to prison was written. I began shoplifting. Before long I was doing burglaries again. Out of control and not wanting to return to prison, I tried to "clean up" on my own. I made calls to numerous "substance abuse centers." I told the drug counselors I was addicted, had already been to prison three times for heroin-related crimes, was doing felonies every day, and could not stop! The response was always the same, a Catch-22 situation: "Do you have insurance?" "No," I answered. "Well," they would say, "If you don't have insurance the charge is $500.00 a day." Right! If I had that much money I wouldn't have to stop doing heroin! Addicts with money get "treated" by medical personnel and spiritual advisors. The rest of us get locked up. . . .

Out of money, addicted to heroin, unable to get drug treatment, and doing crime to support my habit, I was busted again. Now, it was time for a trip inside the Oregon state prison system, most of it spent behind the walls of one of those old, nineteenth-century, maximum-security pens. I served time in Oregon from 1984 to 1990. It was during those years that my perceptions about the world and myself began to change dramatically. . . .

After a couple of years of doing what I had always done in prison (work, hustle, exercise, and get high whenever possible), I found myself becoming bored. Little changes in those places. We ate, slept, showered, worked, and exercised at the same times every day. The food, though good compared to California, got old as well. Only so much can be done with that "mystery meat" they called "hamburger steak," "Swedish meatballs," or "meatloaf," depending on which day it was being served. The constant laughter we engaged in, along with the marijuana or other drugs we managed to use, was always a welcome source of relief. Eventually, though, I was motivated to seek something different to break up the monotony. It was at that time I decided to sign up for college classes in the education department.

PERSONAL TRANSFORMATION THROUGH COLLEGE EDUCATION

In the 1980s, due to the availability of Pell grants, it was possible for Oregon convicts to pursue college educations. Instructors came from the local community. We were able to earn valid, transferable, academic credits for our course work. During my stay it was possible to obtain up to a bachelor's degree. This source of funding has since been discontinued for prisoners (Tregea, [Ross and Richards, 2003]). . . .

Having the opportunity to be formally educated was amazing. . . . Our teachers were, for the most part, dedicated, competent, and caring people. Besides teaching, they treated us like human beings, as equals. Once we left the education floor we were again subjected to the rules and realities of prison life. Nevertheless, in class, at least temporarily, we got a reprieve from the prison oppression.

For nearly two years I attended classes as a full-time student. During this period my self-concept and ideas about life began taking a radical shift. Perhaps the greatest impact came from taking cultural anthropology classes, which helped me recognize how the diversity of the human experience reflected the varieties of cultures found throughout the world. Each culture makes sense and works according to its own meanings, values, and customs. Here was evidence that life involved much more than freeways, cars, fast food, drugs, prisons, and being a "stand-up guy." I began to get a sense of history; that the way things are has everything to do with what came before. Ultimately, I began to question my own way of thinking.

. . . Never before had I thought of myself within a broad sociohistorical context. Seeing prison as a distinct culture, as one that was basically synonymous with the world of the street . . . was something I recognized almost immediately. The "reruns in the yard" stories I had been hearing since my earliest prison days were now boring, shallow, and meaningless. My perception of others became noticeably different. Just as my initial use of heroin propelled me into an alien social world, the new ideas and thoughts I was exposed to in school were, in effect, altering my reality and preparing me for a future I never imagined.

In retrospect, it seems clear that the major effect of my prison college experience was an ability to critically examine my self-conceptions and views of the world.[4] What I began to see was troublesome. At that point I saw myself as a white, mid-30s aged convict, a heroin addict from California. My friends were other white convicts. We spent the majority of our time talking bad about others and reinforcing our convict self-images with the use of humor and stories about the streets. I began to realize that my status and place in prison was made possible because of the identity and meaning system I had learned to embrace. Trusting others outside my social circle had become nearly impossible. For the most part, we either hated or distrusted anyone we saw as different. This, combined with having a sense of being part of an elite group to whom I felt great loyalty, characterized my perspective. These thoughts led me to realize that I was basically cut off from almost everyone on the planet. My new-found ideas provided motivation to continue seeking a way out of my dilemma.

After my prison classes ended, I continued the introspection process by reading books about spirituality and self-awareness. . . . Over time, I learned that my thoughts, feelings, and emotions were a reflection of my self-concept, perceptions, and desires. Anger, hostility, rage, impatience, envy, and jealousy came about because I wanted things to be different than they were. I learned that how I see others is a reflection of how I see myself. Moreover, what I see in them I *increase* in myself. My consciousness was permanently altered when I realized that the negative, hateful thoughts I projected onto others usually had little effect on them. Instead, I learned, I was the one who felt the effects of my thinking. When I projected anger, I felt anger. When I extended kindness and love, I was answered with kindness and love.

The process of realizing these ideas took time, effort, and motivation. The eventual outcome . . . was an increased sense of empathy for others. Where before I would condemn and criticize the pariahs that lived within the prison (e.g., snitches, child molesters), now I felt empathy for them. Like never before, I saw their pain, suffering, and miserable existence as tragic realities of the human condition. As a result of my efforts and new understandings, my hatred was gradually replaced with compassion.

Ripples from the "War on Drugs" taking place in the wider society became increasingly noticeable during my last few years at OSP. Access to drugs dried up considerably. . . . The guards who previously brought in marijuana had been caught and fired. Instead, those who smuggled drugs into the institution brought in methamphetamine and heroin, because they were easier to conceal and had more value. Drug testing became part of institutional policy. This led to many of us spending months in disciplinary segregation units (the hole) for having drug-contaminated urine. Though I still got high occasionally, I spent most of my time clean, exercising, hanging out in the yard, reading, and getting to know myself.

My motivation to learn through formal education, growing older, and changing perceptions, among other things, led to an unanticipated experience that today I would call a major turning point. . . . About 90 days before I was scheduled for release on parole, I injected a good dose of heroin (I had gone for several months without using any). The first thing I thought of after perceiving the effects of the drug was, "I can't believe I wasted so much of my life for this feeling." The next thing I realized, and this thought seemed unquestionably clear, was "this stuff isn't giving me anything. Instead, it's taking away from what I have." For the first time, I realized I liked being straight more than the way I felt using heroin. My world turned upside down. . . .

My parole plans were vague. Unlike times in the past, I did not feel anxious about getting out. . . . My contacts and orientation with the world beyond the prison walls, other than those I had maintained with my family and convict associations, were tenuous. Somehow, I sensed that I would never have to spend more time behind bars. Yet, how this would be possible was unclear. I realized I was institutionalized, that I had never lived as "normal" person, and that making the transition from where I sat in C-block to the outside world would be difficult. One day a thought crossed my mind: "I know I am institutionalized. School is an institution. I like school. Maybe I will get out of prison and go to college. I will just switch institutions."

Withstanding the Initial Impact of Reentry

Leaving prison after all those years was like entering a strange new world. Inside I was a respected convict. I knew where I stood with others, how to act, and what to expect. Once outside in the "free world," everything changed. . . . Irwin (1970: 113–114) described the process:

> The exconvict moves from a state of incarceration where the pace is slow
> and routinized, the events are monotonous but familiar, into a chaotic and
> foreign outside world. The cars, buses, people, buildings, roads, stores,
> lights, noises, and animals are things he hasn't experienced at first hand
> for quite some time. The most ordinary transactions of the civilian have

dropped from his repertoire of automatic maneuvers. Getting on a street-car, ordering something at a hot dog stand, entering a theater are strange. Talking to people whose accent, style of speech, gestures, and vocabulary are slightly different is difficult. The entire stimulus world—the sights, sounds, and smells—are strange.

Walking into a supermarket was like entering Disneyland. All those things—lights, products, lines of people—anything you wanted, right there at your fingertips. And, I'm supposed to pay? Compared to the caged-in prison canteen, this place was wide open. Eating in restaurants was awkward. So many choices. I quickly learned that, unlike in the prison chow hall, making efforts to trade for food was taboo. "Excuse me, would you like to trade those green beans for these mashed potatoes?" After being looked at like I was from Mars and politely being told no, I realized that it's not OK to ask strangers in line at the college admissions office if they want a drink of my soda. The difficulty of my initial entry was mitigated by my family, the 12-step program of Narcotics Anonymous, and associations with people I met at Santa Barbara City College. . . .

My step-mom and a family friend met me at the prison gate to bring me "home." . . . My dad greeted me with a smile and a handshake after we arrived at the house, yet seemed unsettled about my presence. Who could blame him? Here was his 38-year-old heroin addict son coming home after completing his fourth prison sentence. We talked a bit and did our best to communicate. As difficult as that may have been, my folks made it clear that they would do anything they could to support me. The familiarity of the surroundings and their warm welcome was comforting.

Never before had the differences in living conditions between prison and the outside world been so apparent. Of course, this time I had been locked up a long time, having served six-and-a-half years. In prison we had only steel chairs or wooden stools, concrete or tile floors, and thin mattresses on a steel rack. At home everything was soft, with cushioned sofas, carpets, and thick comfortable beds. The walls, instead of penitentiary green, yellow, or brown, were painted in pastel colors and decorated with paintings and family photographs. And, at home there was silence and privacy! No more cell block sounds: the constant noise, screaming, yelling, steel doors slamming shut, and guards aiming flashlights at my head at all hours of the night. Suddenly, I could eat on plates instead of steel trays, shower, sleep, turn off the lights, use the phone, come and go whenever I wanted! Compared to C-block, this was paradise.

Despite the lavish comfort I found in my immediate physical environment, I was still a stranger in a strange land. In order to "make it," I would have to overcome a number of serious obstacles and barriers. This process was facilitated not only by my family but by the 12-step program of Narcotics Anonymous (NA). . . .

My Uncle Joe came to see me my first day home. He had been a member of Alcoholics Anonymous (AA) for several years, and suggested I go with him to a meeting. I agreed. As I entered the meeting place I felt awkward. The group was made up of predominately white, working- and middle-class people who appeared to be members of mainstream society. However, once they started telling stories about themselves and their drinking days, I began to notice similarities instead of the differences between us.

Of particular interest was their focus on spirituality and learning how to become serene instead of insane and selfless rather than self-centered. I was excited to learn that they were talking about the same ideas I had been studying in prison. This realization, and the warm welcome I felt by the time I left, inspired me to "keep coming back."

My first trip to the parole office was routine. "Lock 'em up Tom," as my new PO was called, let me know that he saw me as trouble and would be keeping an eye on me. He said, "One of the conditions of your parole is to attend at least three AA or NA meetings a week." I said, "I don't think that is necessary because I no longer have a drug problem." Chuckling, he said, "Well, that may be true. But you also don't know how to live out here either. Remember the first time you went to jail?" After I said yes, he continued. "When you first went in there [prison] you didn't know what was going on. You had to learn how to survive. You had to learn what you could do and couldn't do. After awhile you knew what was happening and got along quite well." I agreed. "Well," he went on, "this is like that in reverse. Now you have to learn to live in the outside world. The people in those meetings will help you do that if you let them." I had already been introduced to AA by my uncle and liked what I had seen. Tom's directive provided me with additional motivation to participate.

Eventually, Uncle Joe took me to an NA meeting, where people identified as drug addicts instead of alcoholics. I could not really relate to many of them at first; most had not been to prison, were not heroin addicts, or streetwise, and had done things like work all their lives. Yet I immediately felt more comfortable there than I did at AA meetings. The use of language was familiar and likely increased my sense of connection with the group. . . . Before long, I discovered there were people in NA who had backgrounds like myself.

After being out 28 days, I went to an NA convention. . . . Roughly 4,000 recovering addicts from all over southern California were in attendance. . . . I saw Chicanos from East L.A., blacks from South Central, and a whole lot of exconvicts.

. . . It was almost like being in a prison yard (except there were women). . . . The difference, though, was that here people were hugging each other, regardless of their race, talking about doing things to stay clean, helping other addicts, and getting their lives together.

. . . I sat in a room with about 1,500 people and listened to an old Chicano heroin addict (with 15 years clean) who had spent years in prison share his experience, strength, and hope with the audience. As might be expected, I could relate to almost everything he said. He honestly talked about the joys and pains he had experienced since being clean. His story, like the presentations by my convict criminologist colleagues at the ASC, gave me hope, a sense of purpose, and a feeling of being a part of the people in the room.

. . . The people I met at NA meetings served as intermediaries between prison and the outside world. They linked my past to the present and gave me direction for the future. . . .

Finding a real job was difficult. My record of employment was not exactly favorable, and filling out applications seemed less than promising. What can you say when asked about where you worked during the past 10 years, skills, how much you were paid, and why you left your last job? I figured that not much credibility was given for knowing how to stand in lines, lift weights, play dominoes, or tell war stories in the prison yard. I decided that honesty was the best way to go, so on several occasions, I admitted working for the state department of corrections as a "furniture factory finishing man" "firefighter," "tier sweeper," and "file clerk," for wages that never exceeded $3.00 a day. After several rejections, I finally landed a driving job for a new car dealership. The only thing they were interested in was the status of my driver's license. I assured them I had a perfect record, not a single ticket in seven years! The job was mine, but within two weeks the business folded.

My next stop was a temporary service agency. Once again I was honest while completing the application. Before long, I was sitting in front of an attractive woman who said, "I have helped exconvicts get jobs before and I've been burned. I had a guy in here one time who threatened my life and scared the holy hell outta me. If you ever threaten me in any way, I guarantee, I'll get you arrested. And know this, the district attorney is one of my best friends. I can get you a job beginning in the morning, but you must never tell the people where I send you anything about your past or where you came from. Remember, you are working for me, not them." Nice lady. The next day I began earning the minimum wage for a business that provided mail services. For eight hours a day we stuffed papers into envelopes as fast as possible. Most everyone who worked there drank alcohol during breaks. Several had been to prison.

STARTING COMMUNITY COLLEGE

Before the beginning of the semester, I made several trips to Santa Barbara City College (a two-year community college) to take assessment tests, meet with counselors, fill out stacks of forms, choose which classes to take, and apply for financial aid. These journeys to campus were stressful because there were so many people, strange conversations, new places to go, and much to do. I remember walking through campus, with hundreds of people rushing to their next class, and becoming so overwhelmed that I had to pull off to the side, stop, breathe awhile, and get hold of myself. Fortunately, several people I met during these expeditions lessened the strain.

Part of my student aid came in the form of work-study. . . . I walked into the campus transfer center, an office that exists to help students move on to four-year colleges, and met a woman who became a very close friend. I told her I was an exconvict trying to do good and would not let her down if she gave me the job. Later, she told me how intimidated she felt by my presence during that first meeting. She claimed that my level of intensity, language, and brutal honesty was discomforting. Luckily, she recognized that her feelings were due to her own insecurities and expectations and decided to give me a chance.

Once the semester began, I settled into a routine, something convicts do well. There was a time to be at work, in class, attend NA meetings, or go to sleep. Feelings of alienation were lessening with time. Positive social support surrounded me almost everywhere I went. Because of the efforts I was making, the opportunities I had, and the help of those around me, I was actually "doing good" on the outside. For the first time in my adult life, I was developing a straight routine. . . .

My new routine left me with a sense of living in two different worlds. I learned that others from NA, including a few exconvicts, were also students at City College. We would see each other on campus, drink coffee together, and compare what we were doing to our past lives in the streets or in the prison yard. Seeing them was always a boost and reminded me that I was not alone. They were welcome links with my past, helping me move ahead.

That following summer I met Debbie, my wife, and Annie, her nine-year-old daughter. Before long we were all living together. . . . Debbie has been good for me because, among other things, . . . [s]he has helped me learn everything from how to pay bills to what kind of clothes I should wear. Lovingly, she has pointed out that striped pants and checkered shirts do not match, and that it is not OK to remove a fake tooth from my mouth and set it on a restaurant table while I eat. For three years she told me I should put a shirt on when I enter a supermarket. "Why?" I wondered. It was hot. I never wore a shirt in the prison yard when it was hot. One day she finally got through. She said, "Look at it like this. How many other guys do you see in the store without their shirts on? Especially ones with tattoos all over their bodies?" Ding. Ding. Lights going off in my head. I got it that time. . . .

In 1992, I transferred to the University of California, Santa Barbara (UCSB), as a sociology major. While I was there, the person who had the greatest impact on me was Denise Bielby, a professor who knew little about crime, drugs, or convicts. She was my instructor in a yearlong senior seminar—another guide out of nowhere. . . . One day, as I was sitting in her office while she read something I had written, she looked up and said, "Chuck, you write well. I think you should seriously consider getting into a Ph.D. program after you graduate." Her words of validation surprised me and made me feel uncomfortable. What she was saying was not consistent with my outside world negative self-evaluation. Convicts are no good. Convicts don't get Ph.D.'s. According to mainstream standards, convicts don't do *anything* well. Previously, I had received good grades and words of praise from others, but it never had much meaning. Somehow, I imagined that the only reason they were telling me I was doing good was so I would not start shooting heroin again. Nevertheless, . . . [h]er words encouraged me to think about graduate school.

. . . As fate would have it, I got accepted at the University of California at Irvine (UCI). For the next five years, I commuted between Santa Barbara and Orange County, California, in pursuit of a Ph.D.

GRADUATE SCHOOL: "MAKING IT" WITH A LITTLE HELP FROM MY FRIENDS

My time at UCI was spent learning what the "experts" think and say about the general subjects of criminology, law, and society. Although the beliefs and ideas of my instructors varied, they all supported my efforts and treated me with respect. . . . Regardless of which course I took or with whom I interacted, I never kept my views or where I came from a secret. Then, as now, I complained about what I see to be the major missing "factor" in most criminological research. That is, most statistical and theoretical research presented and quoted in journals, books, and classes has little to do with the real-life situations of human beings.

. . . Several times I was given the opportunity to do guest lectures. On these occasions I talked about my life, heroin addiction, prison, and always attempted to humanize the people who inhabit these deviant social worlds.

Convicts, like war veterans, or cops, often develop close relationships with each other. Alan Mobley, who did time in the federal prison system, began his graduate education at UCI during my second year. Though our stories are dramatically different, we immediately became friends. In subsequent years, we spent time together talking about what was going on in school, things we had done and seen in prison, and about the ongoing dramas of our lives. Alan was, and is, not only a good friend, but also a solid link to the past. His presence during graduate school was a major means of support. Again, there was a convict in my life doing what I was doing; I was not alone (see Mobley, [Ross and Richards, 2003]).

Irvine's faculty had a positive influence on my education, and especially on my changing self-concept and future. . . . Paul Jesilow, who acted as my dissertation advisor, had the most lasting impact. . . . I often complained to him about the so-called empirical content of the discipline, which failed to include real-life representations of people who got caught up in crime and the criminal justice system. He encouraged me to follow my heart. Today, as I write, I hear his voice telling me "too many words" or "what's the point?"

. . . Unfortunately, despite the fact the UCI professors taught critical analysis, they were, for the most part, comfortably distant from their subject. . . .

My eyes were really opened at my first American Society of Criminology meeting. I learned that criminology is not only an academic discipline, it is also a profession, and for some people, a business. After living in the "belly of the beast" . . . exposure to these alien-like, privileged social worlds is highly disturbing. My perceptions at this particular event, which reflected my convict background and graduate student status, left me feeling uneasy and out of place. This is common for many graduate students, especially attending a conference for the first time.

Criminology and criminal justice conferences always take place in what appears to me to be lavish, luxurious hotels, replete with extravagant furniture, floor covering, lighting, and restaurants that charge exorbitant prices. "Experts" come from all over the country and world. Social networks are built. Authors of books wander, meeting with old friends and colleagues they may only get to see on these occasions. Their travel and conference expenses, at least in part, are usually paid for by the organizations they represent; for example, universities, research institutes, or government agencies.

Now comes the hard part. Reflecting on John Irwin's earlier statement, *"What the fuck were they doing?"* The value of some of their research is highly debatable. Much of their work, which may have been undertaken as a result of the lure of grant money, does little more than elevate their status. Presentation of "data" is dominated by factor analysis and multivariate correlations. Problems associated with prisons and the lives of people who get released, if mentioned at all, are said to be management related. The widespread damage of crime-related politics and policies is seldom discussed. Issues related to humanity, morality, and virtue are oddly missing.

Early conference encounters were difficult. Panel after panel left me feeling empty inside. Over and over I would think, "Nobody is talking about the people who suffer. Nobody is talking about the truth." What I saw was a group of people benefiting at the expense of human misery beyond their comprehension. The reality of the human condition as it related to those defined as criminal, their definers, and the worlds in which they live was seldom heard. . . . One thing was sure, this was a long way from C-block. And the guys in the yard are still there. The addicts, homeless, poor, and mentally ill on the streets are still suffering. Where is the "data" about their lives?

At my first few conferences, I was assigned to panels based on the type of abstract I submitted. Typically, most of what was said by session participants supported the views of those with interests in maintaining the social order. . . .

At another ACJS session, I talked about the relationship between crime and desperation. Before my presentation we heard from two academics and a man who worked for the National Institute of Justice (NIJ). His sterile, mindless words and unmistakable arrogance turned my stomach. He was clearly far removed from the real lives of people who live on the streets or in prison. Like many other middle-class professionals at the conferences and in the halls of academia, he left me with the impression that he had led a sheltered, antiseptic existence his entire life (J. Ross, 2000).

When I had my chance to speak, I suggested that instead of viewing "criminals" as rational calculating machines . . . , we might try to see them as human beings doing the best they can with what they have to work with. HIV-infected, drug-addicted parents don't choose to leave their home without food while they hustle money for dope. Armed robbers, usually addicts, are not necessarily "seduced into crime.". . . In reality, there are many ways to unravel the causes of criminal behavior, yet any explanations that fail to include politics (crime is politically defined), economics, ideology, and historical context are basically meaningless. Finally, I said, recognizing the desperation involved in many criminal activities might put a different dimension on how we conceptualize criminal behavior. It would, perhaps, allow us to see our own culpability rather than blame it all on "them." During my short talk I noticed the man from the NIJ avoiding my eyes and squirming in his chair as if it was on fire. As soon as I finished, before any questions could be asked, he hurriedly left the room.

I was having a hard time making sense of these conferences. Why am I here? What do I have to offer? Joan Petersilia supported me from the beginning of my graduate school days. Early on she knew my feelings about the failure of criminologists to recognize the dehumanizing conditions of the criminal justice system and the lives of those defined as criminal. She always listened as I told her about my frustrating conference experiences. One day, she suggested I contact some other exconvicts turned academics and attempt to put a panel together for an upcoming ASC meeting. . . . Convict criminology was born, and now I enjoy conferences.

ASSISTANT PROFESSOR

In the fall of 1999, I began working as an assistant professor at the University of Michigan at Flint. . . .

After arriving in Flint, I immediately became involved in the local NA meetings. Doing so helped me to enter a new social network of recovering addicts, who act as a major means of support. As they did in California, they also give me a grounded, nonacademic glimpse into social worlds that revolve around the negative effects of illegal drug use, the law, and imprisonment.

What I do today is a far cry from the controlled environment of the prison. As time passes, I find myself getting increasingly involved in problems that other academics struggle with: interdepartmental conflicts, deadlines, health insurance, retirement funds, car problems, issues about money, and so on. Still, some of the most simple aspects of life, like not having to worry about cell house violence, are not forgotten. Strength is gained by recollecting the past, which is never further than a thought away.

Compared to being a convict, life as an academic is incredible. I live in a nice home with Debbie. The food we eat—though we have to buy it, prepare it, and clean up the dishes afterward (much easier to just get in line)—is of a much higher quality than the mystery meat served behind prison walls. I love my job, and especially enjoy teaching. As I write this I can look out my window at squirrels scurrying around the snow-covered ground. There are no bars on the windows, or guards walking by counting me like I am part of a cattle herd.

The opportunity I have today allows me to tell what I know about the ways many of us, inside prison and out, are living as a result of warped ideologies, politics, economics, racism, sexism, homophobia, social class inequality, and a market economy that generates an extreme form of self-centeredness, rampant competitiveness, and lack of compassion for others.

In prison, I saw men shot by authorities for no reason whatsoever. I have seen convicts stab each other because they felt they must. Failure to do so would have meant being seen as weak, and therefore, no good, in the eyes of other convicts. I have seen men in penitentiary psychiatric units drugged out of their minds because they were deemed "dangerous" by prison doctors. . . . I have seen the hopelessness, degradation, monotony, and real conditions of prisons in this country, and the courage, fortitude, and humor that have helped a few of us survive and maintain some degree of sanity. We need to tell about what we know. Isn't that our job? . . .

It is not always easy for this convict criminologist to be an assistant professor. . . . One particular day, . . . I was invited to a welcoming luncheon at the home of the chancellor. The festivities took place on a spacious lawn area at a mansion-like house. My feelings of alienation deepened as I made my approach. Members of the faculty, or royalty as they appeared to me, were sitting, talking, and eating at colorfully decorated tables. . . . Servers, dressed in white clothes and hats, waited on the tables and helped with the food. Not knowing a single person there, and feeling like I was what they used to call "out of bounds" in prison, I awkwardly scooped up some food, found a table, indulged in some very brief small talk, finished eating, and left within 10 minutes. . . .

That night I went to an NA meeting near downtown Flint. It was held in a church basement in a predominantly black neighborhood, within four miles of the chancellor's house, in an area full of vacated, boarded-up houses. Bars covering the windows and doors of people's homes give them the appearance of miniature jail cells. As happens in many AA and NA meetings where people tell it like it is, stories of pain and hope were shared. Lots of tears and hugs.

Never in California had I heard a woman in an NA meeting talk about one of her children being murdered. That night I heard two people, both black, grieving over the shooting deaths of their adolescent sons. Along with the tears came humorous presentations of life experiences that conveyed a sense of belonging. Tears and laughter are cathartic, a means of healing for people in pain. Nowhere else, except maybe at a funeral, do I hear such truthfulness, people exposing their vulnerability. While in the presence of such honesty, I am not a convict, addict, or academic. During these special moments, at least temporarily, I am just another living, breathing person, nobody special or different. Realizing this helps me see more clearly that underneath our facades, we are all really the same.

INSIDIOUS CONSEQUENCES OF THE PRISON EXPERIENCE: COHORTS AS EVIDENCE

John Irwin recently suggested to me that the ruined lives of the majority of the people we met in our respective prison cohorts is evidence of the damaging effects of imprisonment. I agree. Criminologists have told me that what I saw and talk about is merely anecdotal and, therefore, can have no effect on social policy, which should be the true aim of our work. I disagree. The truth needs to be told. The truth of deviant social worlds—obscured by government-funded statistics, the corporate-owned media, and arrogant middle-class academics—is screaming to be heard.

Stories of people making successful transitions to the streets after spending years behind bars are unusual. The effects of incarceration turn many of us into violent, relatively fearless individuals who hardly care whether we live or die once we get out of prison. While inside, we became psychologically and socially impaired. Once released, those who "do good" generally fall into some conventional social world, usually with the help of family, friends, prisoner assistance programs, and a great deal of individual effort. Many become dependent on families and social welfare. Others cross back and forth, within and outside the law. They may work menial jobs, then drift back into drug habits, spending time in detox wards and county jails. Unknown numbers of us who fail to find some conventional niche gravitate toward dereliction (Austin and Irwin, 2001: 152–157), characterized by homelessness, cheap wine alcoholism, poor health, and despair. We sleep where we can—in bushes, under bridges, on sidewalks, inside cardboard boxes, and in a variety of other locations, beyond the sight of the public. As when we are locked up, we are characterized by many as lazy, morally deficient, and burdensome.

Success stories of my own convict cohort are few and far between. Many died from overdoses. A few were stabbed to death while inside. It was not unusual to hear about a guy who upon getting out of prison was shot to death.

Meanwhile, more and more of us are dying from health problems related to cancer, AIDS, and hepatitis C. Too many, like a friend who was given 32 years to life for possession of a spoon containing traces of heroin residue and less than a quarter gram of cocaine, are doing what is commonly called "all day" by convicts; meaning he will never be released from prison again.

The fear of getting out and the difficulty of "making it" need acknowledgment. From what I have seen, the following words from a friend who wrote me just before being released by a parole board are not unusual for seasoned prisoners:

> . . . I was laying on my rack this morning thinking about the streets, stomach in knots, palms all sweaty. I hate it here. But I'm also scared to get out. Don't know why bro, just makes me scared. Remember how you felt on the van riding to Chino [trip from jail to prison] or wherever? Well, that's how I feel when I'm about to get out. My guts all in a knot. . . .

Within two months after being released, he was murdered in a Phoenix area "homeless camp."

Particularly painful for me was the story of a guy I met in NA. Except for a brief amount of time spent behind bars for heroin possession, he was gainfully employed his entire adult life. When I met him he had just been released from prison and was attending meetings to satisfy his parole officer. The eventual resurgence of his heroin habit led to another drug conviction, which meant he would spend more time living amidst the madness of California prisons. I saw him a few times after he bailed out of jail, waiting for trial, anticipating being returned to prison. His usual, joyful personality was gone. It was as if the life had gotten sucked out of his body. To resolve his dilemma, he killed himself by jumping off a freeway overpass bridge, bouncing off a car traveling between 65 and 70 miles per hour. . . . From what I have seen, tragic stories never seem to end. . . .

I have a few ideas about what might be done to improve the lives of people who spend time in prison and their chances of "doing good" after release. Real solutions would be geared toward improving the social circumstances of those most likely to get incarcerated: the poor, the undereducated, the unemployed—mostly minorities from America's inner cities. Improved employment and educational opportunities, better housing, health care, and a dismantlement of Draconian drug laws would be a good place to start. . . .

As the rate of imprisonment continues to climb, more prisoners are getting out of prison. In 1995, about 463,000 people were released from prison. Estimates indicate those numbers will reach 660,000 by the end of 2000 and hit the 1.2 million mark by 2010. . . . Instead of figuring out how to better "manage" this population, be it inside or outside prison walls, perhaps part of what we can do is study and write about their experiences and lives. Such efforts might help them be seen as human beings instead of animals, as they are continually depicted in the popular culture. By doing so, maybe we can help generate the beginnings of a compassionate criminology, a criminology that does more than help maintain the social order. As Richard Quinney said one time at an ASC panel, "It is not enough to be critical. We must also be proactive."

Addressing the structural impediments (e.g., loss of civil rights, blocked employment opportunities) that hinder the chances of "doing good" after release are important (Richards, 1995a; . . . Richards and Jones, 1997) and should continue. Yet how we see ourselves and how we think others evaluate us after we get out greatly affects our actions. Some typical comments I heard from exconvicts about their release experience illustrate this dilemma. One man, for example, told me, "Everyone looked at me like they were scared to death." He figured they thought, "Jesus Christ. Charles Manson just got out." Another said, "Soon as I got out, I noticed everyone looking at me. It was like everyone knew I'd been to prison. It was like being from another planet." Efforts to reduce such feelings are drastically needed and might be achieved if prisons were more humane.

Encouraging the humanization of the worlds behind bars should be a major concern for all of us. Even prison administrators should be concerned with the unnecessary, counterproductive, punitive practices commonly found in penal institutions across the country. In this regard, prison policies should be geared toward reducing cruel and unusual punishment and increasing the level of prisoner safety.

Moreover, they should provide adequate health care and rehabilitation programs for those who are motivated to help themselves (Murphy, [Ross and Richards, 2003]).

In my view, humanizing *all* contemporary deviant populations should be a fundamental goal of convict criminology. After all, prisoners represent only a fraction of the "dangerous classes," which are increasingly subject to formal social control (Gordon, 1994; Shelden, 2001). We should also remind others that people do change with experience, age, and education. This transformation is facilitated by forgiveness, understanding, and compassion.

Instead of focusing so much on the deviant as the cause of all our social problems, we might benefit by looking at the part each one of us plays in either reducing or increasing human suffering. If harm reduction were our true concern, then "the realization of peace in our own everyday lives [would be] the best social policy" (Quinney, 1995: 148). Our "wars" on drugs and crime are really wars on ourselves. . . .

We all affect each other. Striving to look upon others without condemnation, especially those we fear, is perhaps the greatest harm-reducing effort each of us can make.

Notes

1. See Douglas Hay (1975) for a scathing critique of England's escalation of punishment, especially the death penalty, during the eighteenth century. As is the case today in the United States, those being punished most often came from what was viewed as the "dangerous classes." Also, Hughes (1988) portrays the history of the European colonization of Australia as being rooted in the suffering and brutality of England's convict system of transportation.
2. For more on "making it," which simply means staying out of prison, see Irwin (1970: 88–89) and Jones (2003). See Richards (1995a), Richards and Jones (1997), for an in-depth look at some of the obstacles faced by prisoners after they are released.
3. I "did good" that time for almost two years. Unfortunately, when I attempted to get off methadone I began using heroin again. Shortly thereafter, I returned to prison.
4. Classes that critiqued politics, economics, history, or the law and society were not offered. The effects of the curriculum, a good proportion of which was made up of psychology classes, took my attention inward rather than outward.

References

Austin, James and John Irwin. 2001. *It's About Time.* Belmont, CA: Wadsworth.

Gordon, Diana. 1994. *The Return of the Dangerous Classes: Drug Prohibition and Policy Politics.* New York: Norton.

Hay, Douglas. 1975. *Albion's Fatal Tree.* New York: Pantheon.

Hughes, Robert. 1988. *The Fatal Shore: The Epic of Australia's Founding.* New York: Random House.

Irwin, John, 1970. *The Felon.* Englewood Cliffs, NJ. Prentice-Hall.

Irwin, John, 1980. *Prisons in Turmoil.* Boston: Little, Brown.

Irwin, John, 1985. *The Jail: Managing the Underclass in American Society.* Berkeley: University of California Press.

Jones, Richard S. 2003. Excon: Managing a Spoiled Identity. In Jeffrey I. Ross and Stephen C. Richards, *Convict Criminology.* Belmont, CA: Wadsworth, pp. 191–208.

Maruna, Shadd. 2001. *Making Good: How Ex-Convicts Reform and Rebuild Their Lives.* Washington, DC: American Psychological Association.

Mobley, Alan. 2003. Convict Criminology: The Two-Legged Data Dilemma. In Jeffrey I. Ross and Stephen C. Richards, *Convict Criminology*. Belmont, CA: Wadsworth, pp. 209–225.

Quinney, Richard. 1995. "Social Humanism and the Problem of Crime." *Crime, Law and Social Change* 23: 147–156.

Richards, Stephen. 1995a. *The Structure of Prison Release*. New York: McGraw-Hill.

———. 1995b. *The Sociological Significance of Tattoos*. New York: McGraw-Hill.

Richards, Stephen and Richard Jones. 1997. "Perpetual Incarceration Machine: Structural Impediments to Postprison Success." *Journal of Contemporary Criminal Justice* 13 (1): 4–22.

Ross, Jeffrey Ian. 2000. "Grants-R-US: Inside a Federal Grant-Making Agency." *American Behavioral Scientist* 43 (10): 1704–1723.

[Ross, Jeffrey Ian and Stephen Richards. (Eds.). 2003. *Convict Criminology*. Belmont, CA: Wadsworth.]

Sanders, Clinton. 1988. "Marks of Mischief." *Journal of Contemporary Ethnography* 16 (4): 395–432.

Shelden, Randall. 2001. *Controlling the Dangerous Classes: A Critical Introduction to the History of Criminal Justice*. Boston: Allyn and Bacon.

Tregea, Bill. 2003. Twenty Years Teaching College in Prison. In Jeffrey I. Ross and Stephen C. Richards, *Convict Criminology*. Belmont, CA: Wadsworth, pp. 309–326.

A NEW SUIT BY FARMERS AGAINST THE DEA ILLUSTRATES WHY THE WAR ON DRUGS SHOULD NOT INCLUDE A WAR ON HEMP

Jamison Colburn

Yesterday, two farmers filed suit in the federal district court of North Dakota. They are seeking a declaratory judgment against the Drug Enforcement Administration (DEA) that would allow them to cultivate hemp, a profitable crop with many legal uses.

The DEA, however, is likely to strongly defend the suit. After all, ever since its very inception, the DEA has feared that if it allows "industrial" hemp to be produced, the result will be to seriously undermine its war on drugs, including marijuana. As I will explain, its position has led to a bizarre and, some argue, utterly irrational situation: It makes little sense for the War on Drugs to also include a War on Hemp.

A case decided last year by the U.S. Court of Appeals for the Eighth Circuit illustrates some of this irrationality, but doesn't give the full picture. In this column, I'll provide a chronology of the DEA's war on this plant and its champions; discuss a set of legal questions that, in my view, complicates the agency's war plans; and finally, offer a prediction of hemp's regulatory future.

Source: Findlaw (www.findlaw.com), a Thomson Reuters business. June 19, 2007, http://writ.news .findlaw.com/commentary/20070619_colburn.html. Reproduced by written permission.

THE CANNABIS CONUNDRUM: A CONTROLLED SUBSTANCE WITH HIGHLY BENEFICIAL APPLICATIONS

The Controlled Substances Act (CSA) prohibits the manufacture, distribution, dispensation, or possession of any listed "controlled substance," except as authorized by the CSA or the DEA. Marijuana is included, and even its medicinal use remains flatly prohibited. In 2006, the Supreme Court entertained a Commerce Clause challenge to that latter prohibition, in *Gonzales v. Raich,* but the challengers lost.

This unbending legal regime is a great shame, because the marijuana plant is a botanical superstar. It generates a portfolio of raw materials for products like rope and canvas (which reportedly covered the Conestoga wagons of the Nineteenth Century West), oil, paper, and cellulose.

This is no small matter today: Compared to most tree species, as the U.S. Department of Agriculture has acknowledged, hemp is several times more efficient for producing paper and fiber, is much less dependent upon pesticides and herbicides than crops like cotton, and creates a seed oil high in essential fatty acids. The oil alone has countless applications. Indeed, the U.S. Department of Agriculture even *ordered* cannabis production during World War II in its "Hemp for Victory" program.

So if you're looking for an "assault on reason," a flat ban on this plant—given its multitude of beneficial uses, most of which are fossil fuel-reducing and organic in every sense—certainly fits the bill.

CANNABIS'S EARLY HISTORY: THE 1937 ACT

Of course, the issue with *cannabis sativa* is that some of its varieties are grown to maximize the creation of tetrahydrocannabinols (THC). THC is a psychoactive compound, and, unfortunately, the THC producer is the same genus and species as the botanical wunderkind. They are just different parts of the same plant or, in some instances, different varietals. Unfortunately, throughout American history, the U.S. government has too often acted as if these two features of the plant are inseparable—and that has led to some absurd results.

The cannabis plant was among the first drugs the U.S. Government tried to eradicate in this country, beginning in 1937 with the Marihuana Tax Act. The 1937 law was preceded only by the Harrison Narcotics Tax Act of 1914, which taxed opiates and cocaine, and, of course, the Eighteenth Amendment, imposing Prohibition.

While the 1937 law was formally a tax, it might as well have been a ban, for it made the cost of the plant prohibitively high, and thus effectively prohibited the growing of varieties and foliage to maximize THC ("pot"). Nevertheless, the growing of "hemp"—which has THC concentrations too low to move the needle—was taxed hardly at all.

A Senate Report on the bill made this point quite clear:

> The testimony before the committee showed definitely that neither the mature stalk of the hemp plant nor the fiber produced therefrom contains any drug, narcotic, or harmful property whatsoever and because of that fact the fiber and mature stalk have been exempted from the operation of the law.

Accordingly, the Act specifically excluded "the mature stalks of such plant, fiber produced from such stalks, oil or cake made from the seeds of such plant, any other compound, manufacture, salt, derivative, mixture, or preparation of such mature stalks (except the resin extracted therefrom), fiber, oil, or cake, or the sterilized seed of such plant which is incapable of germination." Put another way, it excludes hemp even as it sweeps in marijuana.

THE ROCKEFELLER ERA AND AFTER: NEW LAWS CONTINUE THE HEMP EXCEPTION

Fast-forward to the Rockefeller era—when the CSA and other drug laws were enacted. Notably, these laws all adopted the 1937 Act's definition of "marihuana," Which, again, was drafted to exclude hemp. Thus, for a time, hemp production continued unabated. But then, complications arose.

The CSA and other laws of the 1960s and '70s had to cope with the *synthetic* production of $C_{21}H_{30}O_2$ (THC). THC and THC-containing products were thus added to "Schedule I" of prohibited drugs, first by a regulation from the DEA's predecessor, the Bureau of Narcotics and Dangerous Drugs, and then via the 1970 Comprehensive Drug Abuse Prevention and Control Act (CDAPCA).

Meanwhile, "marihuana" (with that same original statutory definition from the 1937 Act) remained on the same list, as well—notwithstanding the obvious fact that it was the original source of THC. Thus, like the CSA, the CDAPCA while prohibiting *cannabis sativa,* retained the original, broad exception for hemp fiber, "stalks," "seeds," and any "manufacture" therefrom.

THE ADVENT OF THE DEA—AND THE START OF THE WAR ON HEMP

Then came the DEA—and the first offensives in what would become the war on hemp. It turns out that what Congress thought was "definite" in 1937 is actually a little complicated: The whole cannabis plant contains THC: it occurs in at least trace levels throughout the organism. Thus, even if the THC in hemp seed oil is so low that it cannot possibly induce psychotropic effects, technically, the person who ingests hemp seed oil is still ingesting THC—which Schedule I prohibited. Moreover, the DEA is fond of arguing, to get to the "mature" stage where its productivity is realized, hemp must first sprout through a high-THC (pot) phase—and in that phase, the DEA suggests, it could be poached or simply sold.

During the same era, the pharmaceutical industry found several applications for THC. It developed and marketed a synthetic form under the name Marinol to control nausea and vomiting caused by chemotherapy and stimulate appetite in AIDS patients. (Marinol was rescheduled in 1999 and placed in Schedule III of the CSA, where it may be used by prescription.)

Several inquiries from the public in the late 1990s alerted DEA to the fact that some interpreted the drug laws to exempt "hemp" as such. DEA then tried to "clarify" the CSA, CDAPCA, and its regulations with an "interpretive" rule and a follow-up "legislative" rule asserting that the "THC" entry on Schedule I included both natural and synthetic THC alike. The upshot was that, while the DEA would allow *imported,* non-edible hemp products to remain in commerce, all edible hemp was prohibited, as was all domestic cultivation of *cannabis sativa,* even if it was intended for "industrial" uses.

Yet, in a series of administrative law twists and turns, the Ninth Circuit eventually invalidated those rules. The result was to leave the CSA and CDAPCA as the only laws in effect on the matter.

TODAY'S DEA'S VIEW: IT'S THE THC STUPID!

In the wake of those cases, Justice Department and DEA lawyers maintain that the CDAPCA prohibits *everything* containing THC—whether synthetic or organic—including all parts of the cannabis plant. However, it's highly debatable whether that's true: The federal courts of appeal have divided over the question whether all parts of the cannabis plant are Schedule I controlled substances. Unfortunately, despite the legal ambiguity, the DEA has dug in its heels, acting as if the law were clear, and as if every use of cannabis were created equal.

One case decided in 2006 by the U.S. Court of Appeals for the Eighth Circuit, *United States v. White Plume,* is especially unfortunate. The case arose because in 1998, the Oglala Sioux Tribe amended its tribal law to allow cultivation of "industrial hemp" on tribal lands, and some of its members did so. Rather than prosecute, the government twice destroyed the crop, and then sought a declaratory judgment against White Plume. The district court obliged, as did the Eighth Circuit, which deferred to the DEA's construction of the drug laws and held that all THC-containing articles—including cannabis plants—are Schedule I-prohibited.

What accounts for a decision that prohibited a Native American tribe from growing and selling hemp for harmless industrial purposes? The short answer is that courts are generally inclined to defer to agencies' interpretations of the statutes they are charged with enforcing—in this case, the CDAPCA and CSA.

However, the suit filed yesterday in North Dakota may showcase the consequences of the agency's rigidity on this point. Given such a short growing season, competitors in Canada who are making money on the crop in our globalized agricultural economy, and so many possibilities for this plant, DEA should have to answer for its interpretation of the law in this respect, at least: Isn't there some other kind of trouble we can borrow?

Will Congress change the agency's mind about hemp, or will the courts? The prospect of either happening seems bleak, and that underscores how perverse our drug laws have become. In a time when it is so important to be "green," hemp is one of the "greenest" things around.

Readings on A Crime by Any Other Name . . .

EDITORS' INTRODUCTION

Chapter 2 of *The Rich Get Richer and the Poor Get Prison* examines a variety of ways people in the United States are harmed and it finds that some of the greatest dangers to our well-being are not from acts that are labeled crimes. Readers are asked to compare the harms from crimes with the harms of certain noncriminal behavior as a step in determining whether the harsh response to criminal harms and the gentle approach to noncriminal harms represents intelligent policy. The acts that lead to these *harms* share many elements of criminal conduct—they are harmful acts done knowingly or recklessly—but some tend to be ignored or minimized by the criminal justice system. The inclusion of certain harmful acts within the criminal law—and the exclusion of other harmful acts—does not reflect an objective reality about "dangerous crime." Instead, our concepts of "crime" and the "typical criminal" are socially created through the process of making and enforcing law. The criminal justice system acts as a carnival mirror that magnifies the threat of street crime while minimizing a variety of other harmful behaviors.

In answering the question posed by our original text in the title of its second chapter's opening section, "What's In a Name?", *The Rich Get Richer* (1) analyzes the "typical criminal" to show that criminal justice is a "creative art" that creates the social reality of crime in a way that resembles the distortions of a carnival mirror, (2) responds to the Defenders of the Present Legal Order about why the actions of the powerful should rightly be treated as serious crimes, and (3) reviews evidence about the extent and seriousness of harms from occupational hazards, health care, chemicals, and poverty. Numerous noncriminal harms are discussed and quantified in the book, but they are by no means the only such harms.

The first reading, "When Workers Die: U.S. Rarely Seeks Charges for Deaths in Workplace" by David Barstow, is an article cited in *The Rich Get Richer.* We include it here for detail we could not include in the book about how the Occupational Safety and Health Administration (OSHA) fails to use available criminal penalties when workers die due to willful safety violations. The article reports the results of an eight-month study by the *New York Times* of OSHA's handling of some 1,242 "horror stories—instances in which the agency itself concluded that workers died because of their employer's 'willful' safety violations." In 93 percent of the cases, OSHA did not seek criminal prosecution. This reluctance apparently continued even with regard to employers who repeatedly violated safety rules, even when violations caused multiple deaths, even when "administrative judges found abundant proof of willful wrong-doing." Though, as *The Rich Get Richer* notes, thousands of workers die each year due to unsafe working conditions, it is only a misdemeanor to cause the death of a worker by willfully violating safety laws. A 1988 congressional report commented: "A company official who willfully and recklessly violates federal OSHA laws stands a greater chance of winning a state lottery than being criminally charged." The article discusses a number of cases of worker deaths due to safety violations and the relatively minor penalties that were handed out. It closes with a discussion of efforts to get OSHA to act more aggressively in such cases and to get Congress to increase the penalties—and of the predictable and highly effective resistance that such efforts meet from business and its political allies.

The maximum penalty for a willful safety violation that results in a worker's death is six months in prison. *The Rich Get Richer* uses this fact to bring out how the criminal justice system presents an image of crime in society that, like the image reflected back by a carnival mirror, reflects something real in the world but in a distorted shape and size. *The Rich Get Richer* shows that people stand a considerably greater chance of getting killed as a result of unsafe work conditions than from the violent crimes that the FBI and newspapers focus on. And yet, while poor criminals whose violence results in death face long prison sentences and even the death penalty, executives whose refusal to make their workplaces safe leads to even more deaths than those caused by poor criminals face a six month sentence—less than the sentence for harassing a wild burro on federal land! What image of crime and violence does that create? Does it not suggest that safety violations are a minor threat while poor criminals are the greatest threat? Is this not an example of what *The Rich Get Richer* points to in saying that "the image cast back [by the criminal justice carnival mirror] is false not because it is invented out of thin air but because the proportions of the real are distorted: Large becomes small and small large; grave becomes minor and minor grave"?

In "The U.K.'s 'Corporate Manslaughter' Statute: British versus American Approaches to Making Firms Responsible for Deaths Resulting from Gross Negligence," Anthony Sebok discusses a British legal innovation aimed at holding companies responsible for deaths caused by a firm's negligence. This significant British legislative development, which allows the state to prosecute a corporation for the crime of manslaughter, received almost no media coverage in the United States. Under the British law, the state must prove that the death resulted from a "gross breach of duty owed under the law of negligence" and that this resulted from the way the firm's activities were ordered or organized by senior management. The United Kingdom's Centre for Corporate Accountability notes that "the new offence makes it easier to prosecute large to medium sized organisations for manslaughter, this in our view is progress and would bring improved justice to families." But the Centre expresses concern about the removal from the final law of provisions to hold boards of directors responsible, with the result that the law "fails to motivate sufficiently directors to take action to prevent deaths and injuries, and also allows them to escape accountability when their failures causes death and injury."[1]

Courts can, however, impose unlimited financial penalties on convicted firms, they can require the firms to announce publicly that they have been found guilty of manslaughter, and they can demand that the firms take remedial action to correct the conditions that led to the negligence. Some of these ideas are included in the list of reforms proposed in the Conclusion of *The Rich Get Richer.* The article compares this British approach to the American approach of civil lawsuits aimed at collecting punitive damages.

"The Checklist" by Atul Gawande is another article cited in Chapter 2 of *The Rich Get Richer* as part of the discussion of the number of preventable deaths and diseases that result from—of all things—medical treatment itself. Research shows that medical treatment is the third greatest cause of death in the United States, right after cancer and heart disease. Thus, medical treatment causes harm comparable to the harms caused by common crimes like murder and aggravated assault. *The Rich Get Richer* points out that many of the deaths and diseases due to medical treatment are preventable and argues that the refusal to take the needed preventive measures makes those in charge morally, if not legally, responsible for harm on a scale comparable to that caused by common crimes. "The Checklist" emphasizes this point by showing just how easy it is to prevent these harms, even while recognizing the complexity of medical practice. It documents the power of "a stupid little checklist" for procedures such as putting in a line like a catheter to deliver blood or medications makes a huge difference in preventing infection and saving the lives of patients. Moreover, the article also points out how resistant doctors and hospital directors are to adopting this preventive measure. If those responsible for medical treatment know that a simple procedure could reduce death and disease and refuse to adopt this procedure, are they not morally responsible for the preventable harms that result from this refusal?

In "Popcorn Lung Coming to Your Kitchen? The FDA Doesn't Want to Know," we are told about a dangerous chemical called diacetyl that is used in producing microwave popcorn. Diacetyl is the main chemical used in creating artificial butter flavor. The article's author is David Michaels, who heads the Project on Scientific Knowledge and Public Policy (SKAPP) and is professor of environmental and occupational health at George Washington University's School of Public Health and Health Services. The article shows that, though OSHA has known about the threat that this chemical poses to workers in plants producing microwave popcorn, it has done little to protect those workers. What's more, there is now some evidence of consumers becoming ill from diacetyl fumes released when the popcorn is microwaved.

Diacetyl fumes can cause an irreversible and deadly lung disease, so evidence that *consumers* are contracting this disease "should have resulted in some action by these agencies, but instead, they've done virtually nothing." Diacetyl is thus not just an example of an occupational hazard, but also of the larger issue raised in Chapter 2 of firms that are "waging chemical warfare against America." Much of the article is devoted to describing the responses of the various agencies charged with protecting us against dangerous chemicals after learning about the danger from diacetyl. The Food and Drug Administration (FDA) has dragged its feet and refused to take action. The Environmental Protection Agency (EPA) did a study on the chemicals released in making microwave popcorn but seriously delayed releasing its findings to the public. The Centers for Disease Control and Prevention (CDC) "has done terrific work investigating the causes of lung disease among flavor workers" but has not responded on diacetyl. The Occupational Safety and Health Administration (OSHA) received a petition from two unions, supported by leading scientists, asking it to develop a standard to protect workers from diacetyl exposure. OSHA has failed to establish the standard. If our government does not seem genuinely interested in protecting us, as workers and as consumers, from a serious risk of lung disease, how can we believe that its criminal justice policy is aimed at protecting us? If its criminal justice policy is not aimed at protecting us, then what is it aimed at?

In "Death Sentences in Chinese Milk Case," David Barboza reports a case in which the death penalty was handed down to people involved in causing six deaths and 300,000 ailments in children. Those convicted were adding melamine, a harmful industrial chemical, to protein powder because it causes tests for protein to falsely show high levels of protein. The tainted milk products had an adverse effect on many infants. Other reports on the death sentences note that many Chinese see the lack of government regulation as a major problem. However, although they lack administrative rules and enforcement that have a crime- or harm-prevention function, the Chinese examples clearly show a system that treats corporate actions that knowingly produce death and harm *as crimes*. How would the Defenders of the Present Legal Order respond to the use of the criminal law in these examples?

The presence of the death penalty does add something of a twist to these examples. Our argument in Chapter 2 of *The Rich Get Richer* that more corporate harms should fall within the criminal law is not an argument for the death penalty. Indeed, the articles show the potential link between repressive government and harsh sentencing. The United States is just about the only advanced country that imposes the death penalty at all. European countries have not only given it up as unnecessary to control crime, but often treat it as a violation of human rights. That we share this policy with the communist regime in China ought to make us think deeply about whether our tough policies on crime are fitting for a free and open democratic society. On the other hand, if the United States is to have a death penalty, why should it apply only to street crime and, as Chapter 3 of *The Rich Get Richer* shows, only to the poor who commit homicide? For those who accept the death penalty, the articles should raise questions about whether the punishment should also apply to the rich and powerful whose actions result in deaths of innocent citizens.

Note

1. Centre for Corporate Accountability, "Is the Corporate Manslaughter and Homicide Bill 2006 Worth It?" www.corporateaccountability.org/manslaughter/reformprops/2007/howgood.htm

WHEN WORKERS DIE: U.S. RARELY SEEKS CHARGES FOR DEATHS IN WORKPLACE

David Barstow

Every one of their deaths was a potential crime. Workers decapitated on assembly lines, shredded in machinery, burned beyond recognition, electrocuted, buried alive—all of them killed, investigators concluded, because their employers willfully violated workplace safety laws.

These deaths represent the very worst in the American workplace, acts of intentional wrongdoing or plain indifference that kill about 100 workers each year. They were not accidents. They happened because a boss removed a safety device to speed up production, or because a company ignored explicit safety warnings, or because a worker was denied proper protective gear.

And for years, in news releases and Congressional testimony, senior officials at the federal Occupational Safety and Health Administration have described these cases as intolerable outrages, "horror stories" that demanded the agency's strongest response. They have repeatedly pledged to press wherever possible for criminal charges against those responsible.

These promises have not been kept. Over a span of two decades, from 1982 to 2002, OSHA investigated 1,242 of these horror stories—instances in which the agency itself concluded that workers had died because of their employer's "willful" safety violations. Yet in 93 percent of those cases, OSHA declined to seek prosecution, an eight-month examination of workplace deaths by *The New York Times* has found.

What is more, having avoided prosecution once, at least 70 employers willfully violated safety laws again, resulting in scores of additional deaths. Even these repeat violators were rarely prosecuted.

OSHA's reluctance to seek prosecution, *The Times* found, persisted even when employers had been cited before for the very same safety violation. It persisted even when the violations caused multiple deaths, or when the victims were teenagers. And it persisted even where reviews by administrative judges found abundant proof of willful wrongdoing.

Behind that reluctance, current and former OSHA officials say, is a bureaucracy that works at every level to thwart criminal referrals. They described a bureaucracy that fails to reward, and sometimes penalizes, those who push too hard for prosecution, where aggressive enforcement is suffocated by endless layers of review, where victims' families are frozen out but companies adeptly work the rules in their favor. "A simple lack of guts and political will," said John T. Phillips, a former regional OSHA administrator in Kansas City and Boston. "You try to reason why something is criminal, and it never flies."

In fact, OSHA has increasingly helped employers, particularly large corporations, avoid the threat of prosecution altogether. Since 1990, the agency has quietly downgraded 202 fatality cases from "willful" to "unclassified," a vague term favored by defense lawyers in part because it virtually forecloses the possibility of prosecution.

The Times's examination—based on a computer analysis of two decades of OSHA inspection data, as well as hundreds of interviews and thousands of government records—is the first systematic accounting of how this nation confronts employers who kill workers by deliberately violating workplace safety laws. It identified a total of 2,197 deaths, at companies large and small, from international corporations like Shell Oil to family-owned plumbing and painting contractors in quiet corners of America.

On the broadest level, it revealed the degree to which companies whose willful acts kill workers face lighter sanctions than those who deliberately break environmental or financial laws. For those 2,197 deaths, employers faced $106 million in civil OSHA fines and jail sentences totaling less than 30 years, *The Times* found. Twenty of those years were from one case, a chicken-plant fire in North Carolina that killed 25 workers in 1991.

By contrast, one company, WorldCom, recently paid $750 million in civil fines for misleading investors. The Environmental Protection Agency, in 2001 alone, obtained prison sentences totaling 256 years.

OSHA has often made itself an easy target for criticism. Labor scolds the agency for taking years to write new safety rules. Business ridicules it for nitpicking inspections. But no one disputes OSHA's duty to deter employers from killing workers by deliberately violating safety laws, and few object to the idea that OSHA should at least ask prosecutors to look at such cases. Yet OSHA—whipsawed by criticism, fearful of public embarrassment—has become almost paralyzed by even this task, current and former officials agreed.

In an interview this month, OSHA's administrator, John L. Henshaw, acknowledged that the agency had referred few cases to prosecutors. But he insisted that OSHA seeks criminal sanctions "to the fullest extent that the law provides." And he emphasized that workplace deaths had fallen over the last five years. OSHA has not sought more prosecutions, he said, because officials concluded that most cases simply lacked enough evidence for a conviction. "There's a higher degree of evidence that you need," he said.

While true in some cases, this is only part of the explanation. Before OSHA deems a violation willful, it subjects the case to especially intense scrutiny, sometimes spending thousands of hours amassing evidence. It does so because of the stigma attached, and because the maximum fine for a willful violation is 10 times higher than for almost any other kind of violation. Only 404 of OSHA's 83,539 cited safety violations this fiscal year were labeled willful. "We make sure we have the evidence," said John B. Miles Jr., OSHA's regional administrator for five Southern states.

Yet when it comes to deciding what to do with that evidence, many current and former officials said, the culture of reluctance rules, regardless of which party controls Congress or the White House. Paul Bakewell, who recently retired after 26 years as an OSHA inspector and supervisor in Colorado, said that inspectors meet so much resistance that the very notion of pursuing criminal charges soon disappears—especially since killing a worker is only a misdemeanor under federal law. "I personally didn't think, 'Oh, it's a fatal, it's willful, it should go criminal,'" Mr. Bakewell said, adding, "You just don't need that grief. The honest to God truth is that it's just going to slow you down. They want numbers, lots of inspections, and it will hurt you to do one of these cases."

A TOOL THAT FEW WILL USE

Posters crammed with statistics line the hallway to John Henshaw's office in Washington. "Metrics," he calls them. Numbers drive OSHA's management culture. When Mr. Henshaw speaks of his accomplishments at OSHA, part of the federal Labor Department, he makes his case with numbers—3,000 more inspections this year than in 2000, 9,000 more serious violations. But one number missing from Mr. Henshaw's posters is how often OSHA uses its ultimate enforcement tool, the ability to refer cases to federal or state prosecutors. The omission matters greatly, veterans of the agency said, because at OSHA, what gets counted gets rewarded. And if it is not counted, that sends an unmistakable signal.

When it comes to an interest in prosecuting cases, William M. Murphy, the top OSHA official in Cincinnati until his retirement in 2002, said, "We've never communicated that to the staff."

In the early 1990's, OSHA agreed that inspectors should be trained to work on criminal investigations. The program was discontinued after fewer than 100 employees had the training. In 1994, the agency formed an Enforcement Litigation Strategy Committee to focus resources on cases with "maximum deterrent effect." Deaths involving willful violations were high on the list. The committee disbanded after a few meetings. Two years later, OSHA established a policy requiring its local offices to advise Washington in writing of "cases appropriate for potential criminal prosecution." The policy has not been enforced; OSHA headquarters said it could not find any such written notifications.

The Environmental Protection Agency has more than 200 criminal investigators and works closely with three dozen environmental prosecutors at the Justice Department. But Richard E. Fairfax, OSHA's director of enforcement programs, said he had never met William P. Sellers IV, the one federal prosecutor in Washington who works almost entirely on workplace safety crimes. "I know the name," Mr. Fairfax said in August, "but I'm not placing it."

Indeed, although Mr. Henshaw and his top assistants in Washington insist on approving any proposed fine over $100,000, they said they played virtually no role in deciding when the agency seeks criminal charges. That decision, they said, has been left almost entirely to local and regional OSHA officials and Labor Department lawyers. And yet in at least one region of the country, OSHA inspectors have been instructed in writing not to initiate contact with state law enforcement authorities, whose local laws often offer stronger and more flexible criminal sanctions.

Until presented with results of *The Times* examination, the agency had never done a comprehensive study of how often workers were killed by willful safety violations. *The Times* tried to identify every such workplace death in the last 20 years. It also tracked every prosecution, conviction and jail sentence that resulted from these deaths, and it tallied every civil fine. The deaths were the subject of 1,798 investigations, 1,242 of them by OSHA. The rest were done by the 21 states and one territory with their own versions of OSHA. But with a handful of exceptions these state agencies have been just as hesitant to seek prosecution as the federal OSHA. In all, *The Times* found 196 cases that were referred to state or federal prosecutors, resulting in 81 convictions and 16 jail sentences.

Mr. Henshaw declined to comment specifically on *The Times*'s findings but said he considered it a high priority to seek prosecution for willful violations that kill. "We have a law under the Occupational Safety and Health Act that gives us tools, both civil and criminal, to discharge our responsibility and to correct workplaces," he said. "And that's what we're trying to do."

HIGH HURDLES FROM WITHIN

When people at OSHA explain their reluctance to pursue criminal prosecutions, they sometimes begin by pointing to the example of Ronald J. McCann. Mr. McCann, acting regional administrator in Chicago during the early 1980's, was an early champion of criminal prosecutions. He had a simple, no-nonsense approach: If a death resulted from a willful violation, it should be referred to the Justice Department without delay.

But in the early days of the Reagan administration, he said in a recent interview, that policy brought a clear rebuke from OSHA's new political appointees. Twelve times he sought prosecutions. "They were all thrown out." Soon after, he said, he was removed from his job and transferred so often that he ended up living in a tent to avoid moving his family again.

"We wanted to stop people from killing," said Mr. McCann, now retired. "We wanted to make an example of those few people who do so much harm to society for their own personal gain."

But that impulse—which many OSHA inspectors clearly share—often runs headlong into a deeper instinct to avoid any action that might draw unwelcome scrutiny from Washington. That instinct is reinforced, many OSHA employees say, by an obscure but powerful arm of the Labor Department, the Office of the Solicitor, which oversees the work of the department's 500 or so lawyers.

The solicitor, a political appointee who reports to the labor secretary, makes the final decision on whether to refer a case to the Justice Department. Thomas Williamson Jr., the Labor Department's solicitor under President Bill Clinton, called the solicitor's office a "choke point control"—a mechanism to, among other things, protect the labor secretary's political flanks. And in Mr. Williamson's view, referring cases carries risks OSHA can ill afford. "You lose control of it," he explained. "You start accusing people of crimes and they get acquitted, you're going to destroy the credibility of the agency."

For his part, Mr. Phillips, the former regional administrator, said, "I had more fights with our solicitors than I did with any employer's attorneys."

Joseph M. Woodward, the top OSHA solicitor at the Labor Department, described his office's work as necessary and prudent. "These are cases where somebody has died and you're looking at maybe it was even a deliberate violation of the standard, so they're very high-priority cases," Mr. Woodward said. "It's a very serious charge, and you don't want to make it unless you think that it's warranted, and that you can prevail. So you analyze it under that much higher burden of proof."

But the practical result, current and former OSHA officials say, is that to have even a chance of referral, a case must clear an unwritten threshold that has little to do with actual legal requirements. In interviews, OSHA investigators used words like "smoke screen" and "snow job" to describe the legal objections they encounter. "It can't just be willful, it has to be obscenely willful," said Jeff Brooks, who spent 16 years as an inspector and supervisor before leaving the agency in 2001. "If they didn't purposely with malice seek to kill this person, then you don't prosecute."

What this means, they say, is that prosecutors often never even get to assess cases with compelling evidence of criminal wrongdoing. In 1998, for example, inspectors concluded that willful safety violations had resulted in a worker being crushed to death by a front-end loader in Beaver Falls, Pa. They found that the employer, Venango Environmental, had long known that the machine had defective brakes and steering. An administrative law judge called the case "replete with evidence" that Venango had committed willful safety violations. The case was not referred to prosecutors.

In interviews, a number of federal prosecutors said they would be happy to take on more of these cases. But Joseph A. Dear, who served as OSHA administrator under President Clinton, emphasized that such eagerness was not universal. "After you do all the work, get the file perfect," he said, "you take it to a U.S. attorney, and they say, 'It's a misdemeanor?'"

HUMAN LIFE VS. HARASSED BURRO

When Congress established OSHA in 1970, it made it a misdemeanor to cause the death of a worker by willfully violating safety laws. The maximum sentence, six months in jail, is half the maximum for harassing a wild burro on federal lands.

With more than 5,000 deaths on the job each year, safety experts and some members of Congress have long argued that hundreds of lives could be saved if employers faced a credible threat of prosecution. "A company official who willfully and recklessly violates federal OSHA laws stands a greater chance of winning a state lottery than being criminally charged," said a 1988 Congressional report. Actually, it overstated the odds for much of the country. During the two decades examined by *The Times,* in 17 states, the District of Columbia and three territories, there was not a single prosecution for willful violations that killed 423 workers.

There have been repeated efforts to make it a felony to cause a worker's death. But strong opposition from Republicans and many Democrats doomed every effort. Congress did, however, agree in 1984 as part of a broader sentencing reform package to raise the maximum criminal fine to $500,000 from $10,000. And in 1991, it raised civil fines. But the added deterrent appears modest.

From 1982 until 1991, the median fine for a willful violation that killed a worker was $5,800, according to *The Times* examination. Since 1991, the median has been $30,240.

A much less publicized change has actually eroded any remaining potential for prosecution. Starting in 1990, with a death at a Nebraska meatpacking plant, OSHA began to accede to employer demands that it replace the word "willful" with "unclassified" in citations involving workplace deaths. Unclassified was a term invented by lawyers who specialize in defending corporations against OSHA. Indeed, the word appears nowhere in the law or regulations governing OSHA. But the agency's field manual permits the "unclassified" designation when an employer is willing to correct unsafe conditions "but wishes to purge himself or herself of the adverse public perception attached to a willful" violation.

Mr. Woodward, the top OSHA solicitor, acknowledged that employers "might occasionally" push for unclassified violations to minimize criminal liability. But he defended the arrangement as a useful compromise. Companies, he explained, "might do everything in the world that you wanted them to do as far as fixing the problem and making the workplace safer for the workers." But the big sticking point, he said, was "they didn't want to admit willful."

Major corporations, and their lawyers, have been increasingly successful in persuading the agency to eliminate the word "willful," *The Times* found. The agency has done this even for employers who have repeatedly shown a deliberate disregard for safety laws, resulting in multiple deaths.

The effects of the new policy have been felt by families in several small towns around the country where, over the last decade, refineries and petrochemical plants either owned or co-owned by Shell Oil have blown up because of safety violations. Each town in turn was consumed by the disasters, the funerals and the cleanup. And every time, safety investigators would show up and dig in, filling thick files with the details of how management had disregarded known hazards. Often, the safety violations were exactly the same from plant to plant. And yet in each case, defense lawyers persuaded regulators to label the most flagrant violations unclassified.

In Belpre, Ohio, an explosion in 1994 killed three workers. OSHA called it a "runaway chemical reaction" and blamed poor training, inadequate maintenance, bad equipment and shoddy oversight. Anacortes, Wash., a small town on Puget Sound, shook from the explosions the day before Thanksgiving 1998. Necessary maintenance had been put off, investigators found, and pledges of safety improvements had been neglected. Six men died.

Almost three years later, in Delaware City, a crew was working near a tank filled with spent sulfuric acid at the Motiva Refinery, a plant with a long history of leaks, injuries and deaths. Managers had issued the work order despite employees' warnings that the tank was severely corroded and overdue for maintenance, according to court records and OSHA documents. A welding torch ignited leaking vapors, and the explosion flung Jeffrey Davis, 50, into the tank. The acid consumed all but the steel shanks of his boots. Then last year, a worker was killed at the Shell plant in Geismar, La. OSHA inspectors spent over 12,000 hours documenting a series of preventable safety violations. In all, Shell and partners paid $4.3 million in OSHA fines for the 11 deaths, sums too small to make a meaningful dent in Shell's earnings. There was no admission of wrongdoing, no referral to prosecutors.

"When you are talking settlement, essentially the rules go away," said Robert C. Gombar, a lawyer for Shell in the Anacortes and Delaware City explosions. Mr. Gombar's firm, McDermott, Will & Emery in Washington, advertises on its Web site that it "pioneered" the use of unclassified violations to avoid "unnecessary complication presented by harmful labels." In the Shell cases, Mr. Gombar said, the company simply persuaded OSHA that it should not cite any willful violations. "They know we'll litigate and we'll win," he said.

In a written statement, Shell said that it was treated no differently from any other company and that its "highest priority" was employee safety.

That was not the accountability many of the 11 families had envisioned. Dyna Fry had learned from the evening news that her husband, Woody, was among those killed in Anacortes. She became consumed with piecing together what happened. She said she yearned for a criminal trial so managers would be forced to "make eye contact with my family."

Other Shell widows and relatives felt the same way. "We would have worked in McDonald's for the rest of our lives if it meant anyone would go to jail for this," said Nicole M. Granfors, whose father, Ronald J. Granfors, was killed in Anacortes.

In Delaware, the state's congressman and senators wrote to Mr. Henshaw this year and demanded that he account for "OSHA's inexplicable decision" to reduce the violations in Delaware City. OSHA's handling of the case, they wrote, had compounded "the emotional trauma for the family." In response, OSHA's deputy administrator, R. Davis Layne, wrote that OSHA had simply "exercised its prosecutorial discretion" to settle a contested case. Families, he explained, are not consulted "regarding confidential litigation matters."

But if OSHA saw no potential for a criminal case, Delaware's attorney general, M. Jane Brady, did. In an interview, she recalled the stunned reaction of one Motiva lawyer when she announced her intention to seek charges: "You got to be kidding me."

This summer, Motiva pleaded no contest to criminally negligent homicide and assault, only the second such prosecution in state history. The company was ordered to pay $46,000 in fines, then the maximum under state law, and $250,000 more to a victims fund. Soon after, Delaware changed its law to allow far higher fines.

A RESPONSE BY THE STATES

Once the dominant regulator of workplace safety, the federal government is falling behind a growing number of states. At least four states now require safety inspectors to notify prosecutors of deaths caused by safety violations. Eleven states have increased prison terms beyond the six-month federal maximum. In Michigan, California and Arizona, it is now not only a crime to commit safety violations that kill but also to commit safety violations that cause severe injuries.

Again this year, there is talk of toughening the federal law. Three months ago, in an evaluation of OSHA's handling of deaths among immigrant workers, the Labor Department's inspector general recommended that OSHA study the potential deterrent effect of making it a felony to commit willful violations that kill. In Congress, Senator Jon S. Corzine, a New Jersey Democrat, is proposing legislation to increase the maximum sentence to 10 years from six months.

Like past efforts, this one will meet fierce resistance. "Obviously we're not going to support the expansion of criminal penalties," said Randel K. Johnson, vice president for labor issues at the United States Chamber of Commerce.

At OSHA, Mr. Henshaw recently ordered up some new metrics. After *The Times* sought comment about its analysis, he asked his agency to conduct its own. The results, his aides said, closely mirror those found by *The Times*. They argued, however, that 151 cases could not have been referred to federal prosecutors because the willful violations were of the employer's "general duty" to provide a safe workplace, not of a specific safety standard. Federal law, they said, does not permit referral in such cases. They conceded, though, that such cases could be referred to state and local prosecutors.

Nevertheless, Mr. Henshaw made it clear that he saw no need to change either the law or OSHA's handling of these worst cases of death on the job. "You have to remember," he said, "that our job is not to rack up the individual statistics that some people like to see. Our job is to correct the workplace."

THE U.K.'S "CORPORATE MANSLAUGHTER" STATUTE: BRITISH VERSUS AMERICAN APPROACHES TO MAKING FIRMS RESPONSIBLE FOR DEATHS RESULTING FROM GROSS NEGLIGENCE

Anthony J. Sebok

Last week, the British government agreed to introduce a new law titled the "Corporate Manslaughter Statute." This law is remarkable because it attempts to make companies—not persons—criminally responsible for deaths caused by a firm's gross negligence. In this column, I will examine the law's structure, its history, and finally, I will ask how American law approaches the same problems the Corporate Manslaughter Act is designed to solve.

THE CORPORATE MANSLAUGHTER ACT

The British law allows the state to prosecute a corporation or partnership (an "organization" for short) for the crime of manslaughter if the organization causes the death of a person as the result of its "gross" breach of a duty owed under the law of negligence. However, in order for the state to prove its case, it must prove that a substantial element of the gross breach of duty resulted from the way in which the organization's activities were "managed or organised by its senior management."

Source: Findlaw (www.findlaw.com), a Thomson Reuters business, July 31, 2007, http://writ.news .findlaw.com/sebok/20090731.html. Reproduced by written permission.

The penalties for violating the act are quite interesting. First, a court can impose unlimited financial penalties on the organization, once it is convicted. Second, a court may issue a "publicity order," which requires the organization to publicly announce (through advertisements, it seems) that it has been successfully prosecuted for corporate manslaughter and is subject to any other penalties the court may have ordered.

The third and final potential penalty is that the court can order the organization to publicly take remedial steps to correct the conditions that led to the breach of duty. This penalty could have potentially far-reaching consequences, depending on how the courts choose to interpret it. For example, under this remedy, suppose a court decides that a design defect was the result of conscious indifference to the safety of others (such as in the famous Ford Pinto case). The court could simply order a manufacturer to change the design of their product—a power that no American court currently possesses.

THE IMPETUS FOR THE BRITISH LAW:
SPECTACULAR AND DISTURBING ACCIDENTS

The most direct explanation for the advent of the British law is that there have been a number of spectacular industrial and transportation accidents in the United Kingdom since the Thatcher era of privatization. This is especially true in the area of rail traffic, where the public has become increasingly uneasy about the degree to which the private train operators who took over public lines have placed profit above the public good.

The Southall rail crash of 1997, in which 10 people died in a high-speed train in London, illustrated for many the weakness of the old laws. The company that operated the train, GWT, was prosecuted for common-law manslaughter, but the case failed, despite the voluminous evidence that there was a systematic failure of safety management. Similar disasters involving ferry wrecks and gas works explosions helped reinforce the impression that corporations were not answerable in court because senior management always pointed the finger at someone else.

BRITISH VERSUS AMERICAN LAW
ON CORPORATE RESPONSIBILITY

In the United States, as in England, it is very difficult to hold either organizations or their officers responsible for gross negligence. For example, while many law students learn about the success civil tort plaintiffs had in suing Ford for failing to spend $13 per car to strengthen a gas tank known to be vulnerable to rear-end collisions, few learn that, at the same time, a prosecutor brought a case in criminal negligence against Ford in Indiana—and lost the jury trial.

Government regulation and prosecutions could, in theory, lead to more effective deterrence, but the record suggests that they are not yet a sufficient deterrent force. The Occupational Safety and Health Act (OSHA) authorizes criminal penalties against companies that do not comply with OSHA's requirements. These penalties, on paper, look fearsome—up to a $250,000 fine for an individual, and up to a $500,000 fine for a corporation. But in reality, they are rarely assessed against corporate defendants.

The one thing America has that the United Kingdom does not, is punitive damages. Punitive damages serve, in many ways, the same purpose as the unlimited monetary fines authorized by the Corporate Manslaughter Act. In fact, it may merely be a coincidence, but it should be noted that Britain, through a series of High Court decisions, made it almost impossible for a court to impose punitive damages on a defendant (individual or organization) after 1976. Perhaps the new law is filling in a lacuna left by the retreat from punitive damages in the Commonwealth court systems.

Britain's Corporate Manslaughter Act and America's punitive damages system differ in one significant way, however. Since the Corporate Manslaughter Act is a *public* criminal law, no prosecution of an organization can occur without the permission of the Director of Public Prosecutions. On the other hand, in America, a tort plaintiff is the "master of his own complaint." He does not need permission from the state to pursue private punishment, although he does still need to persuade a jury of his version of the facts of the case and persuade a judge not to dismiss it for legal deficiencies.

In practice, the availability of punitive damages through the jury system places a tremendous amount of autonomy in the hands of private litigants and their lawyers, but the new British law does not really seem to view the lack of "victim autonomy" to be a problem. It may be that British lawmakers assume that the Director of Public Prosecutions will have an agenda that reflects the feelings of the true victims of organizational misfeasance. However, whether this is actually the case remains to be seen, and may become evident in the coming months or years.

In conclusion, the new Corporate Manslaughter Act is a fascinating experiment. Americans who are interested in deterring organizational wrongdoing should watch carefully to see how British judges apply the law, which prosecutions are and are not brought, and whether the law has a measurable, positive impact on either accident costs or liability costs. If the U.S. Supreme Court continues to cut back on the availability of punitive damages under state and federal law, perhaps the gap in deterrence—if there is one—created by the Supreme Court's recent decisions could, in the future, be filled by something like the Corporate Manslaughter Act.

THE CHECKLIST

Atul Gawande

On October 30, 1935, at Wright Air Field in Dayton, Ohio, the U.S. Army Air Corps held a flight competition for airplane manufacturers vying to build its next-generation long-range bomber. It wasn't supposed to be much of a competition. In early evaluations, the Boeing Corporation's gleaming aluminum-alloy Model 299 had trounced the designs of Martin and Douglas. Boeing's plane could carry five times as many bombs as the Army had requested; it could fly faster than previous bombers, and

Source: The *New Yorker,* December 10, 2007. Reprinted by permission of the author.

almost twice as far. A Seattle newspaperman who had glimpsed the plane called it the "flying fortress," and the name stuck. The flight "competition," according to the military historian Phillip Meilinger, was regarded as a mere formality. The Army planned to order at least sixty-five of the aircraft.

A small crowd of Army brass and manufacturing executives watched as the Model 299 test plane taxied onto the runway. It was sleek and impressive, with a hundred-and-three-foot wingspan and four engines jutting out from the wings, rather than the usual two. The plane roared down the tarmac, lifted off smoothly, and climbed sharply to three hundred feet. Then it stalled, turned on one wing, and crashed in a fiery explosion. Two of the five crew members died, including the pilot, Major Ployer P. Hill.

An investigation revealed that nothing mechanical had gone wrong. The crash had been due to "pilot error," the report said. Substantially more complex than previous aircraft, the new plane required the pilot to attend to the four engines, a retractable landing gear, new wing flaps, electric trim tabs that needed adjustment to maintain control at different airspeeds, and constant-speed propellers whose pitch had to be regulated with hydraulic controls, among other features. While doing all this, Hill had forgotten to release a new locking mechanism on the elevator and rudder controls. The Boeing model was deemed, as a newspaper put it, "too much airplane for one man to fly." The Army Air Corps declared Douglas's smaller design the winner. Boeing nearly went bankrupt.

Still, the Army purchased a few aircraft from Boeing as test planes, and some insiders remained convinced that the aircraft was flyable. So a group of test pilots got together and considered what to do.

They could have required Model 299 pilots to undergo more training. But it was hard to imagine having more experience and expertise than Major Hill, who had been the U.S. Army Air Corps' chief of flight testing. Instead, they came up with an ingeniously simple approach: they created a pilot's checklist, with step-by-step checks for takeoff, flight, landing, and taxiing. Its mere existence indicated how far aeronautics had advanced. In the early years of flight, getting an aircraft into the air might have been nerve-racking, but it was hardly complex. Using a checklist for takeoff would no more have occurred to a pilot than to a driver backing a car out of the garage. But this new plane was too complicated to be left to the memory of any pilot, however expert.

With the checklist in hand, the pilots went on to fly the Model 299 a total of 1.8 million miles without one accident. The Army ultimately ordered almost thirteen thousand of the aircraft, which it dubbed the B-17. And, because flying the behemoth was now possible, the Army gained a decisive air advantage in the Second World War which enabled its devastating bombing campaign across Nazi Germany.

Medicine today has entered its B-17 phase. Substantial parts of what hospitals do—most notably, intensive care—are now too complex for clinicians to carry them out reliably from memory alone. I.C.U. life support has become too much medicine for one person to fly.

Yet it's far from obvious that something as simple as a checklist could be of much help in medical care. Sick people are phenomenally more various than airplanes. A study of forty-one thousand trauma patients—just trauma patients—found that they had 1,224 different injury-related diagnoses in 32,261 unique combinations for teams to attend to. That's like having 32,261 kinds of airplane to land. Mapping out the proper steps for each is not possible, and physicians have been skeptical that a piece of paper with a bunch of little boxes would improve matters much.

In 2001, though, a critical-care specialist at Johns Hopkins Hospital named Peter Pronovost decided to give it a try. He didn't attempt to make the checklist cover everything; he designed it to tackle just one problem, the one that nearly killed Anthony DeFilippo: line infections. On a sheet of plain paper, he plotted out the steps to take in order to avoid infections when putting a line in. Doctors are supposed to (1) wash their hands with soap, (2) clean the patient's skin with chlorhexidine anti-septic, (3) put sterile drapes over the entire patient, (4) wear a sterile mask, hat, gown, and gloves, and (5) put a sterile dressing over the catheter site once the line is in. Check, check, check, check, check. These steps are no-brainers; they have been known and taught for years. So it seemed silly to make a checklist just for them. Still, Pronovost asked the nurses in his I.C.U. to observe the doctors for a month as they put lines into patients, and record how often they completed each step. In more than a third of patients, they skipped at least one.

The next month, he and his team persuaded the hospital administration to au-thorize nurses to stop doctors if they saw them skipping a step on the checklist; nurses were also to ask them each day whether any lines ought to be removed, so as not to leave them in longer than necessary. This was revolutionary. Nurses have al-ways had their ways of nudging a doctor into doing the right thing, ranging from the gentle reminder ("Um, did you forget to put on your mask, doctor?") to more force-ful methods (I've had a nurse bodycheck me when she thought I hadn't put enough drapes on a patient). But many nurses aren't sure whether this is their place, or whether a given step is worth a confrontation. (Does it really matter whether a patient's legs are draped for a line going into the chest?) The new rule made it clear: if doctors didn't follow every step on the checklist, the nurses would have backup from the administration to intervene.

Pronovost and his colleagues monitored what happened for a year afterward. The results were so dramatic that they weren't sure whether to believe them: the ten-day line-infection rate went from eleven per cent to zero. So they followed patients for fifteen more months. Only two line infections occurred during the entire period. They calculated that, in this one hospital, the checklist had prevented forty-three infections and eight deaths, and saved two million dollars in costs.

Pronovost recruited some more colleagues, and they made some more check-lists. One aimed to insure that nurses observe patients for pain at least once every four hours and provide timely pain medication. This reduced the likelihood of a patient's experiencing untreated pain from forty-one per cent to three per cent. They tested a checklist for patients on mechanical ventilation, making sure that, for instance, the head of each patient's bed was propped up at least thirty degrees so that oral secretions couldn't go into the windpipe, and antacid medication was given to prevent stomach ulcers. The proportion of patients who didn't receive the recommended care dropped from seventy per cent to four per cent; the occurrence of pneumonias fell by a quarter; and twenty-one fewer patients died than in the previous year. The researchers found that simply having the doctors and nurses in the I.C.U. make their own checklists for what they thought should be done each day improved the consistency of care to the point that, within a few weeks, the average length of patient stay in intensive care dropped by half.

The checklists provided two main benefits, Pronovost observed. First, they helped with memory recall, especially with mundane matters that are easily overlooked in patients undergoing more drastic events. (When you're worrying about what treatment to give a woman who won't stop seizing, it's hard to remember to make sure that the head of her bed is in the right position.) A second effect was to make explicit the minimum, expected steps in complex processes. Pronovost was surprised to discover how often even experienced personnel failed to grasp the importance of certain precautions. In a survey of I.C.U. staff taken before introducing the ventilator checklists, he found that half hadn't realized that there was evidence strongly supporting giving ventilated patients antacid medication. Checklists established a higher standard of baseline performance.

These are, of course, ridiculously primitive insights. Pronovost is routinely described by colleagues as "brilliant," "inspiring," a "genius." He has an M.D. and a Ph.D. in public health from Johns Hopkins, and is trained in emergency medicine, anesthesiology, and critical-care medicine. But, really, does it take all that to figure out what house movers, wedding planners, and tax accountants figured out ages ago?

Pronovost is hardly the first person in medicine to use a checklist. But he is among the first to recognize its power to save lives and take advantage of the breadth of its possibilities. Forty-two years old, with cropped light-brown hair, tenth-grader looks, and a fluttering, finchlike energy, he is an odd mixture of the nerdy and the messianic. He grew up in Waterbury, Connecticut, the son of an elementary-school teacher and a math professor, went to nearby Fairfield University, and, like many good students, decided that he would go into medicine. Unlike many students, though, he found that he actually liked caring for sick people. He hated the laboratory—with all those micropipettes and cell cultures, and no patients around—but he had that scientific "How can I solve this unsolved problem?" turn of mind. So after his residency in anesthesiology and his fellowship in critical care, he studied clinical-research methods.

For his doctoral thesis, he examined intensive-care units in Maryland, and he discovered that putting an intensivist on staff reduced death rates by a third. It was the first time that someone had demonstrated the public-health value of using intensivists. He wasn't satisfied with having proved his case, though; he wanted hospitals to change accordingly. After his study was published, in 1999, he met with a coalition of large employers known as the Leapfrog Group. It included companies like General Motors and Verizon, which were seeking to improve the standards of hospitals where their employees obtain care. Within weeks, the coalition announced that its members expected the hospitals they contracted with to staff their I.C.U.s with intensivists. These employers pay for health care for thirty-seven million employees, retirees, and dependents nationwide. So although hospitals protested that there weren't enough intensivists to go around, and that the cost could be prohibitive, Pronovost's idea effectively became an instant national standard.

The scientist in him has always made room for the campaigner. People say he is the kind of guy who, even as a trainee, could make you feel you'd saved the world every time you washed your hands properly. "I've never seen anybody inspire as he

does," Marty Makary, a Johns Hopkins surgeon, told me. "Partly, he has this conta-
gious, excitable nature. He has a smile that's tough to match. But he also has a way of
making people feel heard. People will come to him with the dumbest ideas, and he'll
endorse them anyway. 'Oh, I like that, I like that, I like that!' he'll say. I've watched
him, and I still have no idea how deliberate this is. Maybe he really does like every
idea. But wait, and you realize: he only acts on the ones he truly believes in."

After the checklist results, the idea Pronovost truly believed in was that checklists could save enormous numbers of lives. He took his findings on the road, showing
his checklists to doctors, nurses, insurers, employers—anyone who would listen. He
spoke in an average of seven cities a month while continuing to work full time in
Johns Hopkins's I.C.U.s. But this time he found few takers.

There were various reasons. Some physicians were offended by the suggestion
that they needed checklists. Others had legitimate doubts about Pronovost's evidence. So far, he'd shown only that checklists worked in one hospital, Johns Hopkins,
where the I.C.U.s have money, plenty of staff, and Peter Pronovost walking the
hallways to make sure that the checklists are being used properly. How about in the
real world—where I.C.U. nurses and doctors are in short supply, pressed for time,
overwhelmed with patients, and hardly receptive to the idea of filling out yet another
piece of paper?

In 2003, however, the Michigan Health and Hospital Association asked
Pronovost to try out three of his checklists in Michigan's I.C.U.s. It would be a huge
undertaking. Not only would he have to get the state's hospitals to use the checklists;
he would also have to measure whether doing so made a genuine difference. But at last
Pronovost had a chance to establish whether his checklist idea really worked.

This past summer, I visited Sinai-Grace Hospital, in inner-city Detroit, and
saw what Pronovost was up against. Occupying a campus of red brick buildings
amid abandoned houses, check-cashing stores, and wig shops on the city's West
Side, just south of 8 Mile Road, Sinai-Grace is a classic urban hospital. It has eight
hundred physicians, seven hundred nurses, and two thousand other medical personnel to care for a population with the lowest median income of any city in the country. More than a quarter of a million residents are uninsured; three hundred thousand
are on state assistance. That has meant chronic financial problems. Sinai-Grace is
not the most cash-strapped hospital in the city—that would be Detroit Receiving
Hospital, where a fifth of the patients have no means of payment. But between 2000
and 2003 Sinai-Grace and eight other Detroit hospitals were forced to cut a third of
their staff, and the state had to come forward with a fifty-million-dollar bailout to
avert their bankruptcy.

Sinai-Grace has five I.C.U.s for adult patients and one for infants. Hassan
Makki, the director of intensive care, told me what it was like there in 2004, when
Pronovost and the hospital association started a series of mailings and conference calls
with hospitals to introduce checklists for central lines and ventilator patients. "Morale
was low," he said. "We had lost lots of staff, and the nurses who remained weren't
sure if they were staying." Many doctors were thinking about leaving, too. Meanwhile,
the teams faced an even heavier workload because of new rules limiting how long the
residents could work at a stretch. Now Pronovost was telling them to find the time to
fill out some daily checklists?

Tom Piskorowski, one of the I.C.U. physicians, told me his reaction: "Forget the paperwork. Take care of the patient."

I accompanied a team on 7 A.M. rounds through one of the surgical I.C.U.s. It had eleven patients. Four had gunshot wounds (one had been shot in the chest; one had been shot through the bowel, kidney, and liver; two had been shot through the neck, and left quadriplegic). Five patients had cerebral hemorrhaging (three were seventy-nine years and older and had been injured falling down stairs; one was a middle-aged man whose skull and left temporal lobe had been damaged by an assault with a blunt weapon; and one was a worker who had become paralyzed from the neck down after falling twenty-five feet off a ladder onto his head). There was a cancer patient recovering from surgery to remove part of his lung, and a patient who had had surgery to repair a cerebral aneurysm.

The doctors and nurses on rounds tried to proceed methodically from one room to the next but were constantly interrupted: a patient they thought they'd stabilized began hemorrhaging again; another who had been taken off the ventilator developed trouble breathing and had to be put back on the machine. It was hard to imagine that they could get their heads far enough above the daily tide of disasters to worry about the minutiae on some checklist.

Yet there they were, I discovered, filling out those pages. Mostly, it was the nurses who kept things in order. Each morning, a senior nurse walked through the unit, clipboard in hand, making sure that every patient on a ventilator had the bed propped at the right angle, and had been given the right medicines and the right tests. Whenever doctors put in a central line, a nurse made sure that the central-line checklist had been filled out and placed in the patient's chart. Looking back through their files, I found that they had been doing this faithfully for more than three years.

Pronovost had been canny when he started. In his first conversations with hospital administrators, he didn't order them to use the checklists. Instead, he asked them simply to gather data on their own infection rates. In early 2004, they found, the infection rates for I.C.U. patients in Michigan hospitals were higher than the national average, and in some hospitals dramatically so. Sinai-Grace experienced more line infections than seventy-five per cent of American hospitals. Meanwhile, Blue Cross Blue Shield of Michigan agreed to give hospitals small bonus payments for participating in Pronovost's program. A checklist suddenly seemed an easy and logical thing to try.

In what became known as the Keystone Initiative, each hospital assigned a project manager to roll out the checklists and participate in a twice-monthly conference call with Pronovost for trouble-shooting. Pronovost also insisted that each participating hospital assign to each unit a senior hospital executive, who would visit the unit at least once a month, hear people's complaints, and help them solve problems.

The executives were reluctant. They normally lived in meetings worrying about strategy and budgets. They weren't used to venturing into patient territory and didn't feel that they belonged there. In some places, they encountered hostility. But their involvement proved crucial. In the first month, according to Christine Goeschel, at the time the Keystone Initiative's director, the executives discovered that the chlorhexidine soap, shown to reduce line infections, was available in fewer than a third of the

I.C.U.s. This was a problem only an executive could solve. Within weeks, every I.C.U. in Michigan had a supply of the soap. Teams also complained to the hospital officials that the checklist required that patients be fully covered with a sterile drape when lines were being put in, but full-size barrier drapes were often unavailable. So the officials made sure that the drapes were stocked. Then they persuaded Arrow International, one of the largest manufacturers of central lines, to produce a new central-line kit that had both the drape and chlorhexidine in it.

In December, 2006, the Keystone Initiative published its findings in a landmark article in *The New England Journal of Medicine.* Within the first three months of the project, the infection rate in Michigan's I.C.U.s decreased by sixty-six per cent. The typical I.C.U.—including the ones at Sinai-Grace Hospital—cut its quarterly infection rate to zero. Michigan's infection rates fell so low that its average I.C.U. outperformed ninety per cent of I.C.U.s nationwide. In the Keystone Initiative's first eighteen months, the hospitals saved an estimated hundred and seventy-five million dollars in costs and more than fifteen hundred lives. The successes have been sustained for almost four years—all because of a stupid little checklist.

Pronovost's results have not been ignored. He has since had requests to help Rhode Island, New Jersey, and the country of Spain do what Michigan did. Back in the Wolverine State, he and the Keystone Initiative have begun testing half a dozen additional checklists to improve care for I.C.U. patients. He has also been asked to develop a program for surgery patients. It has all become more than he and his small group of researchers can keep up with.

But consider: there are hundreds, perhaps thousands, of things doctors do that are at least as dangerous and prone to human failure as putting central lines into I.C.U. patients. It's true of cardiac care, stroke treatment, H.I.V. treatment, and surgery of all kinds. It's also true of diagnosis, whether one is trying to identify cancer or infection or a heart attack. All have steps that are worth putting on a checklist and testing in routine care. The question—still unanswered—is whether medical culture will embrace the opportunity.

Tom Wolfe's "The Right Stuff" tells the story of our first astronauts, and charts the demise of the maverick, Chuck Yeager test-pilot culture of the nineteen-fifties. It was a culture defined by how unbelievably dangerous the job was. Test pilots strapped themselves into machines of barely controlled power and complexity, and a quarter of them were killed on the job. The pilots had to have focus, daring, wits, and an ability to improvise—the right stuff. But as knowledge of how to control the risks of flying accumulated—as checklists and flight simulators became more prevalent and sophisticated—the danger diminished, values of safety and conscientiousness prevailed, and the rock-star status of the test pilots was gone.

Something like this is going on in medicine. We have the means to make some of the most complex and dangerous work we do—in surgery, emergency care, and I.C.U. medicine—more effective than we ever thought possible. But the prospect pushes against the traditional culture of medicine, with its central belief that in situations of high risk and complexity what you want is a kind of expert audacity—the right stuff, again. Checklists and standard operating procedures feel like exactly the opposite, and that's what rankles many people.

It's ludicrous, though, to suppose that checklists are going to do away with the need for courage, wits, and improvisation. The body is too intricate and individual for that: good medicine will not be able to dispense with expert audacity. Yet it should also be ready to accept the virtues of regimentation.

The still limited response to Pronovost's work may be easy to explain, but it is hard to justify. If someone found a new drug that could wipe out infections with anything remotely like the effectiveness of Pronovost's lists, there would be television ads with Robert Jarvik extolling its virtues, detail men offering free lunches to get doctors to make it part of their practice, government programs to research it, and competitors jumping in to make a newer, better version. That's what happened when manufacturers marketed central-line catheters coated with silver or other antimicrobials; they cost a third more, and reduced infections only slightly—and hospitals have spent tens of millions of dollars on them. But, with the checklist, what we have is Peter Pronovost trying to see if maybe, in the next year or two, hospitals in Rhode Island and New Jersey will give his idea a try.

Pronovost remains, in a way, an odd bird in medical research. He does not have the multimillion-dollar grants that his colleagues in bench science have. He has no swarm of doctoral students and lab animals. He's focussed on work that is not normally considered a significant contribution in academic medicine. As a result, few other researchers are venturing to extend his achievements. Yet his work has already saved more lives than that of any laboratory scientist in the past decade.

I called Pronovost recently at Johns Hopkins, where he was on duty in an I.C.U. I asked him how long it would be before the average doctor or nurse is as apt to have a checklist in hand as a stethoscope (which, unlike checklists, has never been proved to make a difference to patient care).

"At the current rate, it will never happen," he said, as monitors beeped in the background. "The fundamental problem with the quality of American medicine is that we've failed to view delivery of health care as a science. The tasks of medical science fall into three buckets. One is understanding disease biology. One is finding effective therapies. And one is insuring those therapies are delivered effectively. That third bucket has been almost totally ignored by research funders, government, and academia. It's viewed as the art of medicine. That's a mistake, a huge mistake. And from a taxpayer's perspective it's outrageous." We have a thirty-billion-dollar-a-year National Institutes of Health, he pointed out, which has been a remarkable powerhouse of discovery. But we have no billion-dollar National Institute of Health Care Delivery studying how best to incorporate those discoveries into daily practice.

I asked him how much it would cost for him to do for the whole country what he did for Michigan. About two million dollars, he said, maybe three, mostly for the technical work of signing up hospitals to participate state by state and coordinating a database to track the results. He's already devised a plan to do it in all of Spain for less.

"We could get I.C.U. checklists in use throughout the United States within two years, if the country wanted it," he said.

So far, it seems, we don't. The United States could have been the first to adopt medical checklists nationwide, but, instead, Spain will beat us. "I at least hope we're not the last," Pronovost said.

POPCORN LUNG COMING TO YOUR KITCHEN? THE FDA DOESN'T WANT TO KNOW

David Michaels

For the past several years, news articles and Congressional hearings have reported on a deadly, irreversible lung disease—bronchiolitis obliterans—that is caused by workers' exposure to food flavoring chemicals, and more specifically by exposure to a butter-flavoring chemical called diacetyl. So far, attention has focused on worker exposure, rather than on possible health problems affecting consumers who pop popcorn in their microwave ovens. That focus may be changing, however, with a warning sent by one of the country's leading lung disease experts.

The CDC, FDA, OSHA, EPA—federal agencies charged with protecting public health—each received a letter in July alerting them to the possible serious respiratory hazard to *consumers* who breathe in fumes from their artificially butter-flavored microwave popcorn. The warning should have resulted in some action by these agencies, but instead, they've done virtually nothing.

It appears that the Bush Administration's efforts to destroy the regulatory system are succeeding; the agencies seem unable to mount a response to information that a well-functioning regulatory system would immediately pursue. The agencies aren't even trying to connect the dots.

In July, Dr. Cecile Rose the chief occupational and environmental medicine physician at National Jewish Medical and Research Center, the most prestigious lung disease hospital in the country, wrote to the FDA, CDC, EPA and OSHA, informing the agencies of a patient she had recently identified "with significant lung disease whose clinical findings are similar to those described in affected workers, but whose only inhalational exposure is as a heavy, daily consumer of butter flavored microwave popcorn."

This letter is a red flag, suggesting that exposure to food flavor chemicals is not just killing workers, but may also be causing disease in people exposed to food flavor chemicals in their kitchens.

In the last seven years, dozens of workers have developed the rare and sometimes fatal disease bronchiolitis obliterans (BO)—also known as "popcorn lung." The sick workers were employed in factories where diacetyl, the primary ingredient in artificial butter flavor, was manufactured or applied to food. Most of these cases have been seen in microwave popcorn factories. Last week, one of the country's largest popcorn makers announced it was eliminating diacetyl from its butter flavor.

Since I first wrote about the failure of OSHA to protect food industry workers from this deadly exposure, I have been asked by dozens of reporters whether it is safe to pop microwave popcorn at home. I explain that there is no evidence that it is dangerous to breathe the chemicals that come out of popcorn bags after they are

Source: The Pump Handle public health blog, Sept 4, 2007. All emphasis is from the original. Reprinted by permission of David Michaels, The George Washington University School of Public Health.

microwaved, but that the issue has not been studied, so I can't say that it is safe. My colleagues and I at the Project on Scientific Knowledge and Public Policy have been doing our best to push the relevant federal agencies into investigating the problem.

We have not been alone. In the last year, the question of consumer exposure has come up in countless media reports and several congressional hearings, and a powerful member of Congress has raised the issue directly with the Commissioner of the FDA.

Given this background, one would expect the relevant federal agencies to respond quickly to what may be the first documented case of lung disease caused by consumer exposure to artificial butter flavor. What we are faced with, however, is a failure of those agencies to take action, a sign that something is seriously wrong with our public health system. The letter from Dr. Rose should have been sufficient to raise concerns at the agencies involved. There are few physicians in the country who have more experience with lung disease caused by food flavor chemicals than Dr. Rose; she has been a consultant to the Flavor and Extract Manufacturers Association (FEMA)—the association of companies that make food flavorings—for more than a decade and helped develop the industry's Respiratory Safety Program.

Later in this post, I detail the response of each agency. First, it is worth looking at Dr. Rose's letter, in which she described the ways in which this patient's condition resembled that of the workers who developed lung disease after exposure to flavor chemicals, and the reasoning that went into her decision to alert the regulatory agencies:

1. The patient described progressively worsening respiratory symptoms of cough and shortness of breath. Extensive medical, occupational and environmental history taking did not reveal a known cause for these symptoms. The patient did report daily consumption of several bags of extra butter flavored microwave popcorn for several years.
2. Serial pulmonary function testing revealed progressively worsening fixed airflow limitation without a bronchodilator response and with a normal diffusion capacity for carbon monoxide. This is the pattern of lung physiologic abnormalities described in affected workers.
3. High resolution chest CT scan showed bronchial wall thickening, bronchiectasis, mosaic attenuation and expiratory air trapping. This appearance is similar to the imaging abnormalities reported in affected microwave popcorn factory workers.
4. Lung biopsy showed diffuse hyperinflation, a relative absence of small airways, and bronchioles in various stages of obliteration, findings of bronchiolitis obliterans (BO).
5. The patient's clinical course has been consistent with that described in microwave popcorn factory workers with BO, with a progressive decline in FEV (Forced Expiratory Volume in the first second, a marker of airflow obstruction) despite treatment with oral corticosteroids. His lung function appears to have stabilized recently with cessation of exposure to butter flavored microwave popcorn.
6. We measured airborne levels of diacetyl during microwave popcorn preparation in the patient's home and found levels similar to those reported in the microwave oven exhaust area in the quality assurance unit of the microwave popcorn manufacturing plant where affected workers were initially described.

This letter represents more than the report of a single isolated case of BO in a person who happens to eat a lot of extra-buttery microwave popcorn. The report comes after years of evidence that diacetyl causes BO in workers at factories where the chemical is produced, mixed and applied to food products. We don't know, in other words, whether this is an unfortunate coincidence or the first identified case of BO among popcorn consumers. It is possible that there are other people who have BO or another, less severe diacetyl-caused obstructive lung disease, but who are being treated by their own personal physicians who do not have Dr. Rose's expertise and familiarity with the outbreak of BO in food industry workers. Are there more cases out there? We don't know, but now is the time to find out.

In her letter, Dr. Rose acknowledged that it is difficult to make judgments based on a single case, but, given "the public health implications" of the possibility this patient's illness was caused by his exposure to butter flavor chemicals at home, she did what any dedicated public health practitioner would do: she notified the agencies that are supposed to protect the public health.

And that's where things seen to have stopped.

The receipt of Dr. Rose's letter is the moment where the FDA, or the CDC, should have said "Whoa! Here is an indication that the problem may go beyond workplaces." The agencies have never looked for BO cases among people who are heavy consumers of popcorn at home, but now they could issue an alert, requesting information from lung disease specialists around the country. Or they could have called a meeting of the technical directors of the popcorn manufacturers to learn about what they know about consumer exposures, especially about the levels of diacetyl released when popcorn with extra butter flavor is popped in a microwave oven. (Documents released by the EPA suggest that ConAgra, manufacturer of the Orville Redenbacher brand, may know quite a lot). At minimum, they could have asked Dr. Rose for more information.

None of the agencies did anything like this. In fact, **their failure to respond adequately is a sign that our public health protection system is in dire need of repair.**

Here's a brief review of what each agency is doing (or not doing) about food flavor chemicals, and, according to Dr. Rose, how they responded (or didn't respond) to the letter.

1. THE FOOD AND DRUG ADMINISTRATION (FDA)

The FDA has been asked several times to examine whether breathing diacetyl poses a risk to consumers. Each time, the agency has refused. Last September, SKAPP petitioned the FDA to remove diacetyl from the "Generally Regarded As Safe" (GRAS) list, pointing out that "there is compelling evidence that breathing diacetyl vapors causes lung disease and there is no evidence of a safe exposure level." In March 2007, the FDA wrote us back, essentially blowing us off.

Then, in May 2007, Congresswoman Rosa L. DeLauro (D-CT), chair of the House of Representatives Appropriations subcommittee that funds the FDA, urged the agency "to consider revoking the generally safe designation for diacetyl and removing it from the market until further testing is completed." FDA Commissioner von

Eschenbach refused to commit the FDA to do anything other than monitor the situation, and there is no evidence they are even doing this.

Frustrated by the FDA's continued failure to take action, Rep. DeLauro added language to the report that accompanied the Agriculture Appropriations Bill, directing the FDA to submit a report on its diacetyl research plan to the committee within 90 days of enactment.

What did the FDA do when it received Dr. Rose's letter in July? According to Dr. Rose, FDA attorneys asked that she resubmit her letter to the docket that has been created for our petition, since evidently, the FDA . . . office to which the letter was sent didn't feel they could do it themselves. (This is the reason the letter is dated July 18th but date stamped August 21, the day it was entered into the docket.)

2. THE ENVIRONMENTAL PROTECTION AGENCY (EPA)

As readers of *The Pump Handle* know from repeated posts on the subject, some time in 2003, the EPA announced that a study on the chemicals released in the popping and opening of packages of microwave popcorn was underway and was expected to be completed by the end of that year (2003). The results of that study still have not been released, although the results have been shared with popcorn manufacturers.

In July, 2006, I wrote to EPA Administrator Stephen L. Johnson, asking for expedited release of the study and objecting to the preferential treatment given to industry. The EPA responded that the study had undergone internal and external review and would soon be sent to industry "solely to ensure that no confidential business information is released." The agency planned to submit the paper to a scientific journal in fall 2006 and anticipated publication by mid-2007.

The scientific community and the public are still waiting for the result. However, last week, the owner of one of the country's leading popcorn manufacturers cited the EPA study as one of the reasons his firm was now selling a butter flavor popcorn made without diacetyl.

What did the EPA do when it received Dr. Rose's letter in July? According to Dr. Rose, the EPA thanked her and said it would treat the letter as a submission under section 8e of the Toxic Substances Control Act. Under this law, the EPA collects and compiles reports on adverse effects of chemicals. At one time, the agency promptly posted them on its website so the reports could be read by interested parties. But the EPA has evidently stopped posting—the last 8e submission posted on the EPA website was submitted in June 2006. So Dr. Rose's letter is apparently collecting dust in some large pile of paper where it apparently remains, unlikely to be released to the public for who knows how long.

3. THE CENTERS FOR DISEASE CONTROL AND PREVENTION (CDC)

Although its mission is "to promote health and quality of life by preventing and controlling disease, injury, and disability," the CDC is not a regulatory agency. It does play a central role in investigating the causes of illnesses and in alerting the public and medical communities about ways to prevent diseases from occurring.

The National Institute for Occupational Safety and Health (NIOSH), a branch of the CDC, has done terrific work investigating the causes of lung disease among flavor workers.

As of last week, CDC had not responded to the letter.

4. THE OCCUPATIONAL SAFETY AND HEALTH ADMINISTRATION (OSHA)

OSHA is charged with protecting the health of workers, so the information in this letter wasn't particularly relevant to their work. Last July, two unions petitioned OSHA for a standard that would protect workers from diacetyl exposure. Dozens of leading scientists supported the petition.

The failure of OSHA to take even minimal steps in the face of a clear and present hazard (dozens of sick workers in popcorn and flavor factories) has been the subject of scathing newspaper articles and editorials and two congressional hearings.

The House of Representatives will soon consider legislation, already passed by the House Education and Labor Committee, requiring OSHA to issue an emergency standard for diacetyl 90 days after the legislation is enacted. FEMA, the flavor industry's trade association, supports the legislation.

The Bush Administration, needless to say, opposes the legislation, and there still is no indication OSHA is actually working on a standard. The only sign of life so far out of OSHA was the recent announcement of a "National Emphasis Program" aimed at popcorn factories. Given that most new cases appear to be occurring in the factories that produce the flavorings used in the production of popcorn and other food products, this is simply too little too late.

Perhaps because Dr. Rose's letter did not contain any information that required OSHA to do anything (it was limited to a report on consumer rather than worker exposure), OSHA evidently did respond promptly, thanking Dr. Rose for her letter.

At one time, the US regulatory agencies were the envy of the world. The agencies were staffed with the best scientists, who did their best to ensure that preventable diseases were actually prevented.

Sadly, much has changed. The newspapers are filled with reports of political hacks running the agencies, over ruling the decisions of career scientists in order to protect perceived corporate interests. The White House Office of Management and Budget has erected a series of barriers impeding those agencies that still want to issue any new measures that will protect the public from pollution and dangerous products.

The anti-regulatory fervor of the Bush Administration is so great that agencies like OSHA will not step in to regulate even when it is requested to by responsible industry, as in this case where the flavor industry supports legislation that will force OSHA to issue a diacetyl standard.

Sadly, the damage to the agencies has been severe. **The anti-regulation policies coming from the White House and the political hacks running the agencies have taken their toll. The agencies have fewer staff and fewer resources. Morale is at its lowest. Many of the best scientists have left and are not being replaced.**

The public will pay the price, for many years to come. Repairing our system of public health protection will be one of the most difficult challenges faced by the next Administration.

UPDATE (9/4/07):

In statement issued today, FEMA [Flavor and Extract Manufacturer's Association] has recommended that "its members who manufacture butter flavors containing diacetyl for use in microwave popcorn consider reducing the diacetyl content of these flavors to the extent possible."

UPDATE (9/5/07):

We've gotten several comments and emails about people who have experienced irritation or difficulty breathing when microwave popcorn is popped. If you are concerned about symptoms you are experiencing, you should discuss them with your doctor; OSHA has posted information that may be useful to physicians.

DEATH SENTENCES IN CHINESE MILK CASE

David Barboza

BEIJING—Chinese courts sentenced two men to death on Thursday for endangering public safety in a tainted-milk scandal that killed at least six children, according to state-run news media. Three other defendants, including a top dairy company executive, were sentenced to life in prison. Another defendant received a suspended death sentence, and 15 others were given prison terms from 2 to 15 years.

The sentences were the first to be handed down in one of the worst food safety scandals in China in decades. The scandals erupted in September, prompting a global recall of Chinese-made dairy products, shaking consumer confidence and devastating the nation's dairy industry.

Some lawyers and victims have accused Beijing of failing to regulate the nation's dairy industry properly. Some critics believe that the government covered up the scandal until after the Olympic Games in Beijing in August.

The Intermediate People's Court in Shijiazhuang, in the northern province of Hebei, said the defendants had intentionally produced or sold dairy products laced with a toxic chemical called melamine, which was used to create the illusion of a higher protein count, but which caused kidney stones and other ailments in about 300,000 children last year.

Zhang Yujun, whom the government called one of the "principal criminals" in the scandal, was sentenced to death. He was convicted of selling 600 tons of melamine-tainted "protein powder" to dairy companies. Another dairy producer, Geng Jinpin, also received the death penalty. A third man, Gao Junjie, received the death penalty with a two-year reprieve, meaning he could be spared execution.

Tian Wenhua, 66, the former chairwoman of the Sanlu Group, one of China's largest dairy companies, was sentenced to life in prison for her failure to stop producing and selling the tainted goods even after her company learned they were flawed. Ms. Tian is the highest-ranking corporate executive to have been brought to trial in the scandal. She pleaded guilty in December and was also fined about $3 million. All the deaths in the scandal so far have been linked to Sanlu, which was found to have sold the milk products with the highest melamine concentrations.

"The sentence against Tian Wenhua is too harsh," Liu Xinwei, Ms. Tian's defense lawyer, said after the verdict, adding, "I don't agree her criminal circumstances were that grave and serious involving this case." Three other former executives at Sanlu were sentenced to 5 to 15 years in prison. One of them, Wang Yuliang, appeared in court in December in a wheelchair after what the Chinese state-run news media said was a failed suicide attempt. He received a 15-year sentence. Two other men who sold tainted protein powder, Zhang Yanzhang and Xue Jianzhong, were sentenced to prison for life, the state-run news agency, Xinhua, reported.

Parents of some victims protested outside the courthouse in Shijiazhuang, where Sanlu is based, saying they were dissatisfied with the verdicts. "I feel sorry for them, but they are just scapegoats," said Liu Donglin, 28, who said his 21-month-old son had kidney stones after drinking tainted milk formula. "The ones who should take the responsibility are the government."

Readings on . . . And the Poor Get Prison

EDITORS' INTRODUCTION

Chapter 3 of *The Rich Get Richer* examines the processes by which our prisons and jails have come to be predominantly occupied by those from the lowest social and economic classes. Following Chapter 2's argument that the criminal law fails to prohibit many serious harmful acts done by the well-off, Chapter 3 argues that the criminal justice system "weeds out the wealthy" and functions in such a way that, for similar crimes, the poor are (1) more likely to be arrested, (2) more likely to be charged, (3) more likely to be convicted, and (4) more likely to be sentenced to longer prison sentences than members of the middle and upper classes. To supplement the little data on class and economic bias in the criminal justice system, the authors also use data on racial disparities, which they argue can be used as a proxy for low economic class because African Americans are disproportionately poor.

"Race at Work: Realities of Race and Criminal Record in the NYC Job Market" reports on a study of hiring decisions, using as testers two groups of job applicants who had been matched for qualifications and varied only in race and the presence of a felony conviction. Authors Devah Pager and Bruce Western found that "employers view minority job applicants as essentially equivalent to whites just out of prison." *The Rich Get Richer* contends that racial discrimination occurs at all steps in the criminal justice process from arrest to sentencing, and that such discrimination, while an evil in its own right, works as well as a mechanism of class bias since blacks who are subjected to the criminal justice system tend be roughly as poor as whites who are subjected to the system. That racial discrimination continues in hiring decisions confirms the continued presence of racial discrimination in U.S. society, and leads to the expectation that it will be found in the criminal justice system as well. The article also supports claims in *The Rich Get Richer* about the bias against ex-cons that makes it difficult for offenders who have paid their debts to society to succeed at going straight. (The Conclusion of this reader includes further discussion of policies to promote reintegration by reducing employment discrimination.)

"Why It Matters: The Connection of 'Driving While Black' to Other Issues of Criminal Justice and Race" is part of an article by David A. Harris reporting the results of studies showing that black drivers are far more frequently stopped by the police than white drivers, and they are often subjected to time-consuming and humiliating searches. Such studies have been reported in *The Rich Get Richer* as evidence of the pervasiveness of racial discrimination in the criminal justice system. Readers may think that being stopped by the police on the highway is a minor bother. This selection goes a great distance to counter this impression by focusing on the broader significance of racial discrimination by the police in traffic stops. The author contends that these practices show that the police effectively treat being black as evidence of probable criminality. However, since most of the stops are done in search of illicit drugs and evidence shows that illegal drug use is no more prevalent among blacks than whites, the disproportionate stopping of blacks cannot be justified as rational police policy. Moreover, since most of the black drivers stopped turn out to be innocent, the racially motivated stops amount to punishment of the innocent. The author contends as well that the practice spreads cynicism about the police, and about the entire criminal justice system, among African Americans. And he argues the practice is unfair even to those few blacks stopped who turn out to possess illegal drugs because of the negative impact the arrest record can have and because of the harm done to communities by so many people being locked up (a topic discussed in Chapter 1 of this reader).

"Ebbers' 25 Year Sentence for Worldcom Fraud Upheld. Good" is a blog entry in response to arguments that Bernard Ebbers' sentence for fraud was too harsh. Paul Leighton's blog is useful for reasons that go beyond understanding this particular criminal process, because it goes deeply into the way sentences are determined. In this case, the probation department submitted to the judge a presentence report that recommended a 30-year sentence. This was based on applying the sentencing guidelines grid that determines a base level for a given offense, and the determination then allows increases and decreases in levels for factors that show the crime to be more or less than normally severe, and other factors, such as whether the offender cooperated with the prosecution and the offender's medical condition. The judge declared a sentence of 25 years, below the guidelines-based recommendation. Nonetheless, this is a longer sentence than some that are given for causing loss of life. Here the blog poses the interesting question of how to evaluate the gravity of a white-collar crime that doesn't lead to loss of life but to a loss of $100 million to more than 50 victims. The blog also points out that, though the sentences given to Ebbers and to Andy Fastow of Enron fame sound severe, they are still more lenient than sentences given out to lower-class crooks, and much lower than sentences given out under three-strikes-and-you're-out laws.

The central contention of Chapter 3 of *The Rich Get Richer* is that the criminal justice system treats poor people who do harmful acts more harshly than rich people who do harmful acts. As the depth and cost of the current financial crisis become clearer, it is evident that large numbers of well-off people were responsible for actions that have caused loss of people's life savings (as stocks and bonds rapidly lose value) and loss of jobs (as businesses, unable to obtain credit, close their doors). It will be some time before we can assess the extent to which parties responsible for these harmful behaviors will be penalized through legal mechanisms. But because this is one of the most significant financial events since the Great Depression—and one that affects us all—an important first step is understanding the process that has led us to this point. Indeed, understanding the causes of the crisis is key to fixing the system. As Nobel prize–winning economist Joseph Stiglitz has noted: "Behind the debates over future policy is a debate over history—a debate over the causes of our current situation," so "it's crucial to get the history straight."[1] One respected financial blogger goes further, commenting that there's now "wild ass covering and blame shifting"[2] that make it more difficult to really appreciate the causes of our current problems.

Toward that end, we include two articles that demonstrate how the crisis was caused by a combination of reckless lending and investing practices, failure of rating agencies truly to evaluate financial instruments before according them high-grade status, and general abdication of responsibility by many government agencies charged with the job of policing banks and markets. Chapter 3 of *The Rich Get Richer* likens the strategy of deregulating financial markets to pulling referees off the field at the Super Bowl, something we would not allow because "we know that players would give in to their worst impulses." The two articles provide an overview of the problem, put human faces on what can be dry financial discussion, and highlight some examples of proposed regulations that would have curbed some of the worst abuses.

The first reading is "A Memo Found in the Street: Uncle Sam the Enabler" by Barry L. Ritholtz, who is CEO of a research firm, a respected financial blogger, and author of *Bailout Nation: How Easy Money Corrupted Wall Street and Shook the World Economy*.[3] The article is a brief and easy-to-follow summary of the steps leading to the financial crisis. It takes the form of a memo from Wall Street to Washington, D.C., admitting that Wall Street must accept much of the blame for the mess: "We on Wall Street . . . ," the author writes, "used excessive leverage, failed to maintain adequate capital, engaged in reckless speculation, created new complex derivatives. We focused on short-term profits at the expense of sustainability. We not only undermined our own firms, we destabilized the financial sector and roiled the global economy, to boot. And we got huge bonuses." But, he continues, "D.C.: We could not have done it without you. We may be drunks, but you were our enablers: Your legislative, executive, and administrative decisions made possible all that we did. Our recklessness would not have reached its soaring heights but for your governmental incompetence."

The second reading, "They Warned Us: U.S. Was Told to 'Expect Foreclosures, Expect Horror Stories,'" by Matt Apuzzo, looks at the crisis from the side of the government agencies whose job it was to regulate the market. Government, under a Bush administration (and accompanied by a Fed chairman, Alan Greenspan) that had limitless faith in the ability of markets to discipline themselves, discouraged sensible regulation of the financial markets, even in the face of warnings that a dangerous bubble was growing. Reluctant regulators were matched by lobbyists representing investment houses and banks that did not want any limits on their ability to construct new ways of packaging and reselling loans. The author writes: "Bowing to aggressive lobbying— along with assurances from banks that the troubled mortgages were OK—regulators delayed action for nearly one year. By the time new rules were released late in 2006, the toughest of the proposed provisions were gone and the meltdown was under way."

Notes

1. Joseph Stiglitz, "Capitalist Fools." *Vanity Fair,* January 2009. www.vanityfair.com/magazine/2009/01/stiglitz200901
2. Barry Ritholtz, "Real Estate, Speculation and 'Occupancy Fraud.'" http://bigpicture.typepad.com/comments/2008/02/real-estate-spe.html
3. His blog can now be found at http://ritholtz.com/blog and his book is published by McGraw-Hill (2009).

RACE AT WORK: REALITIES OF RACE AND CRIMINAL RECORD IN THE NYC JOB MARKET

Devah Pager
Bruce Western

Racial progress since the 1960s has led some researchers and policy makers to proclaim the problem of discrimination solved. Despite low rates of employment among blacks compared to whites, many people are now skeptical that discrimination remains a significant cause of racial inequality in the U.S. labor market. Public opinion polls indicate that Americans today are much less likely to view discrimination as a major problem as were their counterparts in the 1970s. In fact, according to a recent Gallup poll, more than three-quarters of the general public believe that blacks are treated the same as whites in society.

In part, white Americans have turned their attention away from the problems of discrimination because it is difficult to observe. Contemporary forms of discrimination are often subtle and covert, making it difficult for the average observer to recognize their effects. In the present study, we adopt an experimental audit approach to more explicitly identify patterns of discrimination in the low-wage labor market of New York City. By using matched teams of individuals to apply for real entry-level jobs, it becomes possible to directly measure the extent to which race/ethnicity—in the absence of other disqualifying characteristics—reduce employment opportunities among equally qualified applicants.

RESEARCH METHODOLOGY

Our research design involved sending matched teams of young men (called testers) to apply for [341] real entry-level jobs throughout New York City over ten months in 2004. The testers were well-spoken young men, aged 22 to 26; most were college-educated, between 5 feet 10 inches and 6 feet in height, recruited in and around

Source: This report released as part of the NYC Commission on Human Rights conference *Race At Work—Realities of Race and Criminal Record in the NYC Job Market* held on December 9, 2005 at Schomburg Center for Research in Black Culture. Updates to the original provided by the authors. Reprinted by permission of Devah Pager, Princeton University, and Bruce Western, Harvard University.

New York City. They were chosen on the basis of their similar verbal skills, interactional styles and physical attractiveness. Additionally, testers went through a common training program to ensure uniform style of self presentation in job interviews. Testers were assigned matched fictitious resumes representing comparable profiles with respect to educational attainment, quality of high school, work experience, and neighborhood of residence. Testers presented themselves as high school graduates with steady work experience in entry-level jobs. In some conditions, testers presented additional evidence of a felony conviction.[1]

RESULTS

Our first set of results come from the three-person team in which a white, [Latino], and black tester applied to the same set of employers presenting identical qualifications. For each set of visits, we recorded whether testers were offered the job on the spot, or, at some later point, [were] called back for a second interview (which we refer to together as "positive responses.") As we can see in Figure 1, the proportion of positive responses depends strongly on the race of the job applicant. This comparison demonstrates a [clear] racial hierarchy, with whites in the lead, followed by Latinos, with blacks trailing far behind. These outcomes suggest that blacks are only . . . half as likely to receive consideration by employers relative to equally qualified white applicants. Latinos also pay a penalty for minority status, but they are . . . preferred relative to their black counterparts.

Beyond these numerical outcomes, the experiences reported by testers in the course of their interviews with employers were also revealing of the racial dynamics at work. In some cases, our minority testers received clear feedback that they were not welcome or appropriate for a particular work environment. On one occasion, for example, Dathan, an African American tester, reports his experience applying for a position at an upscale jewelry store's booth at a job fair. Waiting for the store representative to finish her conversation with another applicant, he watches her giggling with the blond

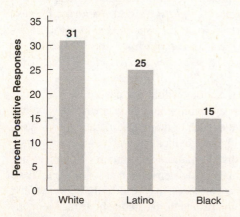

FIGURE 1   Call-Backs or Job Offers by Race/Ethnicity

The total number of employers audited by this team = 252. Positive response rates for Whites and Latinos are significantly different from Blacks (p < .05). Response rates for Latinos are marginally significantly different from Whites (p = .07).

female applicant in front of him. Finally it's Dathan's turn to speak with the representative. He reports the following interaction:

> "[When the rep saw me] her smiley face turned into a serious business face, and I said 'Hi, I'm interested in applying for a position at [your store].' She asked, 'To do what?' I said, 'I have customer service experience and sales experience.'
>
> She said: 'I haven't been with [company X] for too long, but I imagine they want [company X] type of people, who can represent [company X] . . .'"

In this 30 second interaction, the rep had apparently been able to size up Dathan's potential and had decided that he was not "company X type of people." In the rep's view, the employer's status—a prestigious company in a prestigious retail trade—appeared to rule out the possibility of hiring a young black male.

These interactions in which race plays a role provide a small window into the process by which employers regard young African Americans as unsuitable employees. Most commonly, however, stereotyping and discrimination remain invisible to the job applicant. In fact, despite certain fairly striking examples of racial dynamics in testers' interactions with employers, the vast majority of disparate treatment occurred with little or no signs of trouble.

In one case, for example, the three test partners reported experiences that, in the absence of direct comparisons, would have revealed no evidence of discrimination. In recording his experience applying for this retail sales position, Joe, one of our African American testers, reports: *"[The employer] said the position was just filled and that she would be calling people in for an interview if the person doesn't work out."* Josue, his Latino test partner, was told something very similar: *"She informed me that the position was already filled, but did not know if the hired employee would work out. She told me to leave my resume with her."* By contrast, when Simon, their white tester, applied last, his experience was notably different: *" . . . I asked what the hiring process was—if they're taking applications now, interviewing, etc. She looked at my application. 'You can start immediately?' Yes. 'Can you start tomorrow?' Yes. '10 a.m.' She was very friendly and introduced me to another woman (white, 28) at the cash register who will be training me."*

When evaluated individually, these interactions would not have raised any concern. All three testers were asked about their availability and about their sales experience. The employer appeared willing to consider each of them. But in the final analysis, it was the white applicant who walked out with the job. Incidents such as these illustrate the ease with which contemporary acts of discrimination can remain completely undetected. Without a white partner following in their footsteps, Joe and Josue would have had no indication of the degree to which their experiences, in cases like these, were being shaped by racial considerations. And yet, as the results of the study show, race remains highly consequential in determining the opportunities available for low wage work.

In a second set of analyses, we compare the magnitude of race/ethnic discrimination to another prevalent form of stigma among low-wage workers. Recent political discussions and media coverage have highlighted the plight of an increasing number of inmates being released from prison each year. We know that these men face substantial difficulties in securing employment as a result of their criminal background. Comparing the outcome of this group to minorities with no criminal background allows us to assess the relative magnitudes of criminal stigma and minority status.

Figure 2 shows the results from this second three-person team in which the white tester now presents evidence of a felony conviction. His test partners, black and Latino young men, present no criminal background. As we can see in this figure, the rate of positive responses for the white tester are substantially diminished relative to the white tester with no criminal background (from Figure 1). Nevertheless, this white applicant with a felony conviction appears to do . . . better than his black [and Latino] counterpart[s] with no criminal background. These results suggest that employers view minority job applicants as essentially equivalent to whites just out of prison.

Despite the fact that these applicants presented equivalent credentials and applied for exactly the same jobs, race appears to overtake all else in determining employment opportunities.

Calibrating the magnitude of the race effects to the effects of a felony conviction presents a disturbing picture. Blacks remain at the very end of the hiring queue, even in relation to (white) applicants who have just been released from prison. The results here point to the striking persistence of race in the allocation of employment opportunities. Employers faced with large numbers of applicants and little time to evaluate them seem to view race as an adequate means by which to weed out undesirable applicants upon first review.

As just one example, the following case records this team's experience applying for a position at a local auto dealership. Joe, the black tester, applied first and was informed at the outset that the only available positions were for those with direct auto sales experience. When Josue, his Latino partner, applied, the lack of direct auto sales

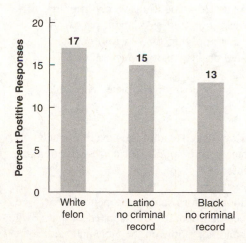

FIGURE 2 **Call-Backs or Job Offers by Race and Criminal Record**

The total number of employers audited by this team = 255. Positive response rates for White felons are not significantly different from Latinos and Blacks. Response rates for Latinos are marginally significantly different from Blacks (p = .05).

experience was less of a problem. Josue reports: *"He asked me if I had any customer service experience and I said not really. . . . He then told me that he wanted to get rid of a few bad apples who were not performing well. He asked me when I could start. . . ."* Josue was told to wait for a call back on Monday. Keith, their white ex-felon test partner, was first given a stern lecture regarding his criminal background. *"I have no problem with your conviction, it doesn't bother me. But if I find out money is missing or you're not clean or not showing up on time I have no problem ending the relationship."* Despite the employer's concerns, and despite Keith having no more sales experience than his test partners, Keith was offered the job on the spot.

This example illustrates the ways in which race can trump even known criminality in certain cases. Indeed, far from racial considerations in employment being a thing of the past, we see that they are alive and well and actively shaping the opportunities available to members of different racial/ethnic groups.

RACE-CODED CHANNELING

The basic outcome of "positive responses" measured in this study quantifies the employers' willingness to consider each applicant type for a job. But the simple distinction between getting a job or not captures only one piece of the employment puzzle. In many cases employers are hiring for more than one position at the same time. Examining how employers match applicants to job types can be further revealing of the assumptions employers hold about various groups of workers.

The testers' narratives, reporting their experiences at the conclusion of each audit, provide vivid illustrations of the kinds of the channeling that takes place. In an audit of a retail clothing company, for example, one of our [Latino] testers, Josue, encounters the following:

> Josue describes the various young white 20-something women running the place. One of the women interviews him and asks about past work experience. She asks him what job he's applying for—"I told her sales associate. . . . [The last serious job listed on Josue's resume was as a sales assistant at a sporting goods store].
>
> She then told me that there was a stock position and asked if I would be interested in that."

Josue ended up getting the stocker job, and was asked to start the next day.

In another case, one of our black testers, Zuri, applied for a sales position at a lighting store. He describes the following interaction:

> When she asked what position I was looking for I said I was open, but that since they were looking for a salesperson I would be interested in that. She smiled, put her head in her hand and her elbow on the table and said, "I need a stock boy. Can you do stock boy?"

Zuri's white and [Latino] test partners, by contrast, were each able to apply for the advertised sales position.

The job applications of Josue and Zuri are both coded as "positive responses" in the initial analyses. Indeed, our key concern is about access to employment of any kind. But this general focus masks some of the racial biases at play. Indeed, the experience of channeling was not limited to a handful of cases. A more systematic analysis of the testers' experiences provides support for these anecdotal experiences. A total of [53] cases of channeling were recorded by the testers.[2] These cases were then individually coded as downward channeling, upward channeling, lateral channeling, or unknown, by comparing the original job title to the suggested job type. Downward channeling is defined as (1) a move from a job involving contact with customers to a job without (e.g., server to busboy); (2) a move from a white collar position to a manual position (e.g., from dispatcher to driver); or (3) a move in which hierarchy can be clearly discerned (e.g., manager to server). Upward channeling is defined as a move in the opposite direction. We focus on these two types of channeling for our current analysis. Instances of channeling in which all members of the team were channeled similarly are eliminated (e.g., the original job was filled and all subsequent job applicants were invited to apply for a different position).

The analysis of these cases reveals fairly striking patterns of racial categorization. Black applicants were channeled into lower positions in [9] cases and never channeled upwards, Hispanics were channeled down in [5] cases and channeled upwards [only twice], whereas whites experienced downward channeling in only [1] case, and only when showing a criminal record (see Table 1), [whereas whites were channeled upwards in at least 6 cases.]

A substantial number of these cases were restaurant jobs in which the tester applied for a position as server but was instead channeled into a position as busboy or dishwasher. Almost all were cases in which the original position required extensive customer contact while the suggested position did not (e.g., salesperson to stocker). While in some cases the limited work experiences reflected on our testers' resumes warranted movement into a lower-level position, the differential incidence by race suggests that these decisions were not based on qualifications alone.

In fact, a surprising degree of channeling among our white testers took place in the opposite direction. In at least [six] cases, white testers were encouraged to apply for jobs that were of a higher-level or required more customer contact than the initial position they inquired about. In one case, for example, a white tester applied for a position as a cleaner but was instead encouraged to apply for a clerical position. In another case the tester requested an application for the dishwasher position, but was instead channeled into applying for a job as waitstaff. In at least one case, a [w]hite tester was encouraged to apply for a management position, despite his paltry level of work experience.

It is not the case, then, that the resumes of testers in this study prevented them from consideration in a wide range of jobs, or left them on the borderline between job classes. In fact, the testers' resumes were constructed so that they would appear highly competitive for the kinds of low-wage jobs we were targeting. Rather, the testers' race or ethnicity appears to be associated with differential levels of skill, competence, or suitability for particular kinds of work. The critical relevance of customer contact in the channeling decisions likewise suggests that employers have assumptions about what their clients expect/prefer in the appearance of those serving them.

TABLE 1   Job Channeling by Race, Ethnicity, & Criminal Background

Original Job Title	Suggested Job
Blacks channeled down	
[Counterperson] ⟶	[Dishwasher/porter]
Server ⟶	Busser
Assistant Manager ⟶	Entry fast food position
Server ⟶	Busboy/Runner
Server ⟶	[Busboy]
Retail Salesperson ⟶	Maintenance
Sales ⟶	not specified (a)
Sales ⟶	Stockboy
[Counterperson] ⟶	[Delivery]
[Latinos] channeled down	
Waitstaff ⟶	Delivery person
[Salesperson] ⟶	[Stock]
[Counterperson] ⟶	Delivery person
Salesperson ⟶	Stock person
Steam Cleaning ⟶	Exterminator
Whites with record channeled down	
Server ⟶	[Busboy]
[Latinos] channeled up	
[Car wash attendant] ⟶	[Manager]
[Warehouse worker] ⟶	[Computer/office]
Whites (with record) channeled up	
Line Cook ⟶	Waitstaff
Mover ⟶	Office/Telesales
Dishwasher ⟶	Waitstaff
Driver ⟶	Auto detailing
[Kitchen job] ⟶	["Front of the house" job]
[Receptionist] ⟶	[Company superior]

(a) employer told tester: "sales might not be right for you . . . "

CONCLUSION

In contrast to public opinion that assumes little influence of discrimination on labor market inequality, we find that black job applicants are only two-thirds as successful as equally qualified Latinos, and . . . half as successful as equally qualified whites. Indeed, black job seekers fare no better than white men just released from prison. Discrimination continues to represent a major barrier to economic self-sufficiency for those at the low end of the labor market hierarchy. Blacks, and to a lesser extent Latinos, are routinely passed over in favor of whites for the most basic kinds of low-wage work. Indeed, discrimination has not been eliminated in the post-civil rights period as some contend, but remains a vital component of a complex pattern of racial inequality.

Notes

1. In this report, we study racial and ethnic discrimination using data from two teams of testers. A total of [4] teams (and [10] testers) were included in [the larger] study, allowing us to study various combinations of race, [ethnicity, and] criminal background. . . . [For a more elaborate discussion of the results, see D. Pager, B. Western, & B. Bonikowski (2009). "Race at Work: Results from a Field Experiment of Discrimination in Low Wage Labor Markets." *American Sociological Review* (forthcoming, October), and D. Pager, B. Western, & N. Sugie (2009). "Sequencing Disadvantage Barriers to Employment Facing Young Black and White Men with Criminal Records." *Annals of the American Academy of Political and Social Sciences, 623*(May), 195–213.

2. In the present study, when an ad listed more than one job opening, members of the audit team would agree upon which job they would apply for. Testers were instructed to communicate their interest [in] the target job, but to express openness to any position the employer may have available. After each visit, testers recorded whether or not they were encouraged to apply for a different position than the one they originally inquired about.

WHY IT MATTERS: THE CONNECTION OF "DRIVING WHILE BLACK" TO OTHER ISSUES OF CRIMINAL JUSTICE AND RACE

David A. Harris

The interviews excerpted here show that racially biased pretextual traffic stops have a strong and immediate impact on the individual African-American drivers involved. These stops are not the minor inconveniences they might seem to those who are not subjected to them. Rather, they are experiences that can wound the soul and cause psychological scar tissue to form. And the statistics show that these experiences are not simply disconnected anecdotes or exaggerated versions of personal experiences, but rather established and persistent patterns of law enforcement conduct. It may be that these stops do not spring from racism on the part of individual officers, or even from the official policies of the police departments for which they work. Nevertheless, the statistics leave little doubt that, whatever the source of this conduct by police, it has a disparate and degrading impact on blacks.

Source: Excerpted from "The Stories, The Statistics, And The Law: Why 'Driving While Black' Matters," *Minnesota Law Review,* 84, 265–326. Copyright 1999 by University of Minnesota Law Science and Technology. Reproduced with permission of David A. Harris, and of University of Minnesota Law Science and Technology via Copyright Clearance Center. Citations renumbered.

But racial profiling is important not only because of the damage it does, but also because of the connections between stops of minority drivers and other, larger issues of criminal justice and race. Put another way, "driving while black" reflects, illustrates, and aggravates some of the most important problems we face today when we debate issues involving race, the police, the courts, punishment, crime control, criminal justice, and constitutional law.

A. THE IMPACT ON THE INNOCENT

The Fourth Amendment to the United States Constitution prohibits unreasonable searches and seizures, and specifies some of the requirements to be met in order to procure a warrant for a search.[1] Since 1961[2]—and earlier in the federal court system[3]—the Supreme Court has required the exclusion of any evidence obtained through an unconstitutional search or seizure. From its inception, the exclusionary rule has inspired spirited criticism. Cardozo himself said that "the criminal is to go free because the constable has blundered,"[4] capturing the idea that the bad guy, caught red handed, gets a tremendous windfall when he escapes punishment because of a mistake in the police officer's behavior. We need not even go all the way back to Cardozo to hear the argument that the exclusion of evidence protects—and rewards—only the guilty.[5]

The justification advanced for the exclusionary rule is that while the guilty may receive the most direct benefit when a court suppresses evidence because of a constitutional violation, the innocent—all the rest of us—are also better off. The right to be free from illegal searches and seizures belongs not just to the guilty, but to everyone. The guilty parties who bring motions to suppress are simply the most convenient vehicles for vindicating these rights, because they will have the incentive—escaping conviction—to litigate the issues. In so doing, the argument goes, the rights of all are vindicated, and police are deterred from violating constitutional rules on pain of failing to convict the guilty. One problem with this argument is that it takes imagination: the beneficiaries of suppressed evidence *other than the guilty who escape punishment* are ephemeral and amorphous. They are everybody—all of us. And if they are everybody, they quickly become nobody, because law-abiding, taxpaying citizens are unlikely to view ourselves as needing these constitutional protections. After all, we obey the law; we do not commit crimes. We can do without these protections—or so we think.

It is not my intention here to recapitulate every argument for and against the exclusionary rule. Rather, I wish to point out a major difference between the usual Fourth Amendment cases and the most common "driving while black" cases. *While police catch some criminals through the use of pretext stops, far more innocent people are likely to be affected by these practices than criminals.* Indeed, the black community as a whole undoubtedly needs the protection of the police more than other segments of society because African-Americans are more likely than others to be victims of crime.[6] Ironically, it is members of that same community who are likely to feel the consequences of pretextual stops and be treated like criminals. It is the reverse of the usual Fourth Amendment case, in that there is nothing ghostlike or indefinite about those whose rights would be vindicated by addressing these police practices. On the contrary, the victims are easy to identify because they are the great majority of black people who are subjected to these humiliating and difficult experiences but who have done absolutely nothing to deserve this treatment—except to resemble, in a literally skin-deep way, a small group of criminals. While whites who have done nothing wrong generally have little need to fear constitutional violations by the police, this is decidedly *untrue* for blacks. Blacks attract undesirable police attention whether they do anything to bring it on themselves or not. This makes "driving while black" a most unusual issue of constitutional criminal procedure: a search and seizure question that directly affects a large, identifiable group of almost entirely innocent people.

B. THE CRIMINALIZATION OF BLACKNESS

The fact that the cost of "driving while black" is imposed almost exclusively on the innocent raises another point. Recall that by allowing the police to stop, question, and sometimes even search drivers without regard to the real motives for the search, the Supreme Court has, in effect, turned a blind eye to the use of pretextual stops on a racial basis. That is, as long as the officer or the police department does not come straight out and say that race was the reason for a stop, the stop can always be accomplished based on some other reason—a pretext. Police are therefore free to use blackness as a surrogate indicator or proxy for criminal propensity. While it seems unfair to view *all* members of one racial or ethnic group as criminal suspects just because *some* members of that group engage in criminal activity, this is what the law permits.

Stopping disproportionate numbers of black drivers because some small percentage[7] are criminals means that skin color is being used as evidence of wrongdoing. In effect, *blackness itself has been criminalized.*[8] And if "driving while black" is a powerful example, it is not the only one. For instance, in 1992, the city of Chicago enacted an ordinance that made it a criminal offense for gang members to stand on public streets or sidewalks after police ordered them to disperse.[9] The ordinance was used to make over forty-five thousand arrests of mostly African-American and Latino youths[10] before Illinois courts found the ordinance unconstitutionally vague.[11] Supporters said that the law legitimately targeted gang members who made the streets of black and Latino neighborhoods unsafe for residents. Accordingly, the thousands of arrests that resulted were a net good, regardless of the enormous amount of police discretion that was exercised almost exclusively against African-Americans and Hispanics.[12] Opponents, such as Professor David Cole, argued that the ordinance had, in effect, created a new crime: "standing while black."[13] In June of 1999, the U.S. Supreme Court declared the law unconstitutional, because it did not sufficiently *limit* the discretion of officers enforcing it.[14]

The arrests under the Chicago ordinance share something with "driving while black": in each instance, the salient quality that attracts police attention will often be the suspect's race or ethnicity. An officer cannot know simply by looking whether a driver has a valid license or carries insurance, as the law requires, and cannot see whether there is a warrant for the arrest of the driver or another occupant of the car. But the officer *can* see whether the person is black or white. And, as the statistics presented here show, police use blackness as a way to sort those they are interested in investigating from those that they are not. As a consequence, every member of the group becomes a potential criminal in the eyes of law enforcement.

C. RATIONAL DISCRIMINATION

When one hears the most common justification offered for the disproportionate numbers of traffic stops of African-Americans, it usually takes the form of rationality, not racism. Blacks commit a disproportionate share of certain crimes, the argument goes. Therefore, it only makes sense for police to focus their efforts on African-Americans. To paraphrase [a] Maryland State Police officer . . . this is not racism—it is good policing.[15] It only makes sense to focus law enforcement efforts and resources where they will make the most difference. In other words, targeting blacks is the rational, sound policy choice. It is the efficient approach, as well.

As appealing as this argument may sound, it is fraught with problems because its underlying premise is dubious at best. Government statistics on drug offenses, which are the basis for the great majority of pretext traffic stops, tell us virtually nothing about the racial breakdown of those involved in drug crime. Thinking for a moment about arrest data and victimization surveys makes the reasons for this clear. These statistics show that blacks are indeed overrepresented among those arrested for homicide, rape, robbery, aggravated assault, larceny/theft, and simple assault crimes.[16] Note that because they directly affect their victims, these crimes are at least somewhat likely to be reported to the police[17] and to result in arrests. By contrast, drug offenses are much less likely to be reported, since possessors, buyers, and sellers of narcotics are all willing participants in these crimes. Therefore, arrest data for drug crimes is highly suspect. These data may measure the law enforcement activities and policy choices of the institutions and actors involved in the criminal justice system, but the number of drug arrests does not measure the extent of drug crimes themselves.[18] Similarly, the racial composition of prisons and jail populations or the racial breakdown of sentences for these crimes only measures the actions of those institutions and individuals in charge; it tells us nothing about drug activity itself.

Other statistics on both drug use and drug crime show something surprising in light of the usual beliefs many hold: blacks may *not*, in fact, be more likely than whites to be involved with drugs. Lamberth's study in Maryland showed that among vehicles stopped and searched, the "hit rates"—the percentage of vehicles searched in which drugs were found—were statistically indistinguishable for blacks and whites.[19] In a related situation, the U.S. Customs Service, which is engaged in drug interdiction efforts at the nation's airports, has used various types of invasive searches from pat downs to body cavity searches against travelers suspected of drug use. The Custom Service's own nationwide figures show that while over forty-three percent of those subjected to these searches were either black or Hispanic, "hit rates" for these searches were actually *lower* for both blacks and Hispanics than for whites.[20] There is also a considerable amount of data on drug use that belies the standard beliefs.[21] The percentages of drug users who are black or white are roughly the same as the presence of those groups in the population as a whole. For example, blacks constitute approximately twelve percent of the country's population. In 1997, the most recent year for which statistics are available, thirteen percent of all drug users were black.[22] In fact, among black youths, a demographic group often portrayed as most likely to be involved with drugs, use of all illicit substances has actually been *consistently lower* than among white youths for *twenty years running.*[23]

Nevertheless, many believe that African-Americans and members of other minority groups are responsible for most drug use and drug trafficking. Carl Williams, the head of the New Jersey State Police dismissed by the Governor in March of 1999, stated that "mostly minorities" trafficked in marijuana and cocaine, and pointed out that when senior American officials went overseas to discuss the drug problem, they went to Mexico, not Ireland.[24] Even if he is wrong, if the many troopers who worked for Williams share his opinions, they will act accordingly. And they will do so by looking for drug criminals among black drivers. Blackness will become an indicator of suspicion of drug crime involvement. This, in turn, means that the belief that blacks are disproportionately involved in drug crimes will become a self-fulfilling prophecy. Because police will *look* for drug crime among black drivers, they will *find* it disproportionately among black drivers. More blacks will be arrested, prosecuted, convicted, and jailed, thereby reinforcing the idea that blacks constitute the majority of drug offenders. This will provide a continuing motive and justification for stopping more black drivers as a rational way of using resources to catch the most criminals. At the same time, because police will focus on black drivers, white drivers will receive less attention, and the drug dealers and possessors among them will be apprehended in proportionately smaller numbers than their presence in the population would predict.

The upshot of this thinking is visible in the stark and stunning numbers that show what our criminal justice system is doing when it uses law enforcement practices like racially-biased traffic stops to enforce drug laws. African-Americans are just 12% of the population and 13% of the drug users, but they are about 38% of all those arrested for drug offenses, 59% of all those convicted of drug offenses, and 63% of all those convicted for drug trafficking.[25] While only 33% of whites who are convicted are sent to prison, 50% of convicted blacks are jailed,[26] and blacks who are sent to prison receive higher sentences than whites for the same crimes. For state drug defendants, the average maximum sentence length is fifty-one months for whites and sixty months for blacks.[27]

D. THE DISTORTION OF THE LEGAL SYSTEM

Among the most serious effects of "driving while black" on the larger issues of criminal justice and race are those it has on the legal system itself. The use of pretextual traffic stops distorts the whole system, as well as our perceptions of it. This undermines the system's legitimacy, which effects not only African-Americans but every citizen, since the health of our country depends on a set of legal institutions that have the public's respect.

1. Deep Cynicism

Racially targeted traffic stops cause deep cynicism among blacks about the fairness and legitimacy of law enforcement and courts. Many of those African-Americans interviewed for this Article said this, some in strong terms. Karen Brank said she thought that her law-abiding life, her responsible job, her education, and even her gender protected her from arbitrary treatment by the police. She thought that these stops happened only to young black men playing loud music in their cars. Now, she feels she was "naive," and has considerably less respect for police and all legal institutions.[28] For James, who looks at himself as someone who has toed the line and lived an upright life, constant stops are a reminder that whatever he does, no matter how well he conducts himself, he will still attract unwarranted police attention.[29] Michael describes constant police scrutiny as something blacks have to "play through," like athletes with injuries who must perform despite significant pain.[30]

Thus, it is no wonder that blacks view the criminal justice system in totally different terms than whites do. They have completely different experiences within the system than whites have, so they do not hold the same beliefs about it. Traffic stops of whites usually concern the actual traffic offense allegedly committed; traffic stops of blacks are often arbitrary, grounded not in any traffic offense but in who they are. Since traffic stops are among the most common encounters regular citizens have with police, it is hardly surprising that pretextual traffic stops might lead blacks to view the whole of the system differently. One need only think of the split-screen television images that followed the acquittal in the O.J. Simpson case—stunned, disbelieving whites, juxtaposed with jubilant blacks literally jumping for joy—to understand how deep these divisions are. Polling data have long shown that blacks believe that the justice system is biased against them. For example, in a Justice Department survey released in 1999, blacks were more than twice as likely as whites to say they are dissatisfied with the police.[31] But this cynicism is no longer limited to blacks; it is now beginning to creep into the general population's perception of the system. Recent data show that a majority of *whites* believe that police racism toward blacks is common.[32] The damage done to the legitimacy of the system has spread across racial groups, and is no longer confined to those who are most immediately affected.

Perhaps the most direct result of this cynicism is that there is considerably more skepticism about the testimony of police officers than there used to be. This is especially true in minority communities. Both the officer and the driver recognize that each pretextual traffic stop involves an untruth. When a black driver asks a police officer why he or she has been stopped, the officer will most likely explain that the driver committed a traffic violation. This may be literally true, since virtually no driver can avoid committing a traffic offense. But odds are that the violation is not the real reason that the officer stopped the driver. This becomes more than obvious when the officer asks the driver whether he or she is carrying drugs or guns, and for consent to search the car.[33] If the stop was really about enforcement of the traffic laws, there would be no need for any search. Thus, for an officer to tell a driver that he or she has been stopped for a traffic offense when the officer's real interest is drug interdiction is a lie—a legally sanctioned one, to be sure, but a lie nonetheless. It should surprise no one, then, that the same people who are subjected to this treatment regard the testimony and statements of police with suspicion, making it increasingly difficult for prosecutors to obtain convictions in any case that depends upon police testimony, as so many cases do. The result may be more cases that end in acquittals or hung juries, even factually and legally strong ones.[34]

2. The Effect on the Guilty

As discussed above, one of the most important reasons that the "driving while black" problem represents an important connection to many larger issues of criminal justice and race is that, unlike many other Fourth Amendment issues, the innocent pay a clear and direct price. Citizens who are not criminals are seen as only indirect beneficiaries of Fourth Amendment litigation in other contexts because the guilty party's vindication of his or her own rights serves to vindicate everyone's rights. Law-abiding blacks, however, have a direct and immediate stake in redressing the "driving while black" problem. While pretextual traffic stops do indeed net some number of law breakers, innocent blacks are imposed upon through frightening and even humiliating stops and searches far more often than the guilty. But the opposite argument is important, too: "driving while black" has a devastating impact upon the guilty. Those who are arrested, prosecuted, and often jailed because of these stops, are suffering great hardships as a result.

The response to this argument is usually that if these folks are indeed guilty, so what? In other words, it is a good thing that the guilty are caught, arrested, and prosecuted, no matter if they are black or white. This is especially true, the argument goes, in the black community, because African-Americans are disproportionately the victims of crime.[35]

But this argument overlooks at least two powerful points. First, prosecution for crimes, especially drug crimes, has had an absolutely devastating impact on black communities nationwide. In 1995, about one in three black men between the ages of 20 and 29 were under the control of the criminal justice system—either in prison or jail, on probation, or on parole.[36] In Washington, D.C., the figure is 50% for all black men between the age of eighteen and thirty-five.[37] Even assuming that all of those caught, prosecuted, convicted and sentenced are guilty, it simply cannot be a good thing that such a large proportion of young men from one community are adjudicated criminals. They often lose their right to vote, sometimes permanently.[38] To say that they suffer difficulties in family life and in gaining employment merely restates the obvious. The effect of such a huge proportion of people living under these disabilities permanently changes the circumstances not just of those incarcerated, but of everyone around them.

This damage is no accident. It is the direct consequence of "rational law enforcement" policies that target blacks. Put simply, *there is a connection between where police look for contraband and where they find it*. If police policy, whether express or implied, dictates targeting supposedly "drug involved" groups like African-Americans, and if officers follow through on this policy, they will find disproportionate numbers of African-Americans carrying and selling drugs. By the same token, they will *not* find drugs with the appropriate frequency on whites, because the targeting policy steers police attention away from them. This policy not only discriminates by targeting large numbers of innocent, law abiding African-Americans; it also discriminates between racial groups among the guilty, with blacks having to bear a far greater share of the burden of drug prohibition.

3. The Expansion of Police Discretion

As the discussion of the law involving traffic stops and the police actions that often follow showed, police have nearly complete discretion to decide who to stop. According to all of the evidence available, police frequently exercise this discretion in a racially-biased way, stopping blacks in numbers far out of proportion to their presence on the highway. Law enforcement generally sees this as something positive because the more discretion officers have to fight crime, the better able they will be to do the job.

Police discretion cannot be eliminated; frankly, even if it could be, this would not necessarily be a desirable goal. Officers need discretion to meet individual situations with judgment and intelligence, and to choose their responses so that the ultimate result will make sense. Yet few would contend that police discretion should be *limitless*. But this is exactly what the pretextual stop doctrine allows. Since *everyone* violates the traffic code at some point, it is not a matter of *whether* police can stop a driver, but *which driver* they want to stop. Police are free to pick and choose the motorists they will pull over, so factors other than direct evidence of law breaking come into play. In the "driving while black" situation, of course, that factor is race. In other law enforcement areas in which the state has nearly limitless discretion to prosecute, the decision could be based on political affiliation, popularity, or any number of other things. What these arenas have in common is that enforcement depends upon external factors, instead of law breaking.

Arguments examining law enforcement discretion have great resonance in the wake of the impeachment of President Clinton. The President was pursued by Independent Counsel Kenneth Starr for four years. Starr had an almost limitless budget, an *infinite* investigative time frame, and an ever-expandable mandate to investigate a particular set of individuals for any possible criminal activity, rather than to investigate particular offenses. In other words, Starr had nearly complete discretion. This was foreseen in 1988 by Justice Scalia in his dissent in *Morrison v. Olsen,*[39] the case in which the Supreme Court held the independent counsel statute constitutional. In a long final section of his opinion, Scalia decried the Independent Counsel Act not only as unconstitutional but also as bad policy, precisely because it gave the prosecutor nearly unlimited discretion. Among the words Justice Scalia chose to express this idea were those of Justice Robert Jackson, who, as Attorney General, talked about prosecutorial discretion in a speech to the Second Annual Conference of United States Attorneys. Jackson could just as easily have been discussing police discretion to make traffic stops; in fact, he used that very activity as an illustration.

> Law enforcement is not automatic. It isn't blind. One of the greatest difficulties of the position of prosecutor is that he must pick his cases, because no prosecutor can even investigate all of the cases in which he receives complaints. . . . *We know that no local police force can strictly enforce the traffic laws, or it would arrest half the driving population on any given morning.* . . .
>
> If the prosecutor is obliged to choose his case, it follows that he can choose his defendants. Therein is the most dangerous power of the prosecutor: that he will pick people that he thinks he should get, rather than cases that need to be prosecuted. With the law books filled with a great assortment of crimes, a prosecutor stands a fair chance of finding at least a technical violation of some act on the part of almost anyone. In such a case, it is not a question of discovering the commission of a crime and

then looking for the man who has committed it, it is a question of picking the man and then searching the law books, or putting investigators to work, to pin some offense on him. . . . It is here that law enforcement becomes personal, and the real crime becomes that of being unpopular with the predominant or governing group, being attached to the wrong political views, or being personally obnoxious to or in the way of the prosecutor himself.[40]

By substituting "the police" for "the prosecutor" in this excerpt, one gets a strong sense of the unfairness of pretextual traffic stops. The person subjected to a pretextual stop is not targeted for his or her law breaking activity, but for other reasons—in this case, membership in a particular racial or ethnic group thought to be disproportionately involved in drug crimes. And the law leaves police absolutely free to do this.[41]

4. Sentencing

"Driving while black" also distorts the sentences that African-Americans receive for crimes. Research shows that blacks receive longer sentences than whites for the same crimes.[42] One might hope that, with the advent of guidelines systems designed to limit judicial discretion in sentencing through the use of strictly applied nonracial criteria, this discrepancy might begin to disappear, but it has not.[43]

A recent federal sentencing decision illustrates the point. In December of 1998, Judge Nancy Gertner of the Federal District Court for the District of Massachusetts sentenced a defendant named Alexander Leviner for the crime of being a felon in possession of a firearm.[44] Under the Federal Sentencing Guidelines, a major determinant of the sentence a defendant receives is his or her record of prior offenses. The worse the record, the greater the offender score; the greater the offender score, the longer the sentence.[45] Judge Gertner found that Leviner's record consisted "overwhelmingly" of "motor vehicle violations and minor drug possession offenses."[46] Since all of the available evidence indicated that African-Americans experience a proportionally greater number of traffic stops than whites,[47] Judge Gertner reasoned that allowing Leviner's offender score to be inflated by these traffic stop-related offenses represented a continuation of the racial discrimination implicit in the prior offenses into the sentencing process.[48] The judge felt this was improper, and as a result accorded Leviner a "downward departure"—a cut in the usual sentence he could expect, given his criminal record.[49]

It is not clear whether Judge Gertner's decision will survive an appeal.[50] It may be true that police, *in general,* discriminate against black motorists in their use of traffic stops. But this does not mean that any of the particular stops Leviner experienced in the past were the result of bias. Thus, an appellate court may not find Leviner deserving of the downward departure. Nevertheless, Judge Gertner's opinion points out something important, and not just in Leviner's case. "Driving while black" can have grave consequences not just immediately, when drivers may be at best irritated and at worst arrested or abused, but in the long term, as a minor criminal record builds over time to the point that it comes back to haunt a defendant by enhancing considerably the sentence in some future proceeding. This is simply less likely to happen to whites.

E. DISTORTION OF THE SOCIAL WORLD

"Driving while black" distorts not only the perception and reality of the criminal justice system, but also the social world. For example, many African-Americans cope with the possibility of pretextual traffic stops by driving drab cars and dressing in ways that are not flamboyant so as not to attract attention.[51] More than that, "driving while black" serves as a spatial restriction on African-Americans, circumscribing their movements. Put simply, blacks know that police and white residents feel that there are areas in which blacks "do not belong." Often, these are all-white suburban communities or upscale commercial areas. When blacks drive through these areas, they may be watched and stopped because they are "out of place." Consequently, blacks try to avoid these places if for no other reason than that they do not want the extra police scrutiny.[52] It is simply more trouble than it is worth to travel to or through these areas. While it is blacks themselves who avoid these communities, and not police officers or anyone else literally keeping them out, in practice it makes little difference. African-Americans do not enter if they can avoid doing so, whether by dint of self-restriction or by government policy.

Another recent example shows even more clearly how "driving while black" can distort the social world. In 1998, the federal government launched "Buckle Up America" in an effort to increase seat belt use.[53] The goal of this national campaign was to make the failure to wear seat belts a primary offense in all fifty states.[54] In many states, seat belt laws are secondary offenses—infractions for which the police cannot stop a car, but for which they can issue a citation once the car is stopped for something else and the seat belt violation is discovered.[55] If seat belt laws are made primary instead of secondary laws, the reasoning is that this would increase seat belt use, which would save thousands of lives per year. Since studies have shown that young African-Americans and Hispanics are more likely to die in automobile accidents than whites because of failure to wear seat belts,[56] any effort to increase seat belt use would likely benefit the black and Hispanic communities more than any other groups.

Given that less frequent use of seats belts has a high cost in the lives and suffering of people of color, one would think that any responsible black organization would do everything possible to support efforts like Buckle Up America. And that is what made the position taken by the National Urban League on the issue so puzzling, at least at first blush. The Urban League told the Secretary of Transportation that its "affiliates' willingness to fully embrace [the] campaign began to stall" because of concern that primary seat belt enforcement laws would simply give police another tool with which to harass black drivers.[57] The League said it could not sign on to the campaign without assurances "that the necessary protections will be put in to ensure that black people and other people of color specifically are not subject to arbitrary stops by police under the guise of enforcement of seat belt laws."[58]

This is a truly disturbing distortion of social reality. Faced with a request to join a campaign to save lives through encouraging the use of a known and proven safety device, the use of which might require some greater degree of traffic enforcement, the decision is not easy for African-Americans. On the contrary, it presents an agonizing choice: encourage the seat belt campaign to save lives and hand the police another reason to make arbitrary stops, or oppose the campaign because of the danger of arbitrary police action, knowing that blacks will be injured and killed in disproportionate numbers because they use seat belts less frequently than others do. Stated simply, it is a choice whites do not have to make.

F. THE UNDERMINING OF COMMUNITY-BASED POLICING

Until recently, police departments concentrated on answering distress calls. The idea was to have police respond to reports of crime relayed to them from a central dispatcher. In essence, the practice was reactive; the idea was to receive reports of crimes committed and respond to them.[59]

But over the past few years, modern policing has moved away from the response model. It was thought to be too slow and too likely to isolate *officers* from the people and places in which they worked. The new model is often referred to as community policing. Though the term sometimes seems to have as many meanings as people who use it, community policing does have some identifiable characteristics. The idea is for the police to serve the community and become part of it, not to dominate it or occupy it. To accomplish this, police become known to and involved with residents, make efforts to understand their problems, and attack crime in ways that help address those difficulties. The reasoning is that if the police become part of the community, members of the public will feel comfortable enough to help officers identify troubled spots and trouble makers. This will make for better, more proactive policing aimed at problems residents really care about, and engender a greater degree of appreciation of police efforts by residents and more concern for neighborhood problems by the police.[60]

In many minority communities, the history of police/community relations has been characterized not by trust, but by mutual distrust. In *Terry v. Ohio*,[61] the fountain head of modern street-level law enforcement, the Supreme Court candidly acknowledged that police had often used stop and frisk tactics to control and harass black communities.[62] As one veteran African-American police officer put it, "Black people used to call the police 'the law.' They *were* the law. . . . The Fourth Amendment didn't apply to black folks because it only applied to white folks."[63] For blacks, trusting the police is difficult; it goes against the grain of years of accumulated distrust and wariness, and countless experiences in which blacks have learned that police are not necessarily there to protect and serve *them*.

Yet, it is obvious that community policing—both its methods and its goals— depends on mutual trust.[64] As difficult as it will be to build, given the many years of disrespect blacks have suffered at the hands of the police, the community must feel that it can trust the police to treat them as law-abiding citizens if community policing is to succeed.[65] Using traffic stops in racially disproportionate numbers will directly and fundamentally undermine this effort. Why should law-abiding residents of these communities trust the police if, every time they go out for a drive, they are treated like criminals? If the "driving while black" problem is not addressed, community policing will be made much more difficult and may even fail. Thus, aside from the damage "driving while black" stops inflict on African-Americans, there is another powerful reason to change this police behavior: it is in the interest of police departments themselves to correct it.

Notes

1. U.S. CONST. amend. IV.
2. *See* Mapp v. Ohio, 367 U.S. 643, 655 (1961).
3. *See* Weeks v. United States, 232 U.S. 383, 393 (1914), *overruled by Mapp,* 367 U.S. 643.
4. People v. Defore, 150 N.E. 585,587 (N.Y. 1926).
5. *See generally* Akhil Reed Amar, *Fourth Amendments First Principles,* 107 HARV. L. REV. 757, 793–800 (1994) (arguing that the exclusionary rule makes murderers better off at the expense of society); David Blumberg, *The Case Against the Exclusionary Rule,* 14 HUM. RTS. 41, 45 (1987) (finding that "the suppression of unconstitutionality seized evidence . . . makes it more likely that the outcome will be an incorrect one, that a guilty defendant will go free or receive an unduly lenient punishment"); Gary S. Goodpaster, *An Essay on Ending the Exclusionary Rule,* 33 HASTINGS L.J. 1065, 1068 (1982) (arguing that although the exclusionary rule generally does not free the guilty, it may help them receive reduced sentences); Dallin H. Oaks, *Studying the Exclusionary Rule in Search and Seizure,* 37 U. CHI. L. REV. 665, 736–39 (1970) (noting that the exclusionary rule is subject to the criticism that it frees the guilty); Richard A. Posner, *Rethinking The Fourth Amendment,* 1981 SUP. CT. REV. 49, 53 (arguing that the exclusionary rule gives criminals "a right to conceal evidence of their crimes," a result not intended by the Fourth Amendment); James E. Spiotto, *Search and Seizure: An Empirical Study of the Exclusionary Rule and Its Alternatives,* 2 J. LEGAL STUD. 243, 276 (1973) (explaining that the exclusionary rule provides a remedy only for those arrested and charged with a crime).
6. *See, e.g.,* ANDREW HACKER, TWO NATIONS: BLACK AND WHITE, SEPARATE, HOSTILE, UNEQUAL 183 (1992) (finding that blacks accounted for 50.8% of murder victims in 1990); U.S. DEPT OF JUSTICE, CRIMINAL VICTIMIZATION IN THE UNITED STATES 1993, at 15 (1996) (showing by empirical study that the rate of victimization of blacks exceeds the rates for other racial groups).
7. *See Developments in the Law—Race and the Criminal Process,* 101 HARV. L. REV. 1472, 1508 (1988) (reporting that in any particular year 97.9% of blacks and 99.5% of whites are not arrested).
8. *See, e.g.,* KATHERINE K. RUSSELL, THE COLOR OF CRIME 122 (1998) (stating that the current use of racial labels for black crime implies that "there is something about blackness that 'explains' criminality"); *see also* Samuel G. Freedman, *Is The Drug War Racist?,* ROLLING STONE, May 14, 1998, at 35–36 (interviewing Glen Loury and Orlando Patterson, two African-Americans described as "leading public intellectuals" in America, in which Loury declares that "we're criminalizing a whole class of young black men"). The following passage helps explain why treating people as criminal suspects on the basis of racial characteristics is morally repugnant, even if based on a statistical justification:

> In the United States at present, there are real and large differences among ethnic and racial groups in their average performance in school and in their rates of committing violent crimes. (The statistics, of course, say nothing about heredity or any other putative cause.) . . . A good statistical category-maker could develop racial stereotypes and use them to make actuarially sound but morally repugnant decisions about individual cases. This behavior is racist not because it is irrational (in the sense of statistically inaccurate) but because it flouts the moral principle that it is wrong to judge an *individual* using the statistics of a racial or ethnic *group.* The argument against bigotry, then, does not come from the design specs for a rational statistical categorizer. It comes from a rule system, in this case a rule of ethics, that tells us when to turn our statistical categorizers off.

STEVEN PINKER, HOW THE MIND WORKS 313 (1997); *see also* Phillip Martin, *Officials Trying To Determine If Racial Profiling Tactics Are Being Employed By Federal Law Enforcement Officials; Arguments Exist that Both Support and Refute Crime Statistics* (National Public Radio broadcast, June 10, 1999) (stating that while police justify profiling based on arrest statistics, these statistics actually measure police activity instead of offense rates and overlook the fact that 98% of all blacks are not arrested in any year) (transcript on file with author).

9. *See* Chicago Gang Congregation Ordinance, CHI. MUN. CODE § 8-4-015 (1992).

10. *See* Joan Biskupic, *High Court to Review Law Aimed at Gangs,* WASH. POST, Dec. 7, 1998, at A4 (reporting that while the law was enforced, 45,000 people, mostly African-Americans and Hispanics, were arrested); David G. Savage, *High Court May Move Back on "Move On" Laws,* L.A. TIMES, Oct. 5, 1998, at A1 (noting that 45,000 arrests were made from the passage of the law until 1995); Lynn Sweet, *Court to Sort Out Loitering Law,* CHI. SUN-TIMES, Dec. 6, 1998, at 14 (stating that about 43,000 arrests were made of mostly blacks and Hispanics under the law).

11. For the full procedural history of the case before it reached the U.S. Supreme Court, see *City of Chicago v. Morales,* 687 N.E.2d 53, 57–59 (Ill. 1997), *aff'd,* 119 S. Ct. 1849 (1999).

12. *See* Tracey L. Meares & Dan M. Kahan, *The Wages of Antiquated Procedural Thinking: A Critique of* Chicago v. Morales, 1998 U. CHI. LEGAL F. 197, 212–13. The arrest of mostly minority group members under the ordinance will have many negative effects, including the "enervation" of the stigma that might otherwise attach to being arrested, the disproportionate involvement of blacks and other minorities in the criminal justice system, and reinforcement of white distrust and suspicion of all African-American men, but the authors feel nonetheless that "the ordinance is an example of a policy tool that is a tolerably *moderate* way to steer children away from criminality." *Id.* at 213. Moreover, they assert that residents of crime-ridden minority neighborhoods understand these downsides and still agree. *See id.* In an earlier version of the argument, Kahan asserts that though the law may have a disproportionate impact on minorities, "giving up on the gang-loitering law will result in more, not less, racial disparity. When we deprive the police of effective law-enforcement tools, it is the members of these groups that suffer most." Dan M. Kahan, *Defending the Gang-Loitering Law,* CHI. TRIB., Dec. 31, 1995, at 19.

13. David Cole, *"Standing While Black,"* NATION, Jan. 4, 1999, at 24 ("Chicago calls the offense 'gang loitering,' but it might more candidly be termed 'standing while black.'"). Professor Paul Butler recently wrote that police followed him in his own neighborhood up onto the front porch of his home in Washington, D.C. because the officers apparently had some doubts about whether a black man should be walking in the area; he called his own "offense" "walking while black." Paul Butler, *Walking While Black: Encounters with the Police on My Street,* LEGAL TIMES, Nov. 10, 1997, at 23. The police relented only when his neighbor came out and vouched for him. *See id.* at 24.

14. *See* City of Chicago v. Morales, 119 S. Ct. 1849, 1861 (1999) (holding that despite the ordinance's features that purported to limit police discretion, its broad sweep violated the requirement that a legislating body establish at least minimal guidance to govern enforcement of a criminal law under *Kolender v. Lawson,* 461 U.S. 352, 358 (1983)).

15. *See* [Michael Fletcher, *Driven to Extremes: Black Men Take Steps to Avoid Police Stops,* WASH. POST, Mar. 29, 1996, at A22]; *see also* [Michael A. Fletcher, *Criminal Justice Panel Defines Racial Issues,* WASH. POST, May 20, 1998, at A13] (noting that one panelist testifying before the President's race advisory board argued that police should use "'profiles' that include race because it is efficient to scrutinize groups who have higher crime rates").

16. *See* BUREAU OF JUSTICE STATISTICS, U.S. DEPT OF JUSTICE, SOURCEBOOK OF CRIMINAL JUSTICE STATISTICS 1997, at 338 (1997).

17. Homicides are much more likely to be reported then rapes.

18. *See* Delbert S. Mot, *Lies, Damn Lies, and Arrest Statistics,* 2–8, Sutherland Award Presentation, American Society of Criminology (Center for the Study of Prevention of Violence, Institute of Behavioral Science, University of Colorado at Boulder 1995) (on file with author) (criticizing the use of arrest statistics to understand criminal behavior); John Kitsuse & Aaron Cicourel, *A Note on the Use of Official Statistics,* 11 SOC. PROBS. 131, 136-37 (1963) (noting that statistics on arrest, disposition, and incarceration may measure the behavior of criminal justice agencies within the system, but not the behavior of criminals themselves).

19. Lamberth, [Report of Dr. John Lamberth, Plaintiff's Expert] at 7-8. [Wilkins v. Maryland State Police (No. MJG-93-468) (D. Md. 1996) (on file with author)]. In a very helpful and insightful comment, Professor Richard Friedman pointed out to me that perhaps this lack of statistical difference between black and white hit rates, even though many more blacks were being searched, may mean that in fact police are doing exactly what they should be: responding to very subtle cues and simply finding more blacks carrying contraband because they are engaged in this activity. I disagree; there is simply no evidence that this is so. But even if it were true, the fact that many more blacks who are completely innocent of any wrongdoing must be stopped and searched in order to expose officers to these cues would make this method of operating an unacceptable policy choice.

20. *See* U.S. CUSTOMS SERVICE, PERSONAL SEARCHES OF AIR PASSENGERS RESULTS: POSITIVE AND NEGATIVE, FISCAL YEAR 1998, at 1 (1998) (finding that 6.7% of whites, 6.3% of blacks, and 2.8% of Hispanics had contraband); *see also* David Stout, *Customs Service Will Review Drug-Search Process for Bias,* N.Y. TIMES, Apr. 9, 1999, at A18 (explaining that the Customs Service faces numerous lawsuits alleging discrimination on the basis of race and gender in the use of intrusive searches at airports).

21. Statistics on drug use are interesting for our purposes not just as a more accurate measure than arrest statistics on who may be drug involved, but as a reasonably good measure of the crime of drug possession, since users must at some point be in possession of drugs.

22. *See* SUBSTANCE ABUSE AND MENTAL HEALTH SERVS. NAT'L ADMIN., U.S. DEPT. OF HEALTH AND HUMAN SERVS., NATIONAL HOUSEHOLD SURVEY ON DRUG ABUSE, PRELIMINARY RESULTS FROM 1997, at 13, 58 tbl.1A (finding that thirteen percent of all illicit drug users were black).

23. *See* NATIONAL INST. ON DRUG ABUSE, DRUG USE AMONG RACIAL-ETHNIC MINORITIES, 64–66 figs. 1–5 (1997) (showing past-year use of marijuana, inhalants, cocaine, and LSD by black twelfth graders lower than use by whites in every year from 1977 to 1997, and tobacco use by blacks lower since 1982); *see also* BUREAU OF JUSTICE STATISTICS, U.S. DEPT OF JUSTICE, DRUGS, CRIME, AND THE JUSTICE SYSTEM 28 (1992) (reporting similar findings). It is important to note that these statistics only count those still in school; those who have dropped out or who were not in school on the particular day the information was gathered were not included. Therefore, we do not know about the rates of drug use among all young people. There could be a greater degree of drug use among those who have left school than those who have not; of course, this is probably just as true for white dropouts as it is for black dropouts. *See* SUBSTANCE ABUSE AND MENTAL HEALTH SERVS. ADMIN., U.S. DEFT OF HEALTH AND HUMAN SERVS., NATIONAL HOUSEHOLD SURVEY ON DRUG ABUSE, PRELIMINARY ESTIMATES FROM 1995, at 13 (1997) (stating that among white, black, and Hispanic youth, "the rates of use are about the same").

24. *See* Carter & Marsico, *supra* note 16, at 1.

25. *See* BUREAU OF JUSTICE STATISTICS, *supra* note [16], at 338 tbl.4.10, 422 tbl.5.46.

26. *See id.* at 426 tbl.5.51(citing figures for 1994).

27. *See id.* at 428 tbl.5.55 (citing figures for 1994).

28. Interview with Karen Brank, [in Toledo, Ohio (Aug. 21, 1998)].

29. *See* Interview with James, [in Toledo, Ohio (Oct. 30, 1998). James asked that his last name not be used in any publication].

30. Interview with Michael, [in Toledo, Ohio (Oct. 1, 1998). Michael, 41, is an African-American male who has been subjected to pretextual traffic stops. As with some of the other individuals quoted here, Michael asked that his last name not be used].

31. *See* Neil MacFarquar, *Police Get Good Ratings From Most, but Not All, New Yorkers,* N.Y. TIMES, June 5, 1999, at B3 (reporting that a national survey conducted by the Bureau of Justice Statistics and the Office of Community Oriented Police Services of the U.S. Department of Justice indicated that almost two and one-half times as many blacks as whites say they are dissatisfied with their police).

32. *See* [Dan Barry & Marjorie Connelly, *Poll in New York Finds Many Think Police Are Biased,* N.Y. TIMES, Mar. 16, 1999, at Al (stating that less than 25 percent of New Yorkers surveyed believe that police treat blacks and whites equally); David W. Moore & Lydia Saad, *No Immediate Sign That Simpson Trial Intensified Racial Animosity,* GALLUP POLL MONTHLY, Oct. 1995, at 5 (reporting that 68% of blacks and 52% of whites said they believe police racism against blacks is common); Julia Vitullo-Martin, *Fairness, Justice Not Simply a Matter of Black and White,* CHI. TRIB., Nov. 13, 1997, at 31 (noting recent poll by Joint Center for Political and Economic Studies that indicated that more than 80% of blacks and Hispanics, and 56% of whites, agree that police are far more likely to harass and discriminate against blacks than whites); *see also* Michael A. Fletcher, *Criminal Justice Panel Defines Racial Issues,* WASH. POST, May 20, 1998, at A13 (noting that panelists appearing before President Clinton's Race Advisory Board argued, with little dissent, that the criminal justice system exhibits many biases toward blacks and other minorities).].

33. *See* Gary Webb, *DWB,* Esquire, Apr. 1999, at 118, 125.

34. *See* Jeffrey Rosen, *One Angry Woman,* New Yorker, Feb. 24 & Mar. 3, 1997, at 54, 64 (arguing that rising percentage of mistrials may be because, as one senior Justice Department official says, "'[Blacks] see black defendants and white prosecutors. *They get stopped for no reason.* Those are the things that stick out in your mind.'" (emphasis added)); *see also* Roger Parloff, *Race and Juries: If It Ain't Broke. . . ,* AM. LAW., June 1997, at 5. Although Parloff argues persuasively that there does not seem to be any impending crisis caused by a dramatic increase in hung juries or acquittals, he reveals considerable factual support for the proposition that minority communities do exhibit more skepticism toward police that whites do. *See id.* Professor Paul Butler has made a related argument: black jurors ought to use the power of nullification, and refuse to convict obviously guilty black men in certain cases, because of the unjust way in which the system treats blacks. *See* Paul Butler, *Racially Based Jury Nullification: Black Power in the Criminal Justice System,* 105 YALE L.J. 677, 679 (1995).

35. *See* Randall Kennedy, *The State, Criminal Law, and Racial Discrimination: A Comment,* 107 HARV. L. REV. 1255, 1260 n.20 (1994) (arguing for a "politics of distinction," in which law enforcement efforts, even if excessive, against law-breaking blacks are seen not as racial discrimination but as a net benefit to law-abiding blacks, because so much crime is intraracial); *see also* Regina Austin, *The Black Community, Its Lawbreakers, and a Politics of Identification,* 65 S. CAL. L. REV. 1769, 1772 (1992) (explaining this idea as "the difference that exists between the 'better' elements of the [black] community and the stereotypical 'lowlifes' who richly merit the bad reputations the dominant society accords them"). *But see* David Cole, *The Paradox of Race and Crime: A Comment on Randall Kennedy's "Politics of Distinction,"* 83 GA. L. REV. 2547 (1995) (arguing that while Kennedy astutely recognizes the paradox posed by the fact that blacks, who are disproportionately victims of crime by other blacks suffer from both over- and under-enforcement of the criminal law, he is wrong to try to make the false choice of benefiting "good" over "bad" blacks).

36. MARC MAUER & TRACY HULING, YOUNG BLACK AMERICANS AND THE CRIMINAL JUSTICE SYSTEM: FIVE YEARS LATER 4 tbl.2 (1995) (on file with author).

37. ERIC LOTKE, NATIONAL CTR. FOR INSTS. AND ALTERNATIVES, HOBBLING A GENERATION (1997) (on file with author).

38. *See* THE SENTENCING PROJECT, LOSING THE VOTE: THE IMPACT OF FELONY DISENFRANCHISEMENT LAWS IN THE UNITED STATES 2, 8-10 tbl.3 (1998) (on file with author) (arguing that 1.4 million black men are disenfranchised, representing 13% of the adult male black population, and 36% of all those disenfranchised; in seven states, one in four black males is permanently disenfranchised).

39. 487 U.S. 654 (1988).

40. *Id.* at 727–28 (Scalia, J., dissenting) (quoting Robert Jackson, The Federal Prosecutor, Address at the Second Annual Conference of United States Attorneys (Apr. 1, 1940)) (emphasis added).

41. . . . Ironically, the Court's opinion in *Whren,* the case that completely freed the police from any Fourth Amendment-based restriction on their discretion to make traffic stops, was written by Justice Scalia. *See* Whren v. United States, 517 U.S. 806 (1996).

42. Blacks receive longer sentences than whites in federal courts and are more likely to be incarcerated. See BUREAU OF JUSTICE STATISTICS, *supra* note [16], at 395 tbl.5.19 & 396 tbl.5.20. Even controlling for offense level and criminal history, blacks received longer sentences than whites under the Federal Sentencing Guidelines. *See* DAVID B. MUSTARD, RACIAL ETHNIC AND GENDER DISPARITIES IN SENTENCING: EVIDENCE FROM THE FEDERAL COURTS (University of Ga. Econ. Working Paper 97–458), *available at The University of Georgia Department of Economics* (visited Oct. 26, 1999) http://www.terry.uga.edu/~dmustard/dbmcv.htm.

43. *See* MUSTARD, supra note [42].

44. *See* United States v. Leviner, 31 F. Supp. 2d 23, 26 (D. Mass. 1998).

45. *See* A.L.I.-A.B.A., FEDERAL SENTENCING GUIDELINES 1 (1988) ("Factors in determining the appropriate sentence range . . . include . . . the defendant's criminal history.").

46. *Leviner,* 31 F. Supp. 2d at 24.

47. *See id.* at 33 & n.26.

48. *See id.* at 33.

49. *See id.* at 31, 34.

50. The United States has filed an appeal in the case. *See* Petition for Appeal, United States v. Leviner, No. 99-1172 (1st Cir. Mar. 17, 1999) (on file with author).

51. *See* Fletcher, *supra* note 15, at Al (describing ways that blacks attempt to avoid police attention by staying out of black areas); Interview with Kevin, *supra* note 46 (stating that he drives a minivan specifically to avoid police scrutiny).

52. *See* Interview with Karen Brank, *supra* note [28] (stating that she avoids the white suburban community where she was stopped before); Interview with James, *supra* note [29] (stating that he avoids a white suburban area because of its reputation for stopping and harassing black motorists).

53. *See* Warren Brown, *Urban League Quits Seat Belt Drive; Group Cites Fear of Increased Police Harassment of Minorities,* WASH. POST, Dec. 11, 1998, at A14.

54. *See id.*

55. *See, e.g.,* 625 ILL. COMP. STAT. ANN. 5/12-603.1(e) (West Supp. 1999) (stating that police cannot stop a vehicle "solely on the basis of a violation or suspected violation of this Section"); MICH. COMP. LAWS ANN. § 257.710(e)(5) (West Supp. 1999) (stating that enforcement of seat belt requirement may be done only as a "secondary action");

OHIO REV. CODE ANN. § 4513.263(D) (Anderson Supp. 1998) (stating that the police may not stop a motorist solely for a seat belt violation).

56. *See* Susan P. Baker et al., *Motor Vehicle Occupant Deaths Among Hispanic and Black Children and Teenagers,* 152 ARCHIVES OF PEDIATRICS & ADOLESCENT MED. 1209, 1210–11 (1998) (noting that higher rates of death in motor vehicle accidents among young blacks and Hispanics than among whites, which could be attributable to "racial/ethnic and sex differences in the use of safety belts and child restraints"); *see also* CENTER FOR DISEASE CONTROL AND PREVENTION, U.S. DEPT OF HEALTH AND HUMAN SERVS., VITAL AND HEALTH STATISTICS: HEALTH OF OUR NATION'S CHILDREN, SERIES 10: DATA FROM THE NATIONAL HEALTH INTERVIEW SURVEY, No. 191, at 45 tbl.14 (1994) (reporting low rates of seat belt and restraint use for black children); Steve J. Niemcryk et al., *Motor Vehicle Crashes, Restraint Use, and Severity of Injury in Children in Nevada,* 13 AM. J. PREVENTATIVE MED. 109, 111 tbl.2 (1997) (same).

57. Brown, *supra* note [53], at A14.

58. *Id.*

59. *See, e.g.,* William J. Bratton, *New Strategies for Combating Crime in New York City,* 23 FORDHAM URB. L.J. 781, 782 (1996) (describing the dominant mode of policing in the 1970s and 1980s as "largely reactive" or "rapid response" oriented, in which officers were "reacting to 911 calls, random patrol, riding around waiting for something to happen . . . and the reactive investigation," leaving police "ill-prepared" to face greater rates of crime and violence that came with the crack cocaine trade); Bureau of Justice Assistance, U.S. Dep't of Justice, *Understanding Community Policing, A Framework for Action,* MONOGRAPH, Aug. 1994, at 6 (explaining how rapid response policing "became an end in itself" and cut officers off from the community); Veronica Jennings, *Community Policing Is on the Way,* WASH. POST, July 2, 1992, at MI (noting that community policing "puts the emphasis on preventing crime rather than on responding to radio dispatched calls").

60. *See, e.g.,* [DAVID COLE, NO EQUAL JUSTICE: RACE AND CLASS IN THE AMERICAN CRIMINAL JUSTICE SYSTEM . . . (1999)] at 192–93 (defining community policing as an effort to "make the police an integral part of the neighborhoods they serve"); COMMUNITY RELATIONS SERV., U.S. DEPT OF JUSTICE, PRINCIPLES OF GOOD POLICING: AVOIDING VIOLENCE BETWEEN POLICE AND CITIZENS 5 (1993) ("Community policing is a philosophy in which the police engage the community to solve problems . . . based on a collaboration between police and citizens in non-threatening and supportive interactions. These interactions include efforts by police to listen to citizens, take seriously the citizens' definitions of problems, and solve the problems that have been identified."); Bretton, *supra* note [59], at 784–85 (stating that community policing emphasizes "the three P's": partnership with the community, problem solving, and prevention of crime).

61. 392 U.S. 1(1968).

62. *See id.* at 14–15 & n.11.

63. Interview with Ova Tate, [Police Officer, in Toledo, Ohio (Aug. 28, 1998)].

64. *See* COLE, *supra* note [60] at 192–93 ("Where such programs develop effective channels for communication between the police and the community about their respective needs, the programs can play an important role in restoring community trust and overcoming the adversarial relationship too many police departments have with disadvantaged communities.").

65. Unfortunately, strong negative feelings about police among members of minority groups, especially African-Americans, is not a thing of the past. *See* [Dan Barry & Marjorie Connelly, *Poll in New York Finds Many Think Police Are Biased,* N.Y. TIMES, Mar. 16, 1999], at Al (citing a 1999 survey indicating that "fewer than a quarter of all New Yorkers believe police treat blacks and whites evenly").

EBBERS' 25 YEAR SENTENCE FOR WORLDCOM FRAUD UPHELD. GOOD.

Paul Leighton

Much of the attention around corporate fraud has been centered on Enron, which declared the largest corporate bankruptcy in history because of multifaceted fraud. When "Worldcon" declared bankruptcy a month or so later, it displaced Enron and became the biggest corporate bankruptcy (a record it held until Lehman Brothers collapsed). Bernard Ebbers was CEO, found guilty by a jury on multiple counts and sentenced to 25 years. His sentence has just been upheld—and I'm glad, although some other people have questions and concerns.

Specifically, the White Collar Crime Professor's Blog as well as the Second Circuit Sentencing Blog have raised some excellent questions about whether the sentence is excessive. I'm sure many others share their sentiments, so I wanted to give some background on the sentence and respond to concerns raised in the two blogs.

WORLDCON BACKGROUND & EBBERS SENTENCING

The Court of Appeal's decision in *U.S. v Ebbers* briefly reviews the relevant history before pronouncing their bottom line:

> the securities fraud here was not puffery or cheerleading or even a misguided effort to protect the company, its employees, and its shareholders from the capital-impairing effects of what was believed to be a temporary downturn in business. The methods used were specifically intended to create a false picture of profitability even for professional analysts that, in Ebbers' case, was motivated by his personal financial circumstances. Given Congress' policy decisions on sentences for fraud, the sentence is harsh but not unreasonable. (p. 47)

Before I detail the objections and respond to them one at a time, let's just review how the sentence was calculated. In general, the sentencing guidelines are a grid that judges use to look up a sentence based on (a) the severity of the crime and (b) the offender's criminal history. In Ebbers' case:

> The pre-sentence report ("PSR") recommended a base offense level of six, plus sentencing enhancements of 26 levels for a loss over $100 million, of four levels for involving more than 50 victims, of two levels for receiving more than $1 million from financial institutions as a result of the offense, of four levels for leading a criminal activity involving five or more partic-

---

Source: Originally appeared on PaulsJusticeBlog.com. Reprinted by permission of the author.

ipants, and of two levels for abusing a position of public trust, bringing the total offense level to 44 levels. The government also sought a two-level enhancement for obstruction of justice on the basis of Ebbers' having testified contrary to the jury's verdict. With Ebbers' criminal history category of I, the Guidelines range calculated in the PSR was life imprisonment. The Probation Department recommended a 30-year sentence. Judge Jones declined to apply the enhancements for deriving more than $1 million from financial institutions or for obstruction of justice. She also denied Ebbers' motions for downward departures based on the claims that, inter alia, the loss overstated the seriousness of the offense, his medical condition was poor, and he had performed many beneficial community services and good works. She determined that his total offense level was 42 and that the advisory Guidelines range would be 30 years to life. She then sentenced Ebbers to 25 years' imprisonment and three years' supervised release, and imposed a $900 special assessment but no fines.

Sounds to me like he caught a few breaks. They are not necessarily unreasonable, but would probably generate outrage and the downward departures would be more likely to result in an appeal by the government if it was a drug case.

QUESTIONS & ISSUES

The concerns outlined in the White Collar Crime blog are in the bulleted points below, followed by my responses.

- Should a white collar offender who commits an economic crime be receiving a greater sentence than someone who commits a murder?

This general issue also shows up in the comment that "In some cases money losses may be more important when it comes to determining a sentence, then loss of life." While the question form sounds more outrageous, the statement seems reasonable: yes, causing $100 million in losses to more than 50 victims, while leading a criminal activity involving others and a breach of public trust can be worse than a loss of life—especially where the latter was not premeditated (passion, negligence, etc).

I will quickly add that I am pissed off that his sentence is greater than what some other executives receive for deaths that result from *willful* violations of workplace safety. According to a *NY Times* report: "When Congress established OSHA in 1970, it made it a misdemeanor to cause the death of a worker by willfully violating safety laws. The maximum sentence, six months in jail, is half the maximum for harassing a wild burro on federal lands." Counterquestion: why is it that a corporate executive who kills receives less of a sentence than everyone else?

If we are going to engage in arguments on the basis of disparities, consider that Leandro Andrade received 50 years for two incidents of shoplifting videos from K-Mart. Two convictions of burglary in the 1980s counted as strikes 1 and 2; the shoplifting charges became strikes 3 and 4, with each strike carrying a mandatory 25 years. The Supreme Court upheld the sentence, as I discussed in a piece I co-authored with Jeffrey Reiman, "A Tale of Two Criminals: We're Tougher on Corporate Crime, But They

Still Don't Get What They Deserve." That piece compares Andrade with Fastow, who received a ten year maximum sentence in a plea bargain based on 109 felony counts. But if it is OK to argue that murderers get less than Ebbers, I'll ask why these sentences—and lots of drug sentences—are higher than what he received?

• Should being a first offender mean something when it comes to the sentence imposed?

In many ways, I think the blog's comment on the decision shows better perspective: "Being a first offender doesn't mean much if the loss is high—the sentence basically ends up placing the convicted defendant in prison for the rest of his life." The first part of this makes sense and applies to many serious crimes, where there is a limited break for being a first offender. Although I've never before defended the rationality of the guidelines, they did take into consideration he was a first offender, but that was outdone by the fact he was leader of an activity involving others, etc. Given that the fraud was ongoing for more than a year also raises questions about how much of a break you should get for a "first offense."

• Have we failed to consider the potential future harmfulness in sentencing white collar offenders? Do we really need these extreme sentences to deter others who may be contemplating these crimes?

Probably not much thought has gone into the first point about harmfulness of individual offenders. That's not to say they should be considered unlikely to be a problem (because there are many ways to commit frauds), just that it is not an important factor in any criminal sentencing now; it's all about "just deserts."

Counter-question: If future harmfulness is an important factor, then shouldn't it be so for all defendants and not just relevant for white collar offenders?

By the way, in Andrade's shoplifting case, the Supreme Court cited *Rummell v Estelle,* another Supreme Court case upholding a life sentence for three felonies for thefts that totaled less than $230 and never involved force or the threat of force. In contrast to the largest corporate bankruptcy in US history, Justice Louis Powell's dissent in *Rummell* noted that "it is difficult to imagine felonies that pose less danger to the peace and good order of a civilized society than the three crimes committed by the petitioner" (445 US 263, 295).

On the deterrence point, I do tend to believe that smooth-talking, well paid, highly privileged executives will be difficult to deter.

• If you decide to take the risk of trial and don't plead guilty and cooperate with the government, you may be spending the rest of your life in prison if the jury convicts you.

This concern arises because of a statement in the court's decision that: "Under the Guidelines, it may well be that all but the most trivial frauds in publicly traded companies may trigger sentences amounting to life imprisonment—Ebbers' 25-year sentence is actually below the Guidelines level. Even the threat of indictment on wafer-thin evidence of fraud may therefore compel a plea."

The Supreme Court rejected the notion that Andrade's 50 year sentence was "life imprisonment" for stealing videos. Once again, let's be consistent—if we're going to talk of 25 year sentences as life imprisonment, let's do so for all crimes, including a large number of harsh and mandatory ones.

Since the next point deals with the harshness directly, consider the coerced plea bargain argument—that the threat of harsh penalties may improperly compel guilty pleas. Interestingly, the *Criminal Justice Ethics* anthology by me and Jeffrey Reiman includes a 1976 article by Kipnis on this topic ("Criminal Justice and the Negotiated Plea"). He shares the concern about coercion and plea bargains in all criminal cases, and reviews the Supreme Court cases of *North Carolina v Alford* and *Brady v US*. In both cases, defendants accepted very long prison terms to avoid possible/probable death sentences. The Court upheld these as voluntary, even though the defendant in *Alford* said in open court: "We never had an argument in our life and I just pleaded guilty because they said if I didn't they would gas me for it, and that is all" and "You told me to plead guilty, right. I don't—I'm not guilty but I plead guilty." (400 US 28, note 2)

Return to the theme and counterquestion: is the coercion with plea bargaining a problem across a wide range of crimes for which we have harsh sentences, or it is just about poor Bernie Ebbers and corporate crooks? Frankly, I am much less concerned about coercion involving CEOs, who have vast resources at their disposal to challenge government attorneys. Some of the Enron defendants spent $30–40 million. Not only is CEO pay extremely high, but at times their employment contract specifies that the company pays attorney fees (unless the crime involved ripping off the company). In many cases CEO defendants will have more resources for a trial than the local US Attorney will. The situation with street criminals is different, so I continue to be more concerned about coercive plea bargains there.

- Have we gone overboard in sentencing white collar offenders?

Let's add to this several questions from the Second Circuit Sentencing Blog:

- 25 years. Perhaps it is reasonable today. But would it have been reasonable 15 years ago? I don't think so. And, if not, what accounts for the change in view as to why 25 years is reasonable today and not yesterday?

As I argued elsewhere, sentences for white collar criminals are certainly *tougher*. But they have been excessively lenient in the past. We've been getting "tough on crime" for more than 30 years, but how many times have corporate crimes been included? In response to whether 25 years would have reasonable in the past, no. But crimes were also smaller then. The S & L losses didn't approach the losses from Worldcom. Or Enron. Companies are now bigger, more powerful, and their collapse from fraud leaves a much larger financial crater. More people get hurt, and the losses are much more severe, with more powerful ripple effects through associated businesses and the economy in general.

Thus, the question is about balancing the harm done by the crime with the punishment. Is 25 years really excessive for being the head of a fraud that causes the largest corporate bankruptcy in history, which impacts hundreds of thousands of people through employment, retirement funds and other avenues?

My question would be why the government was content with using $100 million as the loss figure, when it could have easily proved a much larger loss? Even if there is some controversy about how exactly to figure losses (see pp. 37–42 of the decision), the appeals court notes (p. 42): "the loss amount is still well above $1 billion, or ten times greater than the $100 million dollar threshold for the 26-level enhancement." In describing several shareholders whose losses were not calculated in, the Court said: "And neither their loss nor those of bondholders—estimated by the Probation Office at $10 billion—is included in the Probation Office's calculations. Even a loss calculation of $1 billion is therefore almost certainly too low, and there is no reasonable calculation of loss to investors that would call for" the calculation of losses to be reheard.

So, the sentence is based on a loss of $100 million, when the loss could easily be a $1 billion or more. And somehow Ebbers has received a raw deal? Please.

• Is this what Congress wanted?

Congress was under a great deal of pressure because of the large number of companies that imploded because of financial and accounting scandals. The U.S. Chamber of Commerce has launched an aggressive campaign to get Congress to relax many provisions of Sarbanes-Oxley. No doubt that at some future point when we have a bit more distance, this will happen. But it will be a bad idea.

A MEMO FOUND IN THE STREET: UNCLE SAM THE ENABLER

Barry L. Ritholtz

To: *Washington, D.C.*
From: *Wall Street*
Re: *Credit Crisis*

Dear D.C.,
Wow, we've made quite a mess of things here on Wall Street: Fannie and Freddie in conservatorship, investment banks in the tank, AIG nationalized. Thanks for sending us your new trillion-dollar bailout.

We on Wall Street feel somewhat compelled to take at least some responsibility. We used excessive leverage, failed to maintain adequate capital, engaged in reckless speculation, created new complex derivatives. We focused on short-term profits at the expense of sustainability. We not only undermined our own firms, we destabilized the financial sector and roiled the global economy, to boot. And we got huge bonuses.

But here's a news flash for you, D.C.: We could not have done it without you. We may be drunks, but you were our enablers: Your legislative, executive, and administrative decisions made possible all that we did. Our recklessness would not have reached its soaring heights but for your governmental incompetence.

This memo provides a brief history of your actions that helped create this crisis.

1997: Federal Reserve Chairman Alan Greenspan's famous "irrational exuberance" speech in 1996 was somehow ignored by, um, Fed Chairman Greenspan. The Fed missed the opportunity to change margin requirements. Had the Fed acted, the bubble would not have inflated as much, and the subsequent crash would not have been as severe.

1998: Long Term Capital Management was undercapitalized, used enormous amounts of leverage to purchase all manner of thinly traded, hard-to-value paper. It failed, and under the authority of the Federal Reserve a "private-sector" rescue plan was cobbled together. Had these bankers suffered big losses from LTCM, they might have thought twice before jumping into the exact same business model of undercapitalized, overleveraged, thinly traded, hard-to-value paper. Instead, they re-affirmed Benjamin Disraeli's famous aphorism: "What we learn from history is that we do not learn from history."

1999: The Financial Services Modernization Act repealed Glass-Steagall, a law that had separated the commercial-banking industry from Wall Street, and the two industries, plus insurance, came together again. Banks became bigger, clumsier, and hard to manage. Apparently, risk-management became all but impossible, even as banks had greater access to larger pools of capital.

2000: The Commodities Futures Modernization Act defined financial commodities such as "interest rates, currency prices, and stock indexes" as "excluded commodities." They could trade off the futures exchanges, with minimal oversight by the Commodity Futures Trading Commission. Neither the Securities and Exchange Commission, nor the Federal Reserve, nor any state insurance regulators had the ability to supervise or regulate the writing of credit-default swaps by hedge funds, investment banks or insurance companies.

2001–'03: Alan Greenspan's Fed dropped federal-fund rates to 1%. Lulled into a false belief that inflation was not a problem, the Fed then kept rates at 1% for more than a year. This set off an inflationary spiral in housing, and a desperate hunt for yield by fixed-income managers.

2003–'07: The Federal Reserve failed to use its supervisory and regulatory authority over banks, mortgage underwriters and other lenders, who abandoned such standards as employment history, income, down payments, credit rating, assets, property loan-to-value ratio and debt-servicing ability. The borrower's ability to repay these mortgages was replaced with the lender's ability to securitize and repackage them.

2004: The SEC waived its leverage rules. Previously, broker/dealer net-capital rules limited firms to a maximum debt-to-net-capital ratio of 12 to 1. This 2004 exemption allowed them to exceed this leverage rule. Only five firms—Goldman Sachs, Merrill Lynch, Lehman Brothers, Bear Stearns and Morgan Stanley—were granted this exemption; they promptly lever[ag]ed up 20, 30 and even 40 to 1.

2005–'07: Unscrupulous home appraisers found that they could attract more business by inflating appraisals. Intrinsic value was ignored, so referrals kept coming in. This helped borrowers obtain financing at prices that were increasingly unsupportable. When honest appraisers petitioned both Congress and the bureaucracy to intervene in the widespread fraud, neither branch of government acted.

There's actually a lot more we could add to these items. We could mention impotent supervision of Fannie and Freddie by the Office of Federal Housing Enterprise Oversight; the negligent oversight on ratings agencies; the Boskin Commission's monkeying around with how inflation gets measured; the "Greenspan Put," etc.

We could mention former Fed Governor Edward Gramlich, who warned about making home loans to people who could not afford them, and who said the runaway subprime-mortgage industry would create problems in housing and the credit markets. But Gramlich was up against a Fed chairman who apparently believed that markets can regulate themselves.

We on Wall Street do not deny our part. We created these securities, we rated them triple-A, we traded them without understanding them. Now that they have gone bad, we are real close to getting the rest of the country to take them off our hands.

Thanks, D.C. None of this would have been possible without you.

Very truly yours,
Wall Street

THEY WARNED US: U.S. WAS TOLD TO "EXPECT FORECLOSURES, EXPECT HORROR STORIES"

Matt Apuzzo

The Bush administration backed off proposed crackdowns on no-money-down, interest-only mortgages years before the economy collapsed, buckling to pressure from some of the same banks that have now failed. It ignored remarkably prescient warnings that foretold the financial meltdown, according to an Associated Press review of regulatory documents.

"Expect fallout, expect foreclosures, expect horror stories," California mortgage lender Paris Welch wrote to U.S. regulators in January 2006, about one year before the housing implosion cost her a job.

Bowing to aggressive lobbying—along with assurances from banks that the troubled mortgages were OK—regulators delayed action for nearly one year. By the time new rules were released late in 2006, the toughest of the proposed provisions were gone and the meltdown was under way.

"These mortgages have been considered more safe and sound for portfolio lenders than many fixed rate mortgages," David Schneider, home loan president of Washington Mutual, told federal regulators in early 2006. Two years later, WaMu became the largest bank failure in U.S. history.

The administration's blind eye to the impending crisis is emblematic of a philosophy that trusted market forces and discounted the need for government intervention

Source: The Associated Press, December 1, 2008. Reprinted by permission.

in the economy. Its belief ironically has ushered in the most massive government intervention since the 1930s. "We're going to be feeling the effects of the regulators' failure to address these mortgages for the next several years," said Kevin Stein of the California Reinvestment Coalition, who warned regulators to tighten lending rules before it was too late.

Many of the banks that fought to undermine the proposals by some regulators are now either out of business or accepting billions in federal aid to recover from a mortgage crisis they insisted would never come. Many executives remain in high-paying jobs, even after their assurances were proved false.

In 2005, faced with ominous signs the housing market was in jeopardy, bank regulators proposed new guidelines for banks writing risky loans. Today, in the midst of the worst housing recession in a generation, the proposal reads like a list of what-ifs:

- Regulators told bankers exotic mortgages were often inappropriate for buyers with bad credit.
- Banks would have been required to increase efforts to verify that buyers actually had jobs and could afford houses.
- Regulators proposed a cap on risky mortgages so a string of defaults wouldn't be crippling.
- Banks that bundled and sold mortgages were told to be sure investors knew exactly what they were buying.
- Regulators urged banks to help buyers make responsible decisions and clearly advise them that interest rates might skyrocket and huge payments might be due sooner than expected.

Those proposals all were stripped from the final rules. None required congressional approval or the president's signature. "In hindsight, it was spot on," said Jeffrey Brown, a former top official at the Office of Comptroller of the Currency, one of the first agencies to raise concerns about risky lending.

Federal regulators were especially concerned about mortgages known as "option ARMs," which allow borrowers to make payments so low that mortgage debt actually increases every month. But banking executives accused the government of overreacting. Bankers said such loans might be risky when approved with no money down or without ensuring buyers have jobs but such risk could be managed without government intervention.

"An open market will mean that different institutions will develop different methodologies for achieving this goal," Joseph Polizzotto, counsel to now-bankrupt Lehman Brothers, told U.S. regulators in a March 2006. Countrywide Financial Corp., at the time the nation's largest mortgage lender, agreed. The proposal "appears excessive and will inhibit future innovation in the marketplace," said Mary Jane Seebach, managing director of public affairs.

One of the most contested rules said that before banks purchase mortgages from brokers, they should verify the process to ensure buyers could afford their homes. Some bankers now blame much of the housing crisis on brokers who wrote fraudulent, predatory loans. But in 2006, banks said they shouldn't have to double-check the brokers. "It is not our role to be the regulator for the third-party lenders," wrote Ruthann Melbourne, chief risk officer of IndyMac Bank.

California-based IndyMac also criticized regulators for not recognizing the track record of interest-only loans and option ARMs, which accounted for 70 percent of IndyMac's 2005 mortgage portfolio. This summer, the government seized IndyMac and will pay an estimated $9 billion to ensure customers don't lose their deposits.

Last week, Downey Savings joined the growing list of failed banks. The problem: About 52 percent of its mortgage portfolio was tied up in risky option ARMs, which in 2006 Downey insisted were safe—maybe even safer than traditional 30-year mortgages. "To conclude that 'nontraditional' equates to higher risk does not appropriately balance risk and compensating factors of these products," said Lillian Gavin, the bank's chief credit officer.

At least some regulators didn't buy it. The comptroller of the currency, John C. Dugan, was among the first to sound the alarm in mid-2005. Speaking to a consumer advocacy group, Dugan painted a troublesome picture of option-ARM lending. Many buyers, particularly those with bad credit, would soon be unable to afford their payments, he said. And if housing prices declined, homeowners wouldn't even be able to sell their way out of the mess. It sounded simple, but "people kind of looked at us regulators as old-fashioned," said Brown, the agency's former deputy comptroller.

Diane Casey-Landry, of the American Bankers Association, said the industry feared a two-tiered system in which banks had to follow rules that mortgage brokers did not. She said opposition was based on the banks' best information. "You're looking at a decline in real estate values that was never contemplated," she said.

Some saw problems coming. Community groups and even some in the mortgage business, like Welch, warned regulators not to ease their rules. "We expect to see a huge increase in defaults, delinquencies and foreclosures as a result of the over selling of these products," Stein, the associate director of the California Reinvestment Coalition, wrote to regulators in 2006. The group advocates on housing and banking issues for low-income and minority residents.

The government's banking agencies spent nearly a year debating the rules, which required unanimous agreement among the OCC, Federal Deposit Insurance Corp., Federal Reserve, and the Office of Thrift Supervision—agencies that sometimes don't agree. The Fed, for instance, was reluctant under Alan Greenspan to heavily regulate lending. Similarly, the Office of Thrift Supervision, an arm of the Treasury Department that regulated many in the subprime mortgage market, worried that restricting certain mortgages would hurt banks and consumers.

Grovetta Gardineer, OTS managing director for corporate and international activities, said the 2005 proposal "attempted to send an alarm bell that these products are bad." After hearing from banks, she said, regulators were persuaded that the loans themselves were not problematic as long as banks managed the risk. She disputes the notion that the rules were weakened.

Marc Savitt, president of the National Association of Mortgage Brokers, said regulators were afraid of stopping a good thing. "If it seems to be working, if it's not broken don't fix it, if everybody's making money, then the good times are rolling and nobody wants to be the one guy to put the brakes on," he said.

In the past year, with Congress scrambling to stanch the bleeding in the financial industry, regulators have tightened rules on risky mortgages. Congress is considering further tightening, including some of the same proposals abandoned years ago.

Readings on To the Vanquished Belong the Spoils

EDITORS' INTRODUCTION

Chapter 4 of *The Rich Get Richer* examines how a failing criminal justice system that neither protects society nor achieves justice is allowed to continue. The chapter notes that the criminal justice system actually fails in three ways: (1) It fails to implement policies that stand a good chance of reducing crime, (2) it fails to identify as crimes the harmful acts of the rich and powerful, and (3) it fails to eliminate economic bias in the criminal justice system itself. In addressing why this is happening, the authors point out that the wealthy are the beneficiaries of the current system's failure. They do not argue that this is a conspiracy but that those who have power to change the system benefit from the way it operates; they can go on performing harmful acts and accumulating wealth without punishment, while the country remains focused on street crime and poor minority criminals.

A key idea is that of *ideology,* widely held false beliefs that serve to justify the status quo and its inequalities. Chapter 4 of *The Rich Get Richer* notes that the "have-nots and have-littles far outnumber the have-plenties" in the United States so the wealthy need the voluntary cooperation of the poor for the inequality to continue. For example, consider the distribution of wealth, meaning the assets people accumulate over their lifetime minus all their debts. For 2004, the last year in which full data is available:[1]

Amount of wealth held by poorest 50% of population	$1.28 trillion
Amount of wealth held by *Forbes* 400	$1.0 trillion
(the 400 richest families = 0.0004% of population)	

Chapter 4 notes that ideology is required so that the have-nots and have-littles believe "that they are not being exploited or treated unfairly by the have-plenties" and that this distribution "is about the best that human beings can create." Table 4.1 illustrates other aspects of the current distribution of wealth like stocks, businesses, and credit card

TABLE 4.1   Shares of Net Worth and Components Distributed By Net Worth Groups, 2004

Wealth Percentile Group	Maximum Net Wealth	Net Wealth (percent)	Stock Ownership (percent)	Business Ownership (percent)	Credit Card Debt (percent)
0–50	$92,900	2.5	0.6	0.3	45.7
50–90	827,600	27.9	10.3	9.2	46.9
90–95	1,393,000	12.0	10.1	5.7	3.6
95–99	6,006,000	24.1	28.2	22.4	3.1
99–100		33.4	50.9	62.3	0.7

Note: The *Forbes* 400, the 400 wealthiest families in the United States, were not included in the Survey of Consumer Finances used to produce Table 4.1. In 2004, the *Forbes* 400 collectively had total wealth of over $1 trillion dollars; the minimum wealth to make the list was $750 million and the wealthiest family had $51 billion in wealth.

Source: Arthur Kennickell, "Currents and Undercurrents: Changes in the Distribution of Wealth, 1989–2004." Federal Reserve Board, 2006. www.federalreserve.gov/pubs/oss/oss2/scfindex.html

debt. The criminal justice system helps create some of this ideology but also has its own inequities that require ideology to be seen as legitimate. One significant issue is minority overrepresentation in arrest, conviction, and imprisonment rates. While *The Rich Get Richer* and the various articles in the reader contain statistics on this point, Table 4.2 highlights some key figures. The readings in this section raise awareness about the failings of the criminal justice system and critique the idea that individual criminals bear full responsibility for their criminal acts, while inequality and other social conditions that contribute to crime are rendered invisible or seen as just.

In "Why Are So Many Americans in Prison? Race and the Transformation of Criminal Justice," Glenn Loury points out that of the more than 2,000,000 people currently locked up in about 5,000 U.S. prisons and jails, only one-third are violent criminals, most are drawn from the disadvantaged parts of U.S. society, and they are "vastly disproportionately black and brown." This enormous number of Americans in confinement is said not to have been due to more crime, but to greater punitiveness, referring both to an increase in the number of prison sentences per arrest, and to an increase in the length of the sentences themselves. "Despite a sharp national decline in crime," the author writes, "American criminal justice has become crueler and less caring than . . . at any other time in our modern history." "Why?" the author asks, and responds by pointing to how the toughening of our criminal justice system continues in a new form the historical process of constraining and stigmatizing nonwhite Americans, a new form that ironically appeared just after the civil rights movement succeeded in getting discrimination on the base of race and skin color outlawed. Just as Chapter 4 of *The Rich Get Richer* argues that criminal justice promotes the idea that the greatest threat to middle-class Americans is from the lower classes (rather than from the harmful acts of the upper classes), Loury argues that imprisonment meshes with other processes of exclusion and labeling to promote the idea of nonwhites as dangerous others from whom the majority of Americans must be protected.

TABLE 4.2   People under Control of the Criminal Justice System, by Gender, Race, and Ethnicity

	Jail (rate per 100,000) Mid-2006	Prison (rate per 100,000) 2008	Percent of Adult Population Ever Incarcerated in Prison, 2001	Percent Ever Going to Prison During Lifetime if Born in 2001
White	170	—	**1.4**	**3.4**
Male	—	727	2.6	5.9
Female	—	93	0.5	0.9
Black	815	—	**8.9**	**18.6**
Male	—	4,777	16.6	32.2
Female	—	349	1.7	5.6
Hispanic	283	—	**4.3**	**10**
Male	—	1,760	7.7	17.2
Female	—	147	0.7	2.2

Note: The Bureau of Justice Statistics no longer regularly reports overall incarceration rates for race and has not recently reported jail incarceration rates by race.

Source: Donna Selman and Paul Leighton, *Punishment for Sale*. Rowman and Littlefield, 2010.

The author suggests that we apply to this situation the theory of justice of the late American moral philosopher John Rawls (a philosopher whose work is discussed at a number of places in *The Rich Get Richer*). Rawls proposes that we can arrive at valid principles of justice by imagining ourselves in an "original position," where all people must agree on the rules to govern their interactions from beyond a "veil of ignorance." The veil means that we must reach agreement on these rules while imagining ourselves ignorant of our particular identities (our class, race, gender, level of wealth and abilities, and so on). The effect of the veil of ignorance is that people deciding in the imaginary original position cannot tailor moral principles to their own situations—rather they must imagine that they could be in anyone's shoes and decide on principles in light of what would be best for anyone. For example, not knowing whether they are rich or poor, they cannot base taxation or welfare policies on their current perspective or self-interest. They have to decide what would be better from the standpoint of anyone, or everyone, in the society. This feature highlights the moral, rather than self-interested, nature of the decision that is to be made in the original position.

Consider in this light practices such as racism or sexism. Ask yourself if you would agree to either of these behind a veil of ignorance—that is, not knowing which race or sex you are. Without such knowledge, forced to judge as if you could be anyone, you would not agree to racism or sexism, because you might well be seriously disadvantaged by either. This shows the unfairness of racism and sexism very clearly by demonstrating that these policies could only be freely chosen by members of the favored race or sex—thus such policies only exist because they have been forced on the disfavored ones. The author goes the next step and argues persuasively that examining disproportionate minority confinement from behind a veil of ignorance would lead to rules acknowledging social responsibility for the consequences of racial discrimination and social exclusion. Recognizing that in the original position we would agree that we need institutions of punishment, Loury asks, "How would we apportion blame and affix responsibility for the cultural and social pathologies evident in some quarters of our society if we envisioned that we ourselves might well have been born into the social margins where such pathology flourishes?" He suggests that when punishing, we would need "to think about whether we have done our share in ensuring that each person faces a decent set of opportunities for a good life. We need to ask whether we as a society have fulfilled our collective responsibility to ensure fair conditions for each person—for each life that might turn out to be our life." Here Loury affirms a basic theme of *The Rich Get Richer and the Poor Get Prison:* "Justice is a two-way street—but criminal justice is a one-way street."

"The Moral Ambivalence of Crime in an Unjust Society" takes the notion that justice is a two-way street one important step further. Jeffrey Reiman argues that citizens' moral obligations to obey a society's laws are conditioned on whether they are treated justly by that society. The more unjustly they are treated, the weaker their obligations to obey the law become. This article looks at an example of criminal victimization (a case of robbery with violence experienced by the author and his wife) and asks what moral judgment should be made about the young men responsible. The author applies a social contract model of moral evaluation. John Rawls's "original position" is a form of social contract theory, but in this article the author looks at the earlier versions of the theory set forth by John Locke (whose writings strongly influenced the U.S. Declaration of Independence) and Thomas Hobbes. If people could be thought of as agreeing in a kind of social contract to the establishment of some form of government, then that form of government could not be tyrannical or oppressive, as people would not agree to be oppressed. This does not imply that governments are established by real contracts, real agreements among citizens; the social contract is a theoretical idea, not a historical one. To say that a government satisfies the requirements of the social contract doctrine is to say that people who were not under a government would find it rational to give up the freedom that they would have outside of states and agree freely to be subject to this kind of government. The author contends that the social contract implies that citizens' duties to obey the law are dependent on their receiving a fair share of benefits of social cooperation from other citizens. Thus, victims of injustice (such as the young criminals by whom he and his wife were victimized) have weaker obligations to obey the law than better-treated citizens do. At the same time, the social contract calls for maintaining peace among citizens and victims of injustice benefit from this peace and thus have obligations to maintain it. The article tries to steer a course between these two competing considerations to reach a measured judgment about the moral nature of crime in unjust societies.

"Much Respect: Toward a Hip-Hop Theory of Punishment" by Paul Butler provides another fresh way of thinking about current criminal justice policy, namely, to consider it through the lens of the enormously popular hip-hop music genre. Started by African Americans in the South Bronx, hip-hop has spread widely to other countries and ethnic groups. It is now more popular in the United States than country music. Closer than any other art form to the experiences of poor black Americans, hip-hop decries the "massive punishment regime" criticized in previous articles and throughout *The Rich Get Richer*. But hip-hop does not deny that there is a need for punishment. Imagining a "hip-hop nation," the author lays out three core hip-hop principles of punishment: "People who harm others should be harmed in return. . . . Criminals are human beings who deserve respect and love. . . . Communities can be destroyed by both crime and punishment."

Interestingly, the author considers looking at punishment from Rawls's "original position" but then suggests that we might get more insight from looking at it from the cultural angle of hip-hop, as an expression of the views of people deeply—and often negatively—affected, the African American underclass. He suggests that from this angle punishment should be aimed at retribution, that it should target the harmful acts of the rich more than those of the poor, that it should not be used against sellers or users of recreational drugs (though numerous hip-hop artists recognize that drugs can cause harm to users and their families), and that it should be used sparingly and imposed by people within a community rather than by outsiders. Viewing society from the vantage point occupied by those at the bottom, hip-hop resonates strikingly with the themes in *The Rich Get Richer and the Poor Get Prison*. Both call for respect for the human dignity of criminals, for fair treatment of both poor and rich wrongdoers, and for a hard look at the collateral damage to communities that massive imprisonment brings.

The original version of "Much Respect" appeared in the *Stanford Law Review* and contained lyrics from many hip-hop songs. We regret that we could not include the lyrics here, due to copyright restraints. Where possible, we have tried to paraphrase key ideas, and we have left many of the references to the lyrics. We hope that students will track down these hip-hop tunes and the original article in which the lyrics are quoted, in order to connect the music to larger concepts of justice.

The final reading, "Wheel of Torture," is a satire of the media by criminologist Robert Johnson from his book *Justice Follies: Parodies from Planet Prison*. The idea of "folly," Johnson tells us, means a "costly undertaking having an absurd or ruinous outcome," while "follies" are "an elaborate theatrical revue consisting of music, dance, and skits." Thus, "justice follies" are "stories, sometimes featuring music, dance and skits, about absurd, ruinous or patently unfair and inequitable features of our justice system." Johnson's use of fiction here gets at the central idea of *The Rich Get Richer*, namely, that criminal justice in the United States is allowed to continue its unfair and inequitable practices because of the image it conveys, because, we might say in Johnson's terms, of the theatrical spectacle it presents.

"Wheel of Torture" is a parody of TV's "Wheel of Fortune" that takes a satirical look at how media coverage of crime emphasizes personal responsibility while denying fundamental aspects of social context that shape the behavior. The game show host and his assistant, Veri White, run through the case of a minority woman whose children burned to death because of a fire set by an arsonist while she was at one of her two jobs. The punitive insistence that poor criminals are individually responsible for their troubles is expressed here when the host points to the fact that the loss of this woman's children is due to her poor choice(!) to live in a high-crime neighborhood, and thus not take advantage of American prosperity. The host whips the audience into a righteous frenzy through a narration that downplays unpleasant aspects of reality that interfere with the audience's delight in shouting "Slutty whore, Slutty whore/ She chose to be poor/ Show her the prison door."

Note

1. Arthur Kennickell, "Currents and Undercurrents: Changes in the Distribution of Wealth, 1989–2004." Federal Reserve Board, 2006. www.federalreserve.gov/pubs/oss/oss2/scfindex.html

---

WHY ARE SO MANY AMERICANS IN PRISON? RACE AND THE TRANSFORMATION OF CRIMINAL JUSTICE

Glenn C. Loury

The early 1990s were the age of drive-by shootings, drug deals gone bad, crack cocaine, and gangsta rap. Between 1960 and 1990, the annual number of murders in New Haven rose from six to 31, the number of rapes from four to 168, the number of robberies from 16 to 1,784—all this while the city's population declined by 14 percent. Crime was concentrated in central cities: in 1990, two fifths of Pennsylvania's violent crimes were committed in Philadelphia, home to one seventh of the state's population. The subject of crime dominated American domestic-policy debates.

Most observers at the time expected things to get worse. Consulting demographic tables and extrapolating trends, scholars and pundits warned the public to prepare for an onslaught, and for a new kind of criminal—the anomic, vicious, irreligious, amoral juvenile "super-predator." In 1996, one academic commentator predicted a "blood-bath" of juvenile homicides in 2005.

And so we prepared. Stoked by fear and political opportunism, but also by the need to address a very real social problem, we threw lots of people in jail, and when the old prisons were filled we built new ones.

But the onslaught never came. Crime rates peaked in 1992 and have dropped sharply since. Even as crime rates fell, however, imprisonment rates remained high and continued their upward march. The result, the current American prison system, is a leviathan unmatched in human history.

According to a 2005 report of the International Centre for Prison Studies in London, the United States—with five percent of the world's population—houses 25 percent of the world's inmates. Our incarceration rate (714 per 100,000 residents) is almost 40 percent greater than those of our nearest competitors (the Bahamas, Belarus, and Russia). Other industrial democracies, even those with significant crime problems of their own, are much less punitive: our incarceration rate is 6.2 times that of Canada,

Source: Boston Review, July/August 2007 issue. Reprinted by permission of the author.

7.8 times that of France, and 12.3 times that of Japan. We have a corrections sector that employs more Americans than the combined work forces of General Motors, Ford, and Wal-Mart, the three largest corporate employers in the country, and we are spending some $200 billion annually on law enforcement and corrections at all levels of government, a fourfold increase (in constant dollars) over the past quarter century.

Never before has a supposedly free country denied basic liberty to so many of its citizens. In December 2006, some 2.25 million persons were being held in the nearly 5,000 prisons and jails that are scattered across America's urban and rural landscapes. One third of inmates in state prisons are violent criminals, convicted of homicide, rape, or robbery. But the other two thirds consist mainly of property and drug offenders. Inmates are disproportionately drawn from the most disadvantaged parts of society. On average, state inmates have fewer than 11 years of schooling. They are also vastly disproportionately black and brown.

How did it come to this? One argument is that the massive increase in incarceration reflects the success of a rational public policy: faced with a compelling social problem, we responded by imprisoning people and succeeded in lowering crime rates. This argument is not entirely misguided. Increased incarceration does appear to have reduced crime somewhat. But by how much? Estimates of the share of the 1990s reduction in violent crime that can be attributed to the prison boom range from five percent to 25 percent. Whatever the number, analysts of all political stripes now agree that we have long ago entered the zone of diminishing returns. The conservative scholar John DiIulio, who coined the term "super-predator" in the early 1990s, was by the end of that decade declaring in *The Wall Street Journal* that "Two Million Prisoners Are Enough." But there was no political movement for getting America out of the mass-incarceration business. The throttle was stuck.

A more convincing argument is that imprisonment rates have continued to rise while crime rates have fallen because *we have become progressively more punitive:* not because crime has continued to explode (it hasn't), not because we made a smart policy choice, but because we have made a collective decision to increase the rate of punishment.

One simple measure of punitiveness is the likelihood that a person who is arrested will be subsequently incarcerated. Between 1980 and 2001, there was no real change in the chances of being arrested in response to a complaint: the rate was just under 50 percent. But the likelihood that an arrest would result in imprisonment more than doubled, from 13 to 28 percent. And because the amount of time served and the rate of prison admission both increased, the incarceration rate for violent crime almost tripled, despite the decline in the level of violence. The incarceration rate for nonviolent and drug offenses increased at an even faster pace: between 1980 and 1997 the number of people incarcerated for nonviolent offenses tripled, and the number of people incarcerated for drug offenses increased by a factor of 11. Indeed, the criminal-justice researcher Alfred Blumstein has argued that *none* of the growth in incarceration between 1980 and 1996 can be attributed to more crime:

> The growth was entirely attributable to a growth in punitiveness, about equally to growth in prison commitments per arrest (an indication of tougher prosecution or judicial sentencing) and to longer time served (an

indication of longer sentences, elimination of parole or later parole release, or greater readiness to recommit parolees to prison for either technical violations or new crimes).

This growth in punitiveness was accompanied by a shift in thinking about the basic purpose of criminal justice. In the 1970s, the sociologist David Garland argues, the corrections system was commonly seen as a way to prepare offenders to rejoin society. Since then, the focus has shifted from rehabilitation to punishment and stayed there. Felons are no longer *persons* to be supported, but *risks* to be dealt with. And the way to deal with the risks is to keep them locked up. As of 2000, 33 states had abolished limited parole (up from 17 in 1980); 24 states had introduced three-strikes laws (up from zero); and 40 states had introduced truth-in-sentencing laws (up from three). The vast majority of these changes occurred in the 1990s, as crime rates fell.

This new system of punitive ideas is aided by a new relationship between the media, the politicians, and the public. A handful of cases—in which a predator does an awful thing to an innocent—get excessive media attention and engender public outrage. This attention typically bears no relation to the frequency of the particular type of crime, and yet laws—such as three-strikes laws that give mandatory life sentences to nonviolent drug offenders—and political careers are made on the basis of the public's reaction to the media coverage of such crimes.

Despite a sharp national decline in crime, American criminal justice has become crueler and less caring than it has been at any other time in our modern history. Why?

The question has no simple answer, but the racial composition of prisons is a good place to start. The punitive turn in the nation's social policy—intimately connected with public rhetoric about responsibility, dependency, social hygiene, and the reclamation of public order—can be fully grasped only when viewed against the backdrop of America's often ugly and violent racial history: there is a reason why our inclination toward forgiveness and the extension of a second chance to those who have violated our behavioral strictures is so stunted, and why our mainstream political discourses are so bereft of self-examination and searching social criticism. This historical resonance between the stigma of race and the stigma of imprisonment serves to keep alive in our public culture the subordinating social meanings that have always been associated with blackness. Race helps to explain why the United States is exceptional among the democratic industrial societies in the severity and extent of its punitive policy and in the paucity of its social-welfare institutions.

Slavery ended a long time ago, but the institution of chattel slavery and the ideology of racial subordination that accompanied it have cast a long shadow. I speak here of the history of lynching throughout the country; the racially biased policing and judging in the South under Jim Crow and in the cities of the Northeast, Midwest, and West to which blacks migrated after the First and Second World Wars; and the history of racial apartheid that ended only as a matter of law with the civil-rights movement. It should come as no surprise that in the post–civil rights era, race, far from being peripheral, has been central to the evolution of American social policy.

The political scientist Vesla Mae Weaver, in a recently completed dissertation, examines policy history, public opinion, and media processes in an attempt to understand the role of race in this historic transformation of criminal justice. She argues—persuasively, I think—that the punitive turn represented a political response to the success of the civil-rights movement. Weaver describes a process of "frontlash" in which opponents of the civil-rights revolution sought to regain the upper hand by shifting to a new issue. Rather than reacting directly to civil-rights developments, and thus continuing to fight a battle they had lost, those opponents—consider George Wallace's campaigns for the presidency, which drew so much support in states like Michigan and Wisconsin—shifted attention to a seemingly race-neutral concern over crime. Once the clutch of Jim Crow had loosened, opponents of civil rights shifted the "locus of attack" by injecting crime onto the agenda. Through the process of frontlash, rivals of civil rights progress defined racial discord as criminal and argued that crime legislation would be a panacea to racial unrest. This strategy both imbued crime with race and depoliticized racial struggle, a formula which foreclosed earlier "root causes" alternatives. Fusing anxiety about crime to anxiety over racial change and riots, civil rights and racial disorder—initially defined as a problem of minority disenfranchisement—were defined as a crime problem, which helped shift debate from social reform to punishment.

Of course, this argument (for which Weaver adduces considerable circumstantial evidence) is speculative. But something interesting seems to have been going on in the late 1960s regarding the relationship between attitudes on race and social policy.

Before 1965, public attitudes on the welfare state and on race, as measured by the annually administered General Social Survey, varied year to year independently of one another: you could not predict much about a person's attitudes on welfare politics by knowing their attitudes about race. After 1965, the attitudes moved in tandem, as welfare came to be seen as a race issue. Indeed, the year-to-year correlation between an index measuring liberalism of racial attitudes and attitudes toward the welfare state over the interval 1950–1965 was .03. These same two series had a correlation of .68 over the period 1966–1996. The association in the American mind of race with welfare, and of race with crime, has been achieved at a common historical moment. Crime-control institutions are part of a larger social-policy complex—they relate to and interact with the labor market, family-welfare efforts, and health and social-work activities. Indeed, Garland argues that the ideological approaches to welfare and crime control have marched rightward to a common beat: "The institutional and cultural changes that have occurred in the crime control field are analogous to those that have occurred in the welfare state more generally." Just as the welfare state came to be seen as a race issue, so, too, crime came to be seen as a race issue, and policies have been shaped by this perception.

Consider the tortured racial history of the War on Drugs. Blacks were twice as likely as whites to be arrested for a drug offense in 1975 but four times as likely by 1989. Throughout the 1990s, drug-arrest rates remained at historically unprecedented levels. Yet according to the National Survey on Drug Abuse, drug use among adults fell from 20 percent in 1979 to 11 percent in 2000. A similar trend occurred among adolescents. In the age groups 12–17 and 18–25, use of marijuana, cocaine, and heroin all peaked in the late 1970s and began a steady decline thereafter. Thus, a decline in drug use across the board had begun a decade before the draconian anti-drug efforts of the 1990s were initiated.

Of course, most drug arrests are for trafficking, not possession, so usage rates and arrest rates needn't be expected to be identical. Still, we do well to bear in mind that the social problem of illicit drug use is endemic to our whole society. Significantly, throughout the period 1979–2000, white high-school seniors reported using drugs at a significantly higher rate than black high-school seniors. High drug-usage rates in white, middle-class American communities in the early 1980s accounts for the urgency many citizens felt to mount a national attack on the problem. But how successful has the effort been, and at what cost?

Think of the cost this way: to save middle-class kids from the threat of a drug epidemic that might not have even existed by the time that drug incarceration began its rapid increase in the 1980s, we criminalized underclass kids. Arrests went up, but drug prices have fallen sharply over the past 20 years—suggesting that the ratcheting up of enforcement has not made drugs harder to get on the street. The strategy clearly wasn't keeping drugs away from those who sought them. Not only are prices down, but the data show that drug-related visits to emergency rooms also rose steadily throughout the 1980s and 1990s.

An interesting case in point is New York City. Analyzing arrests by residential neighborhood and police precinct, the criminologist Jeffrey Fagan and his colleagues Valerie West and Jan Holland found that incarceration was highest in the city's poorest neighborhoods, though these were often not the neighborhoods in which crime rates were the highest. Moreover, they discovered a perverse effect of incarceration on crime: higher incarceration in a given neighborhood in one year seemed to predict higher crime rates in that same neighborhood one year later. This growth and persistence of incarceration over time, the authors concluded, was due primarily to the drug enforcement practices of police and to sentencing laws that require imprisonment for repeat felons. Police scrutiny was more intensive and less forgiving in high-incarceration neighborhoods, and parolees returning to such neighborhoods were more closely monitored. Thus, discretionary and spatially discriminatory police behavior led to a high and increasing rate of repeat prison admissions in the designated neighborhoods, even as crime rates fell.

Fagan, West, and Holland explain the effects of spatially concentrated urban anti-drug-law enforcement in the contemporary American metropolis. Buyers may come from any neighborhood and any social stratum. But the sellers—at least the ones who can be readily found hawking their wares on street corners and in public vestibules—come predominantly from the poorest, most non-white parts of the city. The police, with arrest quotas to meet, know precisely where to find them. The researchers conclude:

> Incarceration begets more incarceration, and incarceration also begets more crime, which in turn invites more aggressive enforcement, which then re-supplies incarceration . . . three mechanisms . . . contribute to and reinforce incarceration in neighborhoods: the declining economic fortunes of former inmates and the effects on neighborhoods where they tend to reside, resource and relationship strains on families of prisoners that weaken the family's ability to supervise children, and voter disenfranchisement that weakens the political economy of neighborhoods.

The effects of imprisonment on life chances are profound. For incarcerated black men, hourly wages are ten percent lower after prison than before. For all incarcerated men, the number of weeks worked per year falls by at least a third after their release.

So consider the nearly 60 percent of black male high-school dropouts born in the late 1960s who are imprisoned before their 40th year. While locked up, these felons are stigmatized—they are regarded as fit subjects for shaming. Their links to family are disrupted; their opportunities for work are diminished; their voting rights may be permanently revoked. They suffer civic excommunication. Our zeal for social discipline consigns these men to a permanent nether caste. And yet, since these men—whatever their shortcomings—have emotional and sexual and family needs, including the need to be fathers and lovers and husbands, we are creating a situation where the children of this nether caste are likely to join a new generation of untouchables. This cycle will continue so long as incarceration is viewed as the primary path to social hygiene.

I have been exploring the issue of causes: of why we took the punitive turn that has resulted in mass incarceration. But even if the racial argument about causes is inconclusive, the racial consequences are clear. To be sure, in the United States, as in any society, public order is maintained by the threat and use of force. We enjoy our good lives only because we are shielded by the forces of law and order, which keep the unruly at bay. Yet in this society, to a degree virtually unmatched in any other, those bearing the brunt of order enforcement belong in vastly disproportionate numbers to historically marginalized racial groups. Crime and punishment in America has a color.

In his fine study *Punishment and Inequality in America* (2006), the Princeton University sociologist Bruce Western powerfully describes the scope, nature, and consequences of contemporary imprisonment. He finds that the extent of racial disparity in imprisonment rates is greater than in any other major arena of American social life: at eight to one, the black–white ratio of incarceration rates dwarfs the two-to-one ratio of unemployment rates, the three-to-one ratio of non-marital childbearing, the two-to-one ratio of infant-mortality rates and one-to-five ratio of net worth. While three out of 200 young whites were incarcerated in 2000, the rate for young blacks was one in nine. A black male resident of the state of California is more likely to go to a state prison than a state college.

The scandalous truth is that the police and penal apparatus are now the primary contact between adult black American men and the American state. Among black male high-school dropouts aged 20 to 40, a third were locked up on any given day in 2000, fewer than three percent belonged to a union, and less than one quarter were enrolled in any kind of social program. Coercion is the most salient meaning of government for these young men. Western estimates that nearly 60 percent of black male dropouts born between 1965 and 1969 were sent to prison on a felony conviction at least once before they reached the age of 35.

One cannot reckon the world-historic American prison build-up over the past 35 years without calculating the enormous costs imposed upon the persons imprisoned, their families, and their communities. (Of course, this has not stopped many social scientists from pronouncing on the net benefits of incarceration without doing so.) Deciding on the weight to give to a "thug's" well-being—or to that of his wife or daughter or son—is a question of social morality, not social science. Nor can social science tell us how much additional cost borne by the offending class is justified in order to obtain a given increment of security or property or peace of mind for the rest of us. These are questions about the nature of the American state and its relationship to its people that transcend the categories of benefits and costs.

Yet the discourse surrounding punishment policy invariably discounts the humanity of the thieves, drug sellers, prostitutes, rapists, and, yes, those whom we put to death. It gives insufficient weight to the welfare, to the humanity, of those who are knitted together with offenders in webs of social and psychic affiliation. What is more, institutional arrangements for dealing with criminal offenders in the United States have evolved to serve expressive as well as instrumental ends. We have wanted to "send a message," and we have done so with a vengeance. In the process, we have created facts. We have answered the question, who is to blame for the domestic maladies that beset us? We have constructed a national narrative. We have created scapegoats, indulged our need to feel virtuous, and assuaged our fears. We have met the enemy, and the enemy is *them*.

Incarceration keeps *them* away from *us*. Thus Garland: "The prison is used today as a kind of reservation, a quarantine zone in which purportedly dangerous individuals are segregated in the name of public safety." The boundary between prison and community, Garland continues, is "heavily patrolled and carefully monitored to prevent risks leaking out from one to the other. Those offenders who are released 'into the community' are subject to much tighter control than previously, and frequently find themselves returned to custody for failure to comply with the conditions that continue to restrict their freedom. For many of these parolees and ex-convicts, the 'community' into which they are released is actually a closely monitored terrain, a supervised space, lacking much of the liberty that one associates with 'normal life.'"

Deciding how citizens of varied social rank within a common polity ought to relate to one another is a more fundamental consideration than deciding which crime-control policy is most efficient. The question of relationship, of solidarity, of who belongs to the body politic and who deserves exclusion—these are philosophical concerns of the highest order. A decent society will on occasion resist the efficient course of action, for the simple reason that to follow it would be to act as though we were not the people we have determined ourselves to be: a people conceived in liberty and dedicated to the proposition that we all are created equal. Assessing the propriety of creating a racially defined pariah class in the middle of our great cities at the start of the 21st century presents us with just such a case.

My recitation of the brutal facts about punishment in today's America may sound to some like a primal scream at this monstrous social machine that is grinding poor black communities to dust. And I confess that these brutal facts do at times incline me to cry out in despair. But my argument is analytical, not existential. Its principal thesis is this: we law-abiding, middle-class Americans have made decisions about social policy and incarceration, and we benefit from those decisions, and that means from a system of suffering, rooted in state violence, meted out at our request. We had choices and we decided to be more punitive. Our society—the society we have made—creates criminogenic conditions in our sprawling urban ghettos, and then acts out rituals of punishment against them as some awful form of human sacrifice.

This situation raises a moral problem that we cannot avoid. We cannot pretend that there are more important problems in our society, or that this circumstance is the necessary solution to other, more pressing problems—unless we are also prepared to say that we have turned our backs on the ideal of equality for all citizens and abandoned the principles of justice. We ought to ask ourselves two questions: *Just what manner of people are we Americans? And in light of this, what are our obligations to our fellow citizens—even those who break our laws?*

To address these questions, we need to think about the evaluation of our prison system as a problem in the theory of distributive justice—not the purely procedural idea of ensuring equal treatment before the law and thereafter letting the chips fall where they may, but the rather more demanding ideal of *substantive racial justice.* The goal is to bring about through conventional social policy and far-reaching institutional reforms a situation in which the history of racial oppression is no longer so evident in the disparate life experiences of those who descend from slaves.

And I suggest we approach that problem from the perspective of John Rawls's theory of justice: first, that we think about justice from an "original position" behind a "veil of ignorance" that obstructs from view our own situation, including our class, race, gender, and talents. We need to ask what rules we would pick if we seriously imagined that we could turn out to be anyone in the society. Second, following Rawls's "difference principle," we should permit inequalities only if they work to improve the circumstances of the least advantaged members of society. But here, the object of moral inquiry is not the distribution among individuals of wealth and income, but instead the distribution of a negative good, punishment, among individuals and, importantly, racial groups.

So put yourself in John Rawls's original position and imagine that *you* could occupy any rank in the social hierarchy. Let me be more concrete: imagine that *you* could be born a black American male outcast shuffling between prison and the labor market on his way to an early death to the chorus of *nigger* or *criminal* or *dummy.* Suppose we had to stop thinking of *us* and *them.* What social rules would we pick if we actually thought that *they* could be *us*? I expect that we would still pick some set of punishment institutions to contain bad behavior and protect society. But wouldn't we pick arrangements that respected the humanity of each individual and of those they are connected to through bonds of social and psychic affiliation? If any one of us had a real chance of being one of those faces looking up from the bottom of the well—of being the least among us—then how would we talk publicly about those who break our laws? What would we do with juveniles who go awry, who roam the streets with guns and sometimes commit acts of violence? What weight would we give to various elements in the deterrence-retribution-incapacitation-rehabilitation calculus, if we thought that calculus could end up being applied to our own children, or to us? How would we apportion blame and affix responsibility for the cultural and social pathologies evident in some quarters of our society if we envisioned that we ourselves might well have been born into the social margins where such pathology flourishes?

If we take these questions as seriously as we should, then we would, I expect, reject a pure ethic of personal responsibility as the basis for distributing punishment.

Issues about responsibility are complex, and involve a kind of division of labor—what John Rawls called a "social division of responsibility" between "citizens as a collective body" and individuals: when we hold a person responsible for his or her conduct—by establishing laws, investing in their enforcement, and consigning some persons to prisons—we need also to think about whether we have done our share in ensuring that each person faces a decent set of opportunities for a good life. We need to ask whether we as a society have fulfilled our collective responsibility to ensure fair conditions for each person—for each life that might turn out to be our life.

We would, in short, recognize a kind of social responsibility, even for the wrongful acts freely chosen by individual persons. I am not arguing that people commit crimes because they have no choices, and that in this sense the "root causes" of crime are social; individuals always have choices. My point is that responsibility is a matter of ethics, not social science. Society at large is implicated in an individual person's choices because we have acquiesced in—perhaps actively supported, through our taxes and votes, words and deeds—social arrangements that work to our benefit and his detriment, and which shape his consciousness and sense of identity in such a way that the choices he makes, which we may condemn, are nevertheless compelling to him—an entirely understandable response to circumstance. Closed and bounded social structures—like racially homogeneous urban ghettos—create contexts where "pathological" and "dysfunctional" cultural forms emerge; but these forms are neither intrinsic to the people caught in these structures nor independent of the behavior of people who stand outside them.

Thus, a central reality of our time is the fact that there has opened a wide racial gap in the acquisition of cognitive skills, the extent of law-abidingness, the stability of family relations, the attachment to the work force, and the like. This disparity in human development is, as a historical matter, rooted in political, economic, social, and cultural factors peculiar to this society and reflective of its unlovely racial history: it is a societal, not communal or personal, achievement. At the level of the individual case we must, of course, act as if this were not so. There could be no law, no civilization, without the imputation to particular persons of responsibility for their wrongful acts. But the sum of a million cases, each one rightly judged on its merits to be individually fair, may nevertheless constitute a great historic wrong. The state does not only deal with individual cases. It also makes policies in the aggregate, and the consequences of these policies are more or less knowable. And who can honestly say—who can look in the mirror and say with a straight face—that we now have laws and policies that we would endorse if we did not know our own situation and genuinely considered the possibility that we might be the least advantaged?

Even if the current racial disparity in punishment in our country gave evidence of no overt racial discrimination—and, perhaps needless to say, I view that as a wildly optimistic supposition—it would still be true that powerful forces are at work to perpetuate the consequences of a universally acknowledged wrongful past. This is in the first instance a matter of interpretation—of the narrative overlay that we impose upon the facts.

The tacit association in the American public's imagination of "blackness" with "unworthiness" or "dangerousness" has obscured a fundamental ethical point about responsibility, both collective and individual, and promoted essentialist causal misattributions: when confronted by the facts of racially disparate achievement, racially disproportionate crime rates, and racially unequal school achievement, observers will have difficulty identifying with the plight of a group of people whom they (mistakenly) think are simply "reaping what they have sown." Thus, the enormous racial disparity in the imposition of social exclusion, civic ex-communication, and lifelong disgrace has come to seem legitimate, even necessary: we fail to see how our failures as a collective body are implicated in this disparity. We shift all the responsibility onto *their* shoulders, only by irresponsibly—indeed, immorally—denying our own. And yet, this entire dynamic has its roots in past unjust acts that were perpetrated on the basis of race.

Given our history, producing a racially defined nether caste through the ostensibly neutral application of law should be profoundly offensive to our ethical sensibilities—to the principles we proudly assert as our own. Mass incarceration has now become a principal vehicle for the reproduction of racial hierarchy in our society. Our country's policymakers need to do something about it. And all of us are ultimately responsible for making sure that they do.

THE MORAL AMBIVALENCE OF CRIME IN AN UNJUST SOCIETY

Jeffrey Reiman

I   OUR CRIME

In the summer of 2005, after thirty-five years of thinking and writing about crime, I was—along with my wife—the victim of one. It happened in the French city of Nice. There they have a crime called *vol à la portière,* "theft through the car door." Teenagers wait for cars with foreign license plates or recently rented or leased cars. They come up along the passenger side of the car and grab a purse or a watch through the window, or they try the doors and, if they are not locked, open them and grab whatever they see. That is what happened to us. After flying all night, we picked up the car that we were leasing for the summer and, before we could lock the doors, before we even figured out how to lock the doors, we stopped at a red light and two teenage boys pulled open the front and rear passenger doors, and grabbed what they saw. The boy who opened the rear door grabbed a carry-on bag. The boy who opened the front door, grabbed my wife's purse off her lap. She tried to hold on to it, but in vain. He yanked it away from her and, in the process, broke her finger. I jumped out of the car and started running after the boys. You can guess the outcome. Do the math. I was 63 at the time, they were 15 or 16. I lost them in the French equivalent of housing projects. Then followed dealing with the police, my wife to the hospital in an ambulance, a

Source: Criminal Justice Ethics, vol. 25, no. 2 (Summer/Fall 2007) pp. 3–15. Reprinted by permission of the Institute for Criminal Justice Ethics, 555 West 57th Street, Suite 607, New York, NY 10019–1029.

summer punctuated by two operations—her finger was not only broken, but dislocated, so that pins had to be put in the bone to make it heal straight, and later the pins had to be taken out—and numerous visits to the hospital to change bandages and talk to the surgeon, and so on.

When this happened—for example, when I was running after the two boys—I must confess that I had violence in my heart. I do not clearly know what I would have done had I caught one of them, but later I came to think that it was lucky that I had not. I might now be in jail in France for murder. Afterwards, in the days that followed, my anger slowly dissipated. I found that I did not hate these boys. I did not feel rage or even much in the way of anger. My wife's feelings were much the same. We would have liked to see them caught and punished, but we knew that was unlikely—and we did not have any strong feelings about that. My wife and I decided that our revenge against the thieves would be not to let their crime ruin our summer, and it did not. I suspect that we had a better summer than they did, even with our trips to the hospital and without the things that were stolen. They were poor kids living in what the French call a *quartier chaud,* what in America we would call a "rough neighborhood."

At the same time, I started to wonder about these feelings and thoughts, in particular, about the dwindling of my anger at our criminals. How should one think and feel *morally* about such criminals? To answer this question, it is necessary to reflect on the moral nature of crime, since that will tell us what the criminal who commits it is morally responsible for.

II THE MORAL NATURE OF CRIME

Some people might think that the moral nature of crime is easy to determine. That the youngsters took our possessions or that a law was broken, they think, is enough to show that a moral wrong was done. But, things are more complicated than that. Consider this:

Suppose you see someone huddling over a bicycle that is chained to a post. You look closer and you see that the person is sawing the chain and, once the chain is severed, you see the person jump on the bike and pedal quickly off. I think that you would believe that you had witnessed a crime, and so would I. But now look at this letter that appeared in a *New York Times Sunday Magazine* column called "The Ethicist":

> A few weeks after my bike was stolen, I saw it locked to a post. I knew it was mine, since I had modified it in various ways and recorded the serial number. I . . . had no qualms about . . . taking it back. Should I have called the police instead?[1]

The Ethicist's reply begins: "You didn't steal anything; you reclaimed your own property." Think about what this means for the imaginary example I sketched. When we saw someone sawing the bicycle chain and riding away, we thought we were witnessing a crime. But then we found out that the bicycle belonged to the taker and was earlier stolen from him by the one from whom he now takes it. That contextual information changes what looked like a crime into the opposite of a crime; it changes it into *restitution,* that is, returning something to its rightful owner.

Here's another example that makes the same point with reference to society as a whole. In his *Lectures on Ethics,* Kant said the following about charitable giving:

> Although we may be entirely within our rights, according to the law of the land and the rules of our social structure, we may nevertheless be participating in general injustice, and in giving to an unfortunate man we do not give him a gratuity but only help to return to him that of which the general injustice of our system has deprived him.[2]

Kant's idea is that, if the distribution of property or wealth in one's society is unjust, then what looks like charity may really be giving a person what is rightfully his—that is, giving him what would be his if the economic distribution were just. Here, contextual knowledge makes what looks like charity into the opposite of charity, more like returning stolen goods than giving a gift. Kant's observation adds something that was not present in the bike example, namely, that the context that changes our judgment may be the injustice of the society as a whole.

If we combine the moral in the bike example with Kant's observation, we get an interesting result: we may think that someone is committing a crime, but if the social context in which the act happened was unjust, what appeared to be a crime may "only help to return to [the apparent thief] that of which the general injustice of our system has deprived him." Knowledge that the act occurred in a context of social injustice makes what seemed to be crime into its opposite. This works in the other direction also. When we think that an act is a crime, we are normally assuming that it takes place in a social context that is just, or at least not so unjust that it would make the act into, say, rightful restitution or justified resistance.[3]

To speak precisely about these matters, it is necessary to distinguish between committing a crime in the legal sense, meaning *violating a criminal law,* and committing a crime in the moral sense, meaning *doing a moral wrong.* There is no question that my wife and I were victims of a crime in the legal sense. To figure out how we should think and feel morally about it, however, we must determine whether we were also victims of a moral wrong. For a crime in the legal sense to have been committed, all that is needed is a violation of the criminal law. Whether it was a crime in the moral sense, however, depends on whether the social context in which it occurred was unjust—and, of course, on whether our criminals were victims of that injustice. The philosophical idea of the social contract can help us to think clearly about these matters, so I want to turn to that, and then I will come back to our crime and how I feel about it.

III   THE SOCIAL CONTRACT MENTAL EXPERIMENT

The social contract asks us to think of our laws as if they are the product of a voluntary and reasonable agreement among all citizens. Though different authors describe this exercise in different ways, it has a general form. We start by imagining a condition in which no one has political or legal authority, commonly called "the state of nature." In this condition, people are to consider and finally agree to some set of political and economic institutions. Since they do not know the future, they must agree to institutions without knowing how they in particular will fare in them. This ignorance gives people in the state of nature a reason to form social institutions that are fair to all citizens, since they could end up with any citizen's fate.

The idea of states being formed in a state of nature is not a historical claim. States do not arise this way, and it is just about impossible that they could. This is because we would already need a state to have enough peace and prosperity to reach a point at which people could discuss and ratify some form of state. As Hume pointed out in his critique of the social contract doctrine, states are normally established by violence, rarely if ever by voluntary agreement.[4]

The social contract is not a historical theory; it is a *mental experiment.* And it is a mental experiment designed to yield a normative conclusion. The state of nature is a mental construct, an imaginary place, and the agreement in it is an imaginary agreement. It does not ask whether you do or did agree to the rules that govern your state's institutions, rather it is a way of asking whether it would be reasonable for you to do so. If it would be, then that is a strong argument that the laws and institutions of your state are just—or just enough—and its authority legitimate enough for citizens to be obligated to obey.

The social contract idea has a long history.[5] It has roots in the biblical notion of the covenant. In ancient Greek philosophy, we find Socrates, in the *Crito,* giving a social-contractarian argument for the wrongness of his escaping from prison though he was unjustly condemned.[6] Feudalism was a system based in principle on the exchange of promises between rulers and subjects. But the social contract really came into its own in the seventeenth century when modern physics, capitalism, and the Protestant Reformation combined to call radically into question the traditional bases of authority. Modern science had the effect of confirming late Medieval ideas that only particular things exist, and thus essences and other general concepts were nothing but ideas in someone's mind. This meant that rules determining the legitimacy of authority did not exist outside of our minds, or possibly God's mind, if only we could determine what God wanted of us—which was looking increasingly problematic.[7] Capitalism pitted the demands of newly wealthy merchants for influence based on their accomplishments against the claims of the traditional nobility to authority based on birth, thereby undermining the traditional bases of social authority. Furthermore, the Protestant Reformation meant that Catholic subjects had Protestant kings and Protestant subjects had Catholic kings, and in both cases the subjects might have thought their rulers were heretics without authority to command. Since virtually no one doubted that people could bind themselves by promising, the social contract emerged as a way of establishing the legitimacy of political authority and the obligation to comply with it, in the face of all these challenges to traditional authority.

One may rightly wonder why the question of what laws it would be reasonable for people to agree to is posed to imaginary people in an imaginary state of nature, rather than just asking the actual people subject to some actual set of laws whether they agree to those laws. The answer is that actual people are likely to be affected by how well they are doing in their current society. If we were to ask the actual citizens of the United States whether they would agree to American institutions and laws, their answers would probably reflect how well they are doing in those institutions and according to those laws. Moreover, their minds have likely been shaped by a lot of propaganda in favor of precisely those laws and institutions. Consequently, actual agreement by actual citizens may tell us only how many are pleased with the way they have fared, or how effective the society has been in getting its citizens to believe that it is the best of all possible worlds. It will not tell us if it is genuinely reasonable for all citizens to comply with the laws and institutions of their country.[8] To get to that, we must ask the theoretical question of whether it would be reasonable for all people to agree to those laws and institutions. And to ask that theoretical question, we must *imagine* posing the question to rational people who do not know how they in particular will be affected by the laws and institutions.

This is what the social contract mental experiment does. The state of nature—an imaginary situation outside and prior to the state—is meant, among other things, to simulate the ignorance of specifics that is necessary in order to reach an agreement that is reasonable to all concerned, irrespective of how they are actually faring.

It was probably not a good idea to label this imaginary situation the "state of *nature.*" This name suggests that we are being asked to imagine a purely natural condition, completely free of human cultural accomplishments. But, since language is a cultural accomplishment and one that is necessary for any group to reach agreement, this cannot work. The state of nature is not really a purely natural state, nor need it be. It is better to think of it negatively, in terms of what it is not. For Locke and Hobbes, the state of nature is the human world *minus* relations of social and political authority. There is no state, no officials with the right to tell people what to do and then to back their commands up with force. Looked at this way, there is nothing mysterious about the state of nature. It is reached by an act of abstraction of which we are surely capable. You imagine that humans stand in relations in which no one has authority over anyone else, and then you ask what would be the reasonable response to this condition. Nothing magical here. It is not very different from abstractions made in other fields, as when Galileo imagined balls rolling down slopes with no friction.

For Hobbes, the state of nature is a "war of all against all" and life in it is "nasty, brutish and short."[9] This is so because there are no institutions with authority to keep your fellows from robbing what you have produced. That in turn gives you a need to protect yourself, which makes it in your interest to attack preemptively because that is more effective than letting others attack at the most favorable moment for them: *The best defense is a good offense.* Since this same logic works in everyone's mind, everyone quickly becomes a threat to everyone else. Each individual knows that others will find it reasonable to attack her preemptively, which gives her an even stronger reason to attack the others preemptively. This in turn gives everyone else an even stronger reason to attack *her* preemptively. And so on. The logic of threat and counterthreat snowballs. Even if you started off as a peaceful person with no desire for more than your own little plot of land, you would soon find it in your interest to attack others preemptively.[10] And since everyone else knows this, it will be in everyone's interest to preemptively attack you before you preemptively attack them, which will increase your incentive to attack them first, and so on, right on up to the war of all against all.

Contrary to a popular view, Hobbes's theory does not depend on an extremely negative view of human nature.[11] No doubt Hobbes had a touch of Calvinist belief in the inherent sinfulness of human beings, but one does not have to believe in natural human evil to arrive at the consequence that Hobbes theorizes. All that is necessary is to imagine that there are no political institutions and no prevailing morality, and that some people may be tempted to take advantage of that fact to rob others. Then, everyone is uncertain, and everyone needs to make preparations for self-defense. This position will lead some to consider preemptive strikes, and then others will fear that they will be the victims of preemptive strikes and, even if at first they would have been willing to wait and see, that will give them an incentive to strike preemptively. And others, knowing this, will have an incentive to preempt that, and so on, right up to the war of all against all.

Given this logic—which Hobbes called an "inference from the passions"[12]—people in Hobbes's state of nature find it reasonable to agree to form a state because it is the means to peace. Since war threatens to make everyone's life nasty, brutish and short, it is reasonable from each person's self-interested standpoint to accept the authority of a sovereign ruler who will enforce rules, protect property, and generally make life safe.

In Locke's version, life in the state of nature is not nasty, brutish and short. Locke believed that there is a basic morality that all reasonable people will recognize, understand and feel compelled to act on.[13] This makes Lockean people more peaceful than Hobbesian ones, because they do not have to fear the escalating logic of threat and counterthreat up to the war of all against all. They do not have to fear this because they can generally assume that everyone else will conform to the basic moral code that Locke thinks will be plain to all.

The problem in Locke's state of nature is that application of the basic moral code will be uncertain. Though the moral law is easily understood by all, says Locke, when their own interests are involved, people tend to see things in ways that serve those interests.[14] They will be less likely to accept your judgment that they are wrong if they have something at stake in believing that they are right. Then, when you try to enforce your judgment, they will resist. You will bring your friends, and they will bring theirs, and soon there will be conflict or frustration or both, even if life is not nasty, brutish and short as it is in Hobbes's state of nature. For Locke, though, as for Hobbes, we leave the state of nature out of self-interest. In Hobbes's case, our self-interest lies in achieving peace; in Locke's, our self-interest lies in achieving justice, that is, in creating the conditions for a more certain protection of our moral rights.

IV   JUSTICE AND THE OBLIGATION TO OBEY THE LAW

Since social contract theory tests the laws and institutions of the state by whether it would be reasonable for people to agree to them in light of their self-interest, that agreement is based on citizens' expectations that they will get something in return for giving up some personal freedom by granting a ruler authority over them. That means that, according to the social contract, a state is legitimate—that is, its citizens are morally obligated to obey its laws—if the benefits to citizens are sufficient to make their obedience, which is the price of those benefits, a reasonable bargain. Under the social contract, the obligation to obey the law is a function of what the citizens get back in return for being law-abiding. And that is where the justice of the system enters to determine the morality of criminal lawbreaking.

Because the social contract makes obligations conditional on receipt of benefits from the rest of society, the doctrine shows us a fact about criminal justice that criminal justice officials almost never acknowledge, namely that, as a form of justice, *criminal justice is a two-way street.* When criminal justice officials focus on the question of how the criminal has failed to fulfill his obligations to society, they gloss over the correlative question of whether the society has fulfilled its obligations to the criminal.

Think of how the obligation to obey the law arises according to the social contract. Take something relatively uncontroversial, say, a law against driving through red lights. This law, like any law, requires that people restrict their freedom. You may not want to stop at a red light, you may be in a hurry, you may think it is quite safe to go through; but, except in a genuine emergency, the law requires you to stop. And the social contract implies that you are morally obligated to do so, morally obligated to limit your freedom of action. The reason for this moral obligation, according to the contract, is that other citizens also limit their freedom by stopping at red lights, and that benefits you. But it is only reasonable for citizens to stop at red lights if they can assume that other citizens will stop as well. There is an exchange of costs and benefits: each citizen pays the cost by restricting his or her freedom, and each citizen gets the benefit of the predictability and safety that results. And all laws can be looked at in the same way. If a law is reasonable, each person benefits from everyone else limiting their freedom according to it, and each person is thus obligated to limit his or her freedom as well.[15]

The principle that underlies this obligation is that of basic fairness.[16] If seven college students share a house and a different one does the dishes each day of the week, when the end of the week comes around the seventh person owes it to the other six to do the dishes because that person has benefited from the others doing the dishes on their days. It would be unfair of that person not to do his or her share on the seventh day, after having accepted the benefits that the others have provided on the earlier days—especially since those others did their share on the expectation that everyone else would as well. This is how the social contract leads us to view our obligation to obey the law. A rarely noted implication of this view is that the obligation to obey the law is not owed to the state. We owe it to our fellow citizens as a reasonable compensation for the sacrifices they make—when obeying the law—that benefit us.

If the obligation to obey the law is the fair return for benefits from others' cooperative efforts, it follows that the duty to obey the laws is conditioned on the justice of the society that those laws govern. I have less of a moral obligation to refrain from violence in a society that leaves me prey to violence. I have less of a moral obligation to respect property in a society that excludes me from the possibility of gaining my own property.

With this, we must face the implications of the fact that many of the people who find themselves convicted of crimes are victims of social injustice. They get less than their rightful share of social benefits. And since the obligation to obey the law is a function of the benefits one receives, it follows that many disadvantaged criminals are not violating their moral obligations to obey the law, at least not to the same extent as advantaged people who commit the same crimes would be, because injustice has reduced their obligation to obey the law.[17]

I am not going to try to determine if the young boys who robbed my wife and me in the summer of 2005 are victims of injustice, though I strongly suspect that they are. To determine definitively if they are victims of injustice would require a more detailed examination of the French legal and economic system than I can undertake here.

My point has been to bring out the relation between the issue of social justice and the question of our criminals' moral obligation to obey the law. Nonetheless, since I believe they have lesser opportunities than other French citizens because of the poverty of their parents and because of discrimination against people of North African heritage, I shall henceforth assume that our criminals are victims of injustice.

Remember how Kant held that giving charity may really be giving people what is rightfully theirs, if the distribution of wealth is unjust. Furthermore, remember how taking the bike looked like a crime, but, in fact, was reclaiming what was someone's own. The social contract forces us to consider that a crime committed by the victims of injustice may also be a matter of reclaiming what is rightfully their own, and thus is not a crime in the moral sense.

I believe that my own feelings about those young criminals, especially the dwindling of my anger, came from my sense that those youngsters have less than they are justly entitled to and that my wife and I probably have more than our fair share.[18] If our young criminals are victims of injustice, then my anger is more appropriately aimed at those in France, or perhaps anywhere in the global economy, who could rectify that injustice but do not. They even share responsibility for the violence that accompanied the crime, since, if the victims of injustice are not as strongly obligated to respect the property of others, then they are not as strongly obligated to leave those others in peaceful possession of that property. It is as if we are holding goods that rightly should be theirs, and they have the right to do what is necessary to get their share back.

This last point may seem questionable. It may easily be supposed that my argument here reaches only to their taking of our property and not to the force that the criminals used to get it. But the issue is more complicated. As I have indicated earlier,[19] not all moral obligations arise via the social contract. Even the victims of injustice have a "natural" (that is, pre-social contract, or pre-state) moral obligation not to inflict violence on my wife or me. However, the existence of institutions, such as a system of property ownership, can alter such natural moral obligations. If I possess property that is not rightly my own (even if I came by it innocently, say, by buying it from someone I believed had the right to sell it), then the state would be permitted to use force to take it from me and give it to its rightful owner. And, if in an unjust society, the state refuses to do this, then the victims of injustice have the moral right to do what the state should have done. This is not to say that the victims of injustice have a right to do anything they want to in order to get the property. They have a right parallel to the state's right in such a case, namely, to use violence that is necessary to rectify the injustice and proportionate to what is at stake. As John Rawls has written, "unjust social arrangements are themselves a kind of extortion, even violence."[20] The victims of extortion and violence have the right to use violence in return.

This analysis clearly works best for property crimes committed by poor people against well-off people. For crimes of the poor against the poor, and for crimes of simple violence not aimed at getting money or goods, it works more indirectly. Victims of injustice have reduced opportunities, less hope, more frustration, and less over-all incentive to go straight. An unjust society shares responsibility for this as well, and thus for the crimes that inevitably result. To my mind, that reduces the criminals' moral responsibility even for crimes against other poor people. That, however, is not my main concern here.[21]

Note, further, what I am *not* saying. I am not saying that disadvantaged criminals are forced to commit crimes, or that they cannot help doing so.[22] I assume throughout that criminals are free and responsible for their actions. What my argument claims is that injustice reduces their moral obligation to obey the law and thereby reduces the moral wrongness of their lawbreaking.

One implication of this claim is that the reduction in the criminals' obligation to obey the law is not normally dependent on what their motives are. They must, of course, have the *mens rea* necessary for their act to be a crime. They must be intending to commit a crime, normally theft. But, aside from this, it matters little what they think they are doing, since the reduction in their obligation is a moral fact, so to speak, a truth independent of their inner states. I have argued this in a qualified way, however, because there are some extraordinary motivations that would negate the reduction in obligation. For example, even if victims of injustice have little or no moral obligation to respect the property of well-off people as well as reduced moral responsibility for crimes against other poor people, they do nonetheless have moral obligations not to harm or otherwise worsen the condition of fellow victims of injustice. Thus, if in robbing us, they thought they were robbing others in the same unjust condition as themselves, they would be morally guilty for that. But, in general, if they intend to commit a crime and they do not believe that they are committing it against someone in similar straits to their own (or worse), their moral obligation is reduced because they are victims of injustice, independent of whatever else they think they are doing.

This conclusion does not amount to a moral license for victims of injustice to commit crimes. The issue is more complex. A judgment on obligatoriness requires balancing numerous considerations. For example, since it is better to cure injustice legally than illegally, if a society is generally open to rectifying its injustices, that is a reason it would be morally wrong to commit a crime even for a victim of injustice. Likewise, the more a society does to rectify injustice, say, by providing health care or other benefits to the poor, the less it is morally acceptable to commit a crime even for a victim of injustice.

But there is more to be said. There is another whole dimension of the moral nature of crime that is illuminated by the social contract, and this will complicate things even more.

V   TRUST, PEACE, AND THE MORAL OBLIGATION TO OBEY THE LAW

The social contract shows us that a society is a kind of cooperative endeavor in which each person benefits from everyone else's willingness to limit his or her liberty and conform to the law. It is an important feature of such mutually advantageous cooperation that people need to know in advance that others will do their part. It is not enough that people in fact stop at red lights. For me to have the full benefit of their doing so, I must be able to rely on their stopping. I must be confident in advance that they will obey the law, even when they think that they could get away with violating it. If I were not confident in advance that others would stop at red lights, I would have to slow down at every intersection as if there were not a light there, and thus I would lose much of the benefit of others' stopping.

With this, the social contract points to another feature of social life that is easy to overlook, namely, that a free social existence is based on *trust*.[23] Everyone's freedom of action is based on their ability to trust that others will restrict their own freedom. I cannot freely walk in those parts of town where I cannot trust people to leave me unharmed. I cannot freely enter into economic exchanges if I cannot trust others to keep their part of the bargain. Our lives are based on a network of trust that we rarely notice, until that network is torn up, until people violate our trust.

It might seem that the social contract in its Hobbesian version is the opposite of a system of trust. After all, Hobbes's argument for the need for a sovereign is based on his view that we cannot trust our fellows' mere promises, and so he insists that verbal agreements be backed up by a powerful ruler who would enforce them by threatening punishment for violations. Hobbes does not ignore the need for trust. Rather, he believes that trust must be based on *fear.*

But this is precisely where Hobbes's theory breaks down. The reason, as Locke clearly saw, is that Hobbes provides no ground for trusting the ruler. Hobbes's ruler is not a party to the contract, nor can he be. The ruler cannot be party to the contract because there is no one to enforce his agreement to it. Since the ruler is the one who uses force to back up agreements, his own promise could not be backed up by force. But this means that the ruler remains in the state of nature with respect to the citizens; his power is unlimited, and thus he remains a danger to all citizens. *The result is that Hobbesian citizens never really get out of the dangerous state of nature.* In fact, it is worse than that, because, in the state of nature, the danger to one person is from other individuals with roughly equal power—but in the Hobbesian state, citizens are vulnerable to the power of a ruler who has an army to back him up.[24]

To be sure, Hobbes's sovereign does have a self-interested reason to protect his subjects generally and to promote their prosperity. Hobbes holds that the sovereign is bound by the law of nature to procure "the safety of the people, [where] by safety is not meant a bare preservation, but also all other contentments of life."[25] But the sovereign is accountable only to God for this duty, not to the people. Moreover, since the ground of the law of nature is everyone's interest in peace, this obligation of the sovereign goes only so far as is necessary to keep the peace.[26] Realistically speaking, then, the sovereign has a self-interested reason to avoid oppressing any large segment of the population, since that might provoke rebellion and cost him his rule. But this gives no individual security, because the sovereign can oppress a few without great risk. Locke saw this clearly and so he wrote, with Hobbes in mind:

> As if when men, quitting the state of Nature, entered into society, they agreed that all of them but one should be under restraint of laws; but that [the ruler] should retain all liberty of the state of Nature, increased with power, and made licentious with impunity. This is to think that men are so foolish that they take care to avoid what mischiefs may be done to them by polecats and foxes, but are content, nay, think it safety, to be devoured by lions.[27]

In order for it to be reasonable to form and belong to a state, it must be possible to trust the ruler and one's fellow citizens. Interestingly, this turns out to be a necessary condition of making government accountable to its citizens. Hobbes could not tolerate such accountability because he thought it would make the ruler's power uncertain. If citizens thought the government had to justify its actions to them, they might refuse to obey certain laws that they thought unjustifiable. Then, other citizens would have reason to fear that the laws might not be obeyed, and they would find it reasonable to protect themselves. And with this, the logic of threat and counterthreat that leads to the war of all against all is on again. Listing the opinions that are dangerous to the peace, Hobbes puts near the top of the list the idea *"That every private man is judge of good and evil actions."* And he contends, "From this false doctrine men are disposed to debate with themselves, and dispute the commands of the commonwealth, and afterwards to obey or disobey them, as in their private judgments they shall think fit. Whereby the commonwealth is distracted and *weakened.*"[28]

Hobbes does not believe the government should be accountable to its citizens because he thinks that citizens will differ widely in their private moral judgments about the government's actions. Some will be moved to disobey while others obey, and this will make obedience uncertain and lead ultimately to anarchy as citizens act to protect themselves against this uncertainty. To avoid Hobbes's conclusion, then, it is necessary that citizens be able to trust that their fellow citizens will hold the government to account in predictable and widely acceptable ways. But how can such trust be established? If fear alone cannot work, what can?

One possibility that could account for trust of one's fellow citizens is that they share a culture that limits the actions that can be acceptably undertaken. However, reliance on a shared culture has a problem today analogous to the problem posed by religious differences in Hobbes's or Locke's time. No contemporary state completely overlaps with a people sharing a single culture today, just as no European state in Hobbes's or Locke's time completely overlapped with a people sharing the same religious beliefs. What was once optimistically called the "nation-state" no longer exists, if it ever did. Practically all states are multinational, as they are multireligious and multicultural.

Another possibility is that there is a set of basic moral principles that all reasonable people can be expected to see and uphold. This is what Locke believed. Accordingly, he could hold that government had to be accountable to its citizens without having to fear that this would lead to anarchy. And, it is fortunate that Locke did believe this—otherwise Jefferson would not have been able to put so many stirring lines from Locke into the *Declaration of Independence.*

It is commonly thought that Locke and Hobbes are diametrically opposed on whether there is a basic, natural, shared morality, but this common view is mistaken. Although Hobbes is not optimistic about people being moved by morality in the state of nature, he does believe that there is a moral law in the state of nature. He lists no fewer than nineteen laws of nature, starting with everyone's obligation to seek peace and do what is reasonable to achieve it. His list includes accepting the same limits on one's freedom as one wants others to accept on theirs, the obligation to be sociable, to treat others as equals, to be ready to pardon past sins, to punish only for deterrence, and in general to follow the *Golden Rule.*[29] Of these nineteen laws of nature, Hobbes writes that they constitute "the true moral philosophy."[30]

Hobbes thought that these laws are really precepts of self-interest or prudence.[31] They are ways of establishing and maintaining peace, and peace is in our self-interest since otherwise life is nasty, brutish and short. But even here Hobbes's distance from Locke is small. Locke also believed that morality was motivated by self-interest, namely, everyone's self-interest in receiving God's heavenly rewards.[32] Hobbes thought of his natural moral laws as God's laws, but he did not think that fear of God's punishments would suffice to make people comply with them.[33] Hobbes discussed the appeal to God as a basis for obedience to the law, but apparently thought that religion was more likely to undermine social peace than to promote it.[34]

Locke was more optimistic on this point, though he too expressed doubts. He believed that if people truly acted on their self-interest, then the infinite felicity of heaven and the endless punishments of hell would always prevail as motivators, and people would always be moral. He noted, however, that this was far from the case and concluded that people tended to act to gain short-term pleasures and avoid short-term pains, rather than to seek the more distant rewards and punishments of the afterlife.[35] For both Hobbes and Locke, then, there is a moral law in the state of nature, moral action is based on self-interest, and fear of God's punishment is of limited value as a motivator.

Even Hobbes's belief that only fear of the sovereign will assure compliance with moral or legal rules must be qualified. He recognized that fear of the sovereign's forces would not stop people willing to rebel, since people willing to rebel were already willing to risk battle with the sovereign's forces. Law enforcement is not enough because a law against rebelling is like a law against lawbreaking. Thus, Hobbes maintained that people must be taught the basis for the sovereign's authority so that they will not be tempted to rebel.[36] In short, they must see that only by respecting the sovereign's authority is peace possible. Peace is the condition of all decent social existence and, accordingly, Hobbes believed that "all men agree on this, that peace is good."[37]

This gives us a fourth possibility—after fear, shared culture, and shared morality—as a basis for the trust necessary for decent social existence, namely, everyone's interest in *peace*. For there to be peace, people must be able to count on their fellows obeying the law, and to provide that reliability, people must be willing to obey the law *even when they disagree with it*. And with everyone wanting peace and knowing these things, everyone has reason to trust that everyone else will obey the law. To read Hobbes as putting forth this fourth possibility further reduces the distance between him and Locke. Now the obligation to obey the law in Hobbes's state can be seen to be based on a positive interest in peace rather than on fear alone.

VI LOCKE, HOBBES, AND THE MORAL AMBIVALENCE OF OUR CRIME

Nonetheless, there is a crucial difference between Locke and Hobbes. Where Locke allows for disobedience based on injustice,[38] Hobbes insists on obedience based on the need for peace. Locke thought that we form the state to achieve justice by securing our rights, while Hobbes thought that we form the state to achieve peace. Each view has a different implication: If the state is formed to secure justice, then *injustice can justify disobedience of the law*. If the state is formed to secure peace, then *injustice cannot justify disobedience of the law* since disobedience of the law is the opposite of peace.

Ironically, Locke and Hobbes each recognized the truth in the other's view. It is clear that for Locke, unless there is peace, justice will be uncertain—that is why people form the state. And it is clear that for Hobbes, without justice, peace will be uncertain—that is why Hobbes counseled the sovereign to treat his subjects according to the natural laws of equity.[39] In fact, there is a two-way relationship here that is a basic truth of social life: *Without peace, there will not be justice because people will be defending themselves preemptively and taking what they can get; without justice, there will not be peace because people will be resentful and willing to chance violence to obtain what they believe is justly theirs.* Hobbes and Locke are both right!

Where does this leave us with regard to the obligation to obey the law? Earlier, I argued for the Lockean view that injustice weakens its victims' obligations to obey the law. I do not take back that argument. But note that, since any existing society will not be perfectly just, there will always be occasions in which a person may accurately believe he has been the victim of injustice in a way that would reduce his obligation to obey the law. In fact, even if a society were perfectly just, a person might still believe himself to be a victim of injustice, though mistakenly. Remember that though Locke thought that people would recognize a common morality, he was aware as well that they would interpret it in ways that served their interests. Consequently, if people were to take their belief that they were victims of injustice as reducing or eliminating their obligation to obey the law, lawbreaking could become widespread. Life in the society would become very uncertain, trust would dissolve, and our freedom would contract accordingly. Thus a decent social existence requires that people refrain from taking their own judgments that they are victims of injustice as justification for breaking the law.

With this, we are brought back to Hobbes. Hobbes was wrong in thinking that a ruler could not both keep the peace and be accountable to the citizenry. But he was right in thinking that people cannot have the right to break the law on the basis of their own private moral judgments. If there were such a right, all citizens would have it. Since people will be biased in their judgments about their own interests, exercising this right will lead to injustice. But, even more crucially, it will undermine others' trust in their fellows' willingness to abide by the law, and this will cause people to take preemptive self-protective actions, and lead ultimately to the war of all against all. If everyone thinks they have the right to disobey the law because of injustice, then there will be no peace.

Thus, the Lockean argument that I made earlier, that injustice reduces the obligations of the victims of injustice, meets a Hobbesian argument coming in the other direction. For decent social life to exist, for freedom to exist, there must be secure peace. For there to be secure peace, citizens must be able to trust that other citizens will not break the law *even if they believe that they are victims of injustice.*

We have here two conflicting moral principles. The Lockean principle is that the *obligation to obey the law is reduced or eliminated for victims of injustice.* The Hobbesian principle is that everyone has an *obligation to obey the law even if they are victims of injustice in order to maintain the secure peace that makes freedom possible for all.* I think that both principles are valid. This is why the moral nature of crime—at least of a crime like ours, one committed against the well off by the unjustly disadvantaged—is *ambivalent.*

These two conflicting principles reflect the fact that we want two basic things from the state—justice and peace—and, while ultimately each is a condition of the other, in the short run they may justify conflicting actions. And there is no formula for determining which principle should dominate in a given case. As I said earlier, that requires a judgment based on balancing numerous considerations. For example, the more obvious and extreme an injustice, the more it will tend to reduce the obligation to obey the law. The more open the society is to reform, the greater will be the obligation to maintain trust by obeying the law.

This brings me back to our crime. Worse than the loss of the stolen goods, worse even than my wife's injury, which happily could be treated and repaired, was the loss of the feeling of freedom that we used to have in the streets of Nice. We were robbed of trust. So, though I still believe that my criminals were victims of injustice, and thus that their obligation to respect our property was reduced by that fact, I also feel that they stole something from us that they did owe us. They disturbed the peace. They made the world a scarier place, and thereby constrained our freedom of movement in a more insidious way than mere chains would do.

I think that I need offer to the reader some statement about what should be done to our criminals were they to be caught and brought to justice. Because of complexities already referred to, this is not an easy task, but here goes. That they are victims of injustice means that our criminals' guilt for stealing our property is reduced. How great that reduction is will depend on how badly victimized they are, on how great or small a chance there is to remedy this victimization legally, and so on—a set of factors too complicated to put into a simple formula. Nonetheless, if my argument is sound, this reduction must be substantial. On the other hand, that our criminals' abiding by the law is a necessary condition of the trust and peace that makes their own freedom possible means that they are morally guilty of violating that peace. In the end, then, I believe that justice would be served if our criminals were primarily punished for violating the peace, and only slightly if at all for stealing our property—as far as these aspects of our crime can be disaggregated. It is perhaps needless to add that it is too much to hope that an actual criminal justice system could function in this way. No actual criminal justice system can be expected to acknowledge that the injustice of the society it defends weakens the obligations of some of its citizens to obey the law, and then to adjust penalties to this fact.

Notes

[This essay is a revised version of a talk that I gave as the Visiting Scholar Lecture at James Madison University, in Harrisonburg, VA, on October 13, 2005; as the keynote address at the Twelfth Annual Graduate Student Conference on "The Perceptions and Politics of Justice" at Duquesne University, in Pittsburgh, PA, on February 17, 2006; and in the Justice Lecture Series at Roger Williams University, in Bristol, RI, on October 12, 2006. I thank the faculty and students at these institutions for their many helpful comments. I thank, as well, Phillip Scribner, who read and responded helpfully to an earlier draft of the paper; and John Kleinig, editor of *Criminal Justice Ethics,* for many challenging questions the responses to which have, I hope, much improved the paper.]

1. "The Ethicist," *New York Times Magazine,* September 25, 2005, 19.
2. Immanuel Kant, *Lectures on Ethics* (Indianapolis, IN: Hackett Publishing Company, 1963), 194.

3. See Jeffrey Reiman, *The Rich Get Richer and the Poor Get Prison: Ideology, Class, and Criminal Justice,* 8th ed. (Boston: Allyn & Bacon, 2007), 174–78, for discussion of the ideological effects of this fact.

4. "The face of the earth is continually changing, by the encrease of small kingdoms into great empires, by the dissolution of great empires into smaller kingdoms, by the planting of colonies, by the migration of tribes. Is there any thing discoverable in all these events, but force and violence? Where is the mutual agreement or voluntary association so much talked of?" David Hume, "Of the Original Contract," in Hume, *Essays: Moral, Political, and Literary,* ed. E. Miller (Indianapolis, IN: Liberty Fund, 1985), 471.

5. On the history of social contract doctrine, generally, see J. W. Gough, *The Social Contract: A Critical Study of its Development,* 2nd ed. (Oxford: Oxford University Press, 1957).

6. In the dialogue, Socrates imagines himself in a conversation with the laws of Athens, in which the laws say: "If any [Athenian] chooses to go to one of our colonies, supposing that he should not be satisfied with us and the state, or to emigrate to any other country, not one of us laws hinders or prevents him from going away wherever he likes, without any loss of property. On the other hand, if any one of you stands his ground when he can see how we administer justice and the rest of our public organization, we hold that by so doing he has in fact undertaken to do anything we tell him." Plato, *Crito,* in *Plato: The Collected Dialogues,* ed. E. Hamilton and H. Cairns (Princeton, NJ: Princeton University Press, 1989), 37 (51d-e).

7. "For since I know that my nature is very weak and limited, whereas the nature of God is immense, incomprehensible, and infinite, this is sufficient for me also to know that he can make innumerable things whose causes escape me. For this reason alone the entire class of causes which people customarily derive from a thing's 'end,' I judge entirely useless in physics. It is not without rashness that I think myself capable of inquiring into the ends of God." René Descartes, *Meditations of First Philosophy,* Meditation IV, in Descartes, *Discourse on Method and Meditations of First Philosophy* (Indianapolis, IN: Hackett Publishing Company, 1998), 82.

8. Of course, asking actual citizens if they approve the laws under which they stand is an essential element of democratic government. In the real world of politics, this—conjoined with constitutional protections for minorities—represents the best available practical approximation of the theoretical test of morality here discussed.

9. Thomas Hobbes, *Leviathan* (Indianapolis, IN: Hackett Publishing Company, 1994), pt. I, chap. 13, 76.

10. "[B]ecause there be some that taking pleasure in contemplating their own power in the acts of conquest, which they pursue farther than their security requires, if others (*that otherwise would be glad to be at ease within modest bounds*) should not by invasion increase their power, they would not be able, long time, by standing only on their defense, to subsist." Id., 75; emphasis added.

11. See note 10 for evidence that Hobbes did not assume that all people were naturally self-aggrandizing.

12. Hobbes, *Leviathan,* pt. I, chap. 13, 77.

13. "How short soever [men's] Knowledge may come of an universal, or perfect Comprehension of whatsoever is, it yet secures their great Concernments, that they have Light enough to lead them to the Knowledge of their Maker, and the sight of their own Duties." John Locke, *An Essay Concerning Human Understanding* (New York: Oxford University Press, 1975), bk. I, chap. 1, sec. 5, 44. And of those duties, Locke writes "The state of Nature has a law of Nature to govern it, which obliges every one, and reason, which is that law, teaches all mankind who will but consult it, that being all equal and independent, no one ought to harm another in his life, health, liberty or possessions."

Locke, *Second Treatise of Civil Government* (New York: Everyman's Library, 1975), chap. 2, sec. 6, 119.

14. "For though the law of Nature be plain and intelligible to all rational creatures, yet men, being biased by their interest, as well as ignorant for want of study of it, are not apt to allow of it as a law binding to them in the application of it to their particular cases." Locke, *Second Treatise*, chap. 9, sec. 124, 180.

15. This is not to say that all obligations arise this way. I am speaking here strictly about the obligation to obey the law as such. There may, for example, be moral obligations not to kill people (outside of self-defense, etc.) and such obligations will bind us not to violate a law against homicide, but not because it is a law. This will raise questions about the status of the violence used in our crime that will be addressed below (see the text accompanying note 19).

16. "The main idea [of the principle of fairness] is that when a number of persons engage in a mutually advantageous cooperative venture according to rules, and thus restrict their liberty in ways necessary to yield advantages for all, those who have submitted to these restrictions have a right to a similar acquiescence on the part of those who have benefited from their submission. We are not to gain from the cooperative labors of others without doing our fair share." John Rawls, *Theory of Justice,* rev. ed. (Cambridge, MA: Harvard University Press, 1999), 96; see also H.L.A. Hart, "Are There Any Natural Rights?" *Philosophical Review* 64 (1955): 185ff.

17. Rawls asserts "that the duty to comply [with laws made by the majority] is problematic for permanent minorities that have suffered injustice for many years." Rawls, *Theory of Justice,* 312. See also Michael Walzer, "The Obligations of Oppressed Minorities," *Obligations: Essays of Disobedience, War and Citizenship* (New York: Simon and Schuster, 1970), 46–70; Bill Lawson, "Crime, Minorities, and the Social Contract," *Criminal Justice Ethics* 9, no. 2 (1990): 14–24; and Jeffrie Murphy, "Marxism and Retribution," *Philosophy & Public Affairs* 2, no. 3 (1973): 217–43. I think, by the way, that, in addition to injustice reducing the obligations of its victims to obey the law, injustice spreads moral responsibility for crimes beyond the victims of injustice who commit them to those who promote injustice (for example, by discriminating on the basis of race) or who benefit from injustice (for example, by earning more than they would if blacks were able to compete in the market without discrimination), but who don't work to correct it. I shall not make this argument here, however.

18. I am, for purposes of this argument, treating myself and my wife as participants in the French economy. This is reasonable in that, though we do not earn our incomes in France, we own property there and we spend a few months there every year. Thus we benefit from French economic and legal institutions and we are subject to French taxes. Moreover, we share membership with the French in the global economy in which the boundaries between national economies mean less and less each day.

19. See note 15, above.

20. Rawls, *Theory of Justice,* 302.

21. Given that the majority of crimes of the sort of which my wife and I were victims are committed by poor people against other poor people, it should be clear that among the unrectified injustices from which many of the disadvantaged suffer is that they pay the lion's share of the price for the injustice that prompts some of their fellows to commit crime. In my view, this only further weakens their obligations to obey the law.

22. See William C. Heffernan and John Kleinig, eds., *From Social Justice to Criminal Justice* (New York: Oxford University Press, 2000) for several essays that debate this point pro and con.

23. Following Hume, Annette Baier argues that the social contract is "an artificially contrived and secured case of mutual trust," in part because "in general we cannot trust at

will." Baier, "Trust and Antitrust," *Ethics* 96 (1986): 245, referring to David Hume, *Treatise of Human Nature* (Oxford: Clarendon Press, 1978), 521–22. Baier faults the contractarian focus on voluntary agreements between equals as leaving out trust between unequals, such as an infant's trust in its mother. No doubt there is something to this, but I am not convinced that what infants have toward their mothers is really trust, since it seems rather only that they have not yet begun to doubt. Trust, says Baier, implies accepting vulnerability ("Trust then . . . is *accepted* vulnerability to another's possible but not expected ill will . . . toward one" [235; my emphasis]). But, accepting vulnerability presupposes an awareness of vulnerability—which is more than we can attribute to infants. Moreover, the trust implied in the social contract is not *willed*. What is willed is the agreement; trust itself is based on something else: in Hobbes's case fear and our interest in peace, in Locke's on a shared basic morality.

24. "[H]e being in a much worse condition that is exposed to the arbitrary power of one man who has the command of a hundred thousand than he that is exposed to the arbitrary power of a hundred thousand single men." Locke, *Second Treatise,* chap. 11, sec. 137, 187.

25. Hobbes, *Leviathan,* pt. II, chap. 30, 219; see also 226.

26. See note 31 below, and accompanying text.

27. Locke, *Second Treatise,* chap. 7, sec. 93, 163.

28. Hobbes, *Leviathan,* pt. II, chap. 29, 212. Hobbes likewise condemned the opinion "That he that hath the sovereign power is subject to the civil laws." Id., 213. Earlier he rejected the notion that the sovereign receives his power from the covenant, since the sovereign is not party to the covenant but must already exist with power to enforce it (*Leviathan,* pt. II, chap. 18, 112). All of these views that Hobbes rejected would justify holding the sovereign accountable to the citizens.

29. Hobbes, *Leviathan,* pt. I, chaps. 14, 15, 79–100.

30. Hobbes, *Leviathan,* pt. I, chap. 15, 100.

31. "These dictates of reason men use to call by the name of laws, but improperly; for they are but conclusions or theorems concerning what conduceth to the conservation and preservation of themselves, whereas law, properly, is the word of him that by right hath command over others. But yet if we consider the same theorems, as delivered in the word of God, that by right commandeth all things, then they are properly called laws." Hobbes, *Leviathan,* pt. I, chap. 15, 100. Interestingly, Hobbes calls these theorems *laws* throughout his discussion of them.

32. "[T]he true ground of morality . . . can only be the Will and Law of a God, who sees men in the dark, has in his hands Rewards and Punishments, and power enough to call to account the Proudest Offender." Locke, *Essay*, bk. I, chap. 3, 69. There is considerable controversy over the question of whether Locke's moral theory requires the notion that moral laws come from God. My own view is that Locke believed that moral laws had to come from God, but that his moral theory has sufficient resources for a secular grounding of morality. See Jeremy Waldron, *God, Locke, and Equality: Christian Foundations in Locke's Political Thought* (New York: Cambridge University Press, 2002). My view is defended in Jeffrey Reiman, "Towards a Secular Lockean Liberalism," *The Review of Politics* 67 (2005): 473–93.

33. Hobbes considered swearing to God as a means of making agreements binding in the state of nature, but soon after insisted that people only have good reason for relying on others keeping their agreements if there is a sovereign who enforces those agreements. Hobbes discussed swearing to God at the end of *Leviathan,* pt. I, chap. 14, 88, and then almost immediately in chap. xv, wrote: "there must be some coercive power to compel men equally to the performance of their covenants, by the terror of some punishment greater than the benefit they expect by the breach of their covenant . . . ; and such power there is none before the erection of a commonwealth" (*Leviathan,* pt. I, chap. 15, 89).

34. See Hobbes, *Leviathan,* pt. I, chap. 11, 67, 71.

35. Locke, *Essay,* bk. II, chap. 21, 255.

36. "And the grounds of [the sovereign's] rights have the rather need to be diligently and truly taught, because they cannot be maintained by any civil law or terror of legal punishment. For a civil law that shall forbid rebellion (and such is all resistance to the essential rights of sovereignty) is not (as a civil law) any obligation but by virtue only of the law of nature that forbiddeth violation of faith; which natural obligation, if men know not, they cannot know the right of any law the sovereign maketh. And for the punishment, they take it but for an act of hostility [i.e., an act of war], which, when they think they have strength enough, they will endeavor by acts of hostility to avoid." Hobbes, *Leviathan,* pt. II, chap. 30, 220.

37. Hobbes, *Leviathan,* pt. I., chap. 15, 100.

38. "And where the body of the people, or any single man, are deprived of their right, or are under the exercise of a power without right, having no appeal on earth they have a liberty to appeal to Heaven whenever they judge the cause of sufficient moment. . . . And this judgment they cannot part with, it being out of a man's power so to submit himself to another as to give him a liberty to destroy him; God and Nature never allowing a man so to abandon himself as to neglect his own preservation." And further: "Who shall be the judge whether the prince or legislative act contrary to their trust? . . . . The people shall be judge; for who shall be judge whether his trustee or deputy acts well according to the trust reposed in him, but he who deputes him and must, by having deputed him, have still a power to discard him when he fails in his trust?" Finally, though God "alone is judge of the right. But every man is judge for himself, as in all other cases so in this, whether another hath put himself in a state of war with him." Locke, *Second Treatise,* chap. 14, sec. 168, 203; chap. 19, sec. 240, 241.

39. "In this [the sovereign's] distribution [of goods], the first law is for division of the land itself, wherein the sovereign assigneth to every man a portion, according as he (and not according as any subject . . .) shall judge agreeable to equity and the common good." Hobbes, *Leviathan,* pt. I, chap. 24, 160. In addition: "The safety of the people requireth further, from him or them that have the sovereign power, that justice be equally administered to all degrees of people, that is, that as well the rich and mighty as poor and obscure may be righted on the injuries done them." Hobbes, *Leviathan,* pt. II, chap. 30, 226.

MUCH RESPECT: TOWARD A HIP-HOP THEORY OF PUNISHMENT

Paul Butler

INTRODUCTION: THE HIP-HOP NATION

This Article imagines the institution of punishment in the hip-hop nation. My thesis is that hip-hop can be used to inform a theory of punishment that is coherent, that enhances public safety, and that treats lawbreakers with respect. Hip-hop can improve the ideology and administration of justice in the United States.

For some time the debate about why people should be punished has been old school: Each one of four theories of punishment—retribution, deterrence, incapacitation, and rehabilitation—has acceded to prominence, and then lost its luster. Hip-hop offers a fresh approach. It first seems to embrace retribution.[1] . . .

Next, however, comes the remix. Hip-hop takes punishment personally. Many people in the hip-hop nation have been locked up or have loved ones who have been. Punishment is an exercise of the state's police power, but it also implicates intimate family relationships. "Shout outs" to inmates—expressions of love and respect to them—are commonplace in the music and visual art. You understand criminal justice differently when the people that you love experience being locked down. . . . [2]

The hip-hop theory of punishment acknowledges that when too many people are absent from their communities because they are being condemned by the government, prison may have unintended consequences. Retribution must be the object of punishment, but it should be limited by important social interests. In a remarkable moment in American history, popular music is weighing the costs and benefits of punishment. As we listen to the radio, watch music videos, dance at clubs, or wear the latest fashion, we receive a message from the "black CNN." [3] Hip-hop exposes the current punishment regime as profoundly unfair. It demonstrates this view by, if not glorifying law breakers, at least not viewing all criminals with the disgust which the law seeks to attach to them. Hip-hop points out the incoherence of the law's construct of crime, and it attacks the legitimacy of the system. Its message has the potential to transform justice in the United States. . . .

At the same time that an art form created by African American and Latino men dominates popular culture, African American and Latino men dominate American prisons. . . . Unsurprisingly then, justice—especially criminal justice—has been a preoccupation of the hip-hop nation. The culture contains a strong descriptive and normative analysis of punishment by the people who know it best.

Bold, rebellious, often profane, the music has multicultural detractors as well as fans. One need not like hip-hop, however, to appreciate its potential to transform. Imagine, for example, that television situation comedies consistently critiqued the government's foreign policy, that country music ridiculed the nation's health care, or that fans at professional sports events were warned that the government was exploiting them. We would anticipate a strong response from the state if powerful critiques of it were widely disseminated. These scenarios are hard to imagine because most of American popular culture is explicitly apolitical. Moreover, there probably would be widespread disagreement among the producers and consumers of the culture about what politics to advocate.

Hip-hop culture is different. Often it is explicitly political. Its politics are not always easy to determine, and on some issues there is great diversity of opinion. On the fairness and utility of American criminal justice, however, the hip-hop nation speaks as one. In the contemporary history of the United States, it is hard to recall another dominant form of popular culture that contains such a strong critique of the state.

Many seem to be listening. The hip-hop nation is gaining political power, and seems more inclined to use it than has historically been the case with youth or artists. I do not suggest, however, that the hip-hop nation will be a potent voting bloc in the near future. My claim is normative. Hip-hop culture makes a strong case for a transformation of American criminal justice: It describes, with eloquence, the problems with the current regimes, and articulates, with passion, a better way. Its message is one that we should heed for reasons both moral and utilitarian.[4]

This Article proceeds as follows. In the next Part, I discuss the relationship between popular culture and criminal law. Part II provides a short history of hip-hop culture, with special attention to the rule-breaking that attended the culture's birth. Part III describes hip-hop's relevance to the the current debate in criminal law scholarship about social norms. Part IV sets forth several elements of a hip-hop theory of criminal law. The Article concludes by comparing hip-hop justice with constructs of justice found in civil rights and critical theory.

I. POPULAR CULTURE AND CRIMINAL LAW

There is a symbiotic relationship between culture and law. Culture shapes the law, and law is a product of culture. Television, for example, has profoundly informed our perceptions of criminal justice in the United States. Most Americans can recite the Miranda warnings, not because they have been arrested, but because television cops advise television "bad guys" of their constitutional rights several times a day.

Television news programs are dominated by stories about crime. . . . The message conveyed is that "street" crime is a major threat to our well-being. . . . The main perpetrators, the news programs suggest, are African American and Latino men. Politicians respond to the purported crisis by getting tough on crime, which includes building more prisons, instituting more severe sentences, imposing harsh punishments upon recidivists, eliminating the discretion of judges to reduce punishment, and federalizing many crimes.[5] One effect of these laws is the disproportionate incarceration of African Americans and, to a lesser extent, Latinos.

Some scholars and activists have suggested that the effect of the cultural depiction of crime is that many Americans have exaggerated concerns about being victimized by black and Latino men. . . . Some lawmakers seem to exploit these concerns for political reasons. . . . One result is that some punishment seems driven by racial stereotypes. . . .

The most frequently cited contemporary example is harsher federal penalties for crack cocaine than powder cocaine.[6] Crack cocaine is powder cocaine that is cooked with baking soda until it forms small solid pieces. Crack is smoked rather than inhaled. It is less expensive than powder cocaine and has a briefer intoxicating effect.

A star basketball player, Len Bias, died as a result of a cocaine overdose in 1986.[7] He was presumed to have ingested crack, although there was actually no evidence as to what form of cocaine he had consumed. Bias was African American, and crack cocaine was thought to be the preferred form in the black community. . . . Bias' death focused the media's attention on crack cocaine. Congress responded with one of the most severe punishment schemes for a drug in American history.[8] It instituted a mandatory sentence for possession of crack cocaine, but not powder cocaine. The punishment for sellers was especially harsh. To receive the same sentence as a crack distributor, a powder distributor must possess one hundred times the quantity of cocaine. . . . For example, the distributor of five grams of crack, which is enough for 25 doses and has a street value of approximately $500, receives the same sentence as the distributor of 500 grams of powder, which is enough for 3,000 doses and is worth $40,000.

There is little scientific support for the proposition that crack cocaine merits more punishment than powder on a harm principle, and virtually no support for the hundred-to-one federal differential. The U.S. Sentencing Commission has proposed that the distinction be reduced. Likewise, President Clinton's drug czar recommended no disparity in punishment,[9] and, during the presidential campaign of 2000, George W. Bush also rejected a distinction.[10] Thus far, however, Congress has refused to budge, in part because of the strong cultural bias against crack cocaine. . . . Culture, not logic or science, is the best explanation for why and how crack users are punished.

This point is not new or particularly surprising. In a democracy we would expect culture to inform law. The potential of hip-hop culture, however, to influence law seems less obvious—perhaps because hip-hop is a product of youth culture and perhaps because it seems to celebrate defiant and even outlaw conduct.[11] I hope to demonstrate that the culture, while rebellious, can be used to inform a principled, rules-based theory of punishment.

Austin Sarat has described punishment as "living in culture through its pedagogical effects. It teaches us how to think about categories like intention, responsibility, and injury, and it models the socially appropriate ways of responding to injuries done to us."[12] Hip-hop offers a fresh way of analyzing persistent unresolved problems in criminal law theory, including how to determine cause, the relationship between responsibility and blame, and the appropriate response of the state to law-breaking. Considering the growing influence of hip-hop culture, and the personal experience of many citizens of the hip-hop nation with criminal justice, its perspective deserves examination.

II. HIP-HOP 101

Hip-hop was begat in one of the poorest and most crime-ridden jurisdictions in the United States: the South Bronx, New York, during the 1970s. It was a place of a desperate, hard-knock creativity, as evidenced by the way its citizens talked, dressed, and danced. Even the teenagers who drew graffiti on the subway thought of themselves as artists, though the police had a different point of view.

A man who spun records for parties—DJ Kool Herc, he called himself—experimented with using two turntables to play copies of the same record.[13] Herc used the turntables like a musical instrument—he made his own songs from other people's recordings. Sometimes Herc would speak rhythmically to his beats (a technique borrowed from his Jamaican heritage). . . . He taped these "raps" for boomboxes, and the music became popular all over New York City. . . .

Herc's work inspired other DJs, including Afrika Bambaataa, a Black Muslim also of Jamaican descent. . . . Bambaataa expanded Herc's musical tracks from disco and house music to virtually any recorded sound, including rock music and television shows. . . . DJs "battled" (engaged in artistic competition) at city parks, and dancers performed in an athletic, bone-popping style called "break-dancing." . . .

For the purposes of my thesis, I want to note four things about the creation of hip-hop. First, many artists took an instrumentalist view of the law. The trespass law did not deter the graffiti artists, the copyright law did not stop the DJs from sampling any music they wanted, and the property law did not prevent DJs from "borrowing" electricity from street lamps at public parks. Second, the culture was more about recycling or remixing than creating out of whole cloth. Third, virtually every hip-hop artist renamed himself or herself; "slave" or "government" names were seldom used to describe the artists. Many hip-hop artists named themselves thinking of the criminal law. A short list includes rappers and groups such as Big Punisher, . . . Canibus, Missy "Misdemeanor" Elliot, . . . Naughty by Nature, OutKast, and Public Enemy. Fourth, rappers were compared, almost from the beginning, to African griots, who also communicated wisdom (or, in the hip-hop lexicon, "dropped science") with drum beats and words.[14]

In 1979, the Sugarhill Gang's *"Rapper's Delight"* became the first hip-hop song to become a national hit.[15] Rap was immediately appropriated by white artists; the next year the new wave group Blondie produced *"Rapture,"* which reached the top of the charts. In the mid-1980s, groups like Run-DMC, the Beastie Boys (a white group that became the best selling and most critically acclaimed hip-hop act of the time), and Salt-N-Pepa (the first female hip-hop act of significance) had popular songs that attracted the attention of MTV, which started, somewhat reluctantly, to show rap videos. . . .

In the late 1980s, mainstream rap music took two divergent directions. Many artists addressed political issues, "resulting in the most overt social agenda in popular music since the urban folk movement of the 1960s." . . . A classic album of this era is Public Enemy's *It Takes a Nation of Millions to Hold Us Back*. . . .

The other direction of rap, however, drew more attention, and sales. "Gangsta rap," which unapologetically depicted outlaw conduct in the innercity, became popular. . . . The group NWA (Niggaz With Attitude) received widespread media attention for its controversial song *"Fuck da Police."* . . .

Hip-hop music continues to exemplify this dichotomy between the politically correct and the world, real or imagined, of some artists. *The Washington Post* has described "two faces of hip-hop," one a "conscious" side "where political, social and cultural issues are hashed out in verse."[16] The other side is "the bling-bling, the music that embraces the glamorous life, the live-now-I-got-mine attitude found in countless hits, and in flashy videos where hootchy mamas bounce their backsides and Busta Rhymes exhorts, 'Pass the Courvoisier.'"[17]

Conscious hip-hop is critically acclaimed, with Lauryn Hill's *The Mis-Education of Lauryn Hill* becoming the first hip-hop album to receive the Grammy award for Record of the Year in 1999. . . . Since then Alicia Keys and OutKast have also won top honors. . . .

Gangsta and "bling bling" rap, on the other hand, have been derided as materialist, sexist, and homophobic,[18] but these forms of hip-hop have their defenders as well. They assert that the lyrics are accurate reflections of some people's experiences or that the lyrics are not the most important, or artistic, element of the music. The scholar Tricia Rose describes hip-hop as a "hidden transcript . . . it uses cloaked speech and disguised cultural codes to comment on and challenge aspects of current power inequalities."[19] Moreover, one person's "conscious" rapper might be another person's gangsta rapper. 50 Cent, who made the best selling album of 2003, is described by some critics as a gangsta rapper, and by others as someone whose music comments, critically, on the costs of violence and materialism.[20]

A. Hip-Hop's Influence: Consumers

The evolution that rap pioneers like Kool Herc and Afrikka Bambaataa probably did not foresee is the extraordinary success of their art form with suburban consumers. Market studies indicate that about seventy-five percent of people who buy hip-hop music are non-black. . . . Over the last decade hip-hop music has surpassed country music in popularity. Hip-hop created the United States' first African American billionaire, Robert Johnson, who sold BET, a cable network that plays hip-hop videos, to Viacom, the corporation that owns MTV.[21]

Hip-hop has had a major impact on fashion, with rap stars like P. Diddy and Jay-Z presiding over houses of fashion that produce top selling men's wear at Macy's and Bloomingdale's.[22] Hip-hop fashion pays homage to the garments that prison inmates wear; it emphasizes loose, baggy clothing.[23] Hip-hop entrepreneurs have branched out into manufacturing and distributing products such as liquor, . . . energy drinks, . . . and gym shoes . . . and have launched marketing and advertising firms. . . .

B. The Academy

Approximately seventy-five colleges and universities offer courses in hip-hop studies.[24] Harvard University's famed Afro-American studies department recently hired a specialist in hip-hop because, according to Professor Henry Louis Gates, "it is one of the most important cultural phenomenons in the second half of the twentieth century. We would be remiss if we did not treat it accordingly."[25] Hip-hop has critics in the academy as well, and some of their critiques have implications for this project's construction of a hip-hop theory of punishment. The Harvard historian Martin Kilson, for example, believes that hip-hop denigrates African American achievements in civil rights.[26] John McWhorter of the University of California condemns hip-hop for being antiauthoritarian.[27]

C. Hip-Hop as a Political Movement

Some members of the hip-hop nation explicitly have embraced politics. The most prominent is Russell Simmons, the multimillionaire coowner of Def Jam, a hip-hop record label.[28] Simmons created the Hip-Hop Summit Action Network ("HSAN"), a nonprofit organization "dedicated to harnessing the cultural relevance of Hip-Hop music to serve as a catalyst for education advocacy and other societal concerns fundamental to the well-being of at-risk youth throughout the United States."[29] One of HSAN's objectives is to register two million new voters for the 2004 presidential election.[30] In one measure of Simmons' influence, all but one of the major Democratic candidates for President in 2004 met with him. . . .

HSAN has emphasized reform of the criminal justice system, including the "total elimination of police brutality and the unjust incarceration of people of color and all others."[31] It seeks "the end and repeal of all repressive legislations [sic], laws, regulations and ordinances such as . . . federal and state mandatory minimum sentencing; trying and sentencing juveniles as adults; sentencing disparities between crack and powdered cocaine use; [and] capitol [sic] punishment . . ." . . .

HSAN focus has been the repeal of New York's Rockefeller drug laws. These laws, first passed in 1973 by Governor Nelson Rockefeller, require long prison sentences for drug crimes.[32] The organization's "Countdown to Fairness" campaign was intended to accomplish repeal of the Rockefeller laws by June 2003. . . . Its campaign was endorsed by the Congressional Black Caucus, the National Urban League, the NAACP, and both Hilary Clinton and Chuck Schumer, New York's United States Senators. . . .

HSAN did not, however, succeed in getting the Rockefeller laws repealed within its stated time frame.[33]

Other efforts to politically organize the hip-hop community include the "Rap the Vote" project and the National Hip-Hop Political Convention.[34] The Internet contains numerous sites dedicated to inspiring activism in the hip-hop nation.[35]

D. The Limits of Hip-Hop's Influence

I want to be careful not to overstate hip-hop's role as a political force in the United States. Compared to its cultural and economic power, hip-hop's political influence is not strong. In fact, hip-hop's primary constituent groups—young people and artists—are well known for their lack of participation in traditional electoral politics. . . . Hip-hop's role in law and policy, at least for now, will be determined more by the strength of its vision than by its community's potency at the ballot box. The rest of this Article is intended to make the case that its vision, though undertheorized, has the potential to transform the United States into a safer, more just society.

III. HIP-HOP AND SOCIAL NORMS

What happens when many of the leaders of popular culture are arrested and incarcerated? For the hip-hop nation, this is not a theoretical question. Many of its most prominent artists have been involved in the criminal justice system. . . . So many have been arrested that the *Village Voice* recently questioned whether the New York Police Department has a secret unit dedicated to hip-hop artists.[36] Police in Miami admitted that they secretly watched and kept dossiers on hip-hop stars who visited South Florida.[37]

A telling example of the role of punishment in the hip-hop nation can be seen in a recent issue of *Source* magazine, which bills itself as the "bible" of hip-hop. The March 2004 cover featured the tag-line: "Hip-Hop Behind Bars: Are Rappers the New Target of America's Criminal Justice System?"[38] The magazine's cover featured mug shots of ten hip-hop artists who are incarcerated or awaiting trial. . . .

The statistics about rap artists reflect the statistics about young African American and Latino men. In the mid-1990s, one study found that one in three young black men were under criminal justice supervision.[39] An African American man born in 1991 has a 29% chance of being imprisoned, compared with a 16% chance for a Latino man, and a 4% chance for a white man.[40] There are more young black men in prison than in college.[41]

The reaction of artists in the hip-hop community to the mass incarceration of African Americans has been to interrogate the social meaning of punishment. Prison, as depicted in rap music, is a placement center for the undereducated, the unemployed, and, especially, aspiring capitalists who, if not locked up, would successfully challenge white elites. . . .

Criminologists and legal scholars recently have emphasized the role of social norms in preventing crime. In the strongest form, the idea is that cultural (or subcultural) forces are more important than criminal law in determining conduct. We care more about how people in our communities label us than how the law does. The appropriate role of criminal law, then, is to support social mores that contribute to public safety. Criminal law fails when it subverts those norms.[42] When, for example, incarceration is not sufficiently stigmatized, it loses its value as deterrence.

To say that hip-hop destigmatizes incarceration understates the point: Prison, according to the artists, actually stigmatizes the government. In a culture that celebrates rebelliousness, prison is the place for unruly "niggas" who otherwise would upset the political or economic status quo. In this sense, inmates are heroic figures[43] [such as] in *"A Ballad for the Fallen Soldier"* [by] Jay-Z . . .

While glorification of outlaws is certainly not limited to hip-hop,[44] the culture's depiction of the criminal as a socially useful actor is different. Hip-hop justifies rather than excuses some criminal conduct. Breaking the law is seen as a form of rebelling against the oppressive status quo. Rappers who brag about doing time are like old soldiers who boast of war wounds.

The hip-hop slang for being arrested demonstrates the culture's view of the almost arbitrary nature of criminal justice. One "catches a case."[45] The language connotes the same combination of responsibility and happenstance as when one "catches" the common cold.

Hip-hop suggests that American punishment is not mainly designed to enhance public safety or for retribution against the immoral. Rather, its critique of punishment echoes that of the philosopher Michel Foucault, who argued that prison is designed to encourage a "useful illegality" that benefits the state. The scholar Robin Kelley notes that "most rappers—especially gangsta rappers—treat prisons as virtual fascist institutions."[46]

That the hip-hop perspective on punishment is the opposite of the way citizens are expected to think is exactly the point. Hip-hop scholar Tricia Rose explains:

[A] large and significant element in rap's discursive territory is engaged in symbolic and ideological warfare with institutions and groups that symbolically, ideologically, and materially oppress African Americans . . . .
Rappers act out inversions of status hierarchies . . . and draw portraits of contact with dominant groups in which the hidden transcript inverts/subverts the public, dominant transcript.[47]

Thus, in order to maintain their self-esteem, the African American men who dominate hip-hop connote that any organization that is composed primarily of people like them must be kind of cool; it matters not whether that organization is the National Basketball Association, Morehouse College, or the state penitentiary. Since these men wield significant influence over what the nation's youth think is cool, it may be only a matter of time before punishment loses its stigma with other Americans as well.

The United States has the . . . highest incarceration rate in the world. . . . Hip-hop artists are the most visible critics of the massive punishment regime.[48] Considering the diversity of the hip-hop nation, their united front on this issue is remarkable.

They disagree about many controversial issues, including capitalism, feminism, gay and lesbian rights, abortion, religion, and immigration. On the social meaning of punishment, however, the hip-hop nation virtually speaks as one. Indeed the central point of agreement between gangsta rap and conscious hip-hop is their joint critique of American criminal justice, especially its heavy reliance on prison.[49]

. . . When popular culture presents prison as a rite of passage, punishment begins to lose its deterrent effect. If punishment is to be meaningful, it must be reinvested with stigma. We could accomplish this by using prison less frequently and more effectively. The next section suggests a way.

IV. PUNISHMENT: THE REMIX

When the prisoners began to speak, they possessed an individual theory of prisons, the penal system, and justice. It is this form of discourse which ultimately matters, a discourse against power, the counter-discourse of prisoners and those we call delinquents. . . .

—Michel Foucault[50]

Every society has seen the need to punish. The hip-hop nation is no different. Three core principles inform its ideas about punishment. First, people who harm others should be harmed in return. Second, criminals are human beings who deserve respect and love. Third, communities can be destroyed by both crime and punishment.

How would these ideas contribute to a theory of punishment? In a sense the hip-hop nation, and especially its black and Latino citizens, are best situated to design a punishment regime. The philosopher John Rawls suggests that law is most just when it is made by people who don't know how they will fare under it.[51] It is impossible, of course, to actually live in Rawls' netherworld. As Rawls recognized, our instinct is to assess public policy from the standpoint of our individual interest. Since, however, minority members of the hip-hop nation are the most likely to be arrested and incarcerated for crimes—and also the most likely to be victims of crimes[52]—they get closer to the netherworld than most of us. Ideally their theory of punishment will value both public safety and fairness to lawbreakers.

This project is not intended to suggest that hip-hop culture has explicitly constructed a theory of punishment. The claim is more limited, but still, I hope, profound. Thousands of hip-hop songs consider crime and punishment. These voices are worth listening to—they evaluate criminal justice from the bottom up.[53] Our current punishment regime has been designed from the top down, and that, in part, explains why many perceive it to be ineffective or unfair. We might punish better if the ghetto philosophers and the classic philosophers met. They address many of the same issues in punishment, including causation, harm, responsibility, excuse, and justification.

We would see that Erykah Badu, Snoop Dogg, and Jeremy Bentham have a lot in common. Immanuel Kant and Jay-Z would get along well, but their differences would be instructive. Not all of the artists are brilliant theorists, although some of them are. They represent, however, a community that has borne the brunt of the world's 200-year experiment with prison. That community knows much, has laid it down on tracks, and now attention must be paid.

We should not look to hip-hop culture for an entirely new justification of punishment. Hip-hop culture does not create out of whole cloth, and neither do the philosophers, scholars, and lawmakers who have articulated the current punishment regime. The art of hip-hop is in the remix. Thus some hip-hop overtly responds to trendy theories of punishment. The "broken window" theory of law enforcement, for example, has had a profound impact on the ghetto and thus on hip-hop culture.[54] Other elements of hip-hop can be interpreted as unconscious shout-outs to scholars of whom the artists probably are not aware. Foucault's influential history of the prison reverberates throughout hip-hop theory, as does the new criminal law scholarship on third party interests in criminal law and the effects of mass incarceration. Hip-hop culture, though, is post-postmodern. In fact, some of its characteristics, especially its embrace of retribution, seem startlingly old-fashioned.

I want to begin a discussion about a hip-hop theory of punishment by focusing on three classic problems in punishment theory. Why do we punish? What should we punish? How should we punish? I will identify six principles from hip-hop culture that address these issues.[55] First, the purpose of punishment should be retribution. Second, punishment should be limited (but not determined) by utilitarian concerns, especially the effect of punishment on people other than the lawbreaker. Third, punishment should be designed to "catch" the harm caused by rich people more than poor people. Fourth, people probably should not be punished for using or selling intoxicants. Fifth, punishment should be imposed only by people within a community, not outsiders. Sixth, prison should be used sparingly as an instrument of punishment.

A. Why Punish?

1. RETRIBUTION AND RESPECT IN HIP-HOP.

Hip-hop lyrics exhibit a strong conviction that wrongdoers should suffer consequences for their acts. . . . The culture abounds with narratives about revenge, retaliation, and avenging wrongs. The narrator in Eve's *"Love is Blind"* kills the man who abuses her close friend.[56]

At the same time, hip-hop culture seems to embrace criminals [as] [i]n Angie Stone's *"Brotha"*[57] . . . This kind of warm acknowledgement of the incarcerated is commonplace in hip-hop, and virtually unheard of in other popular culture, which largely ignores the two million Americans in prison.

The most important civic virtue in the hip-hop nation is respect. One of the culture's contributions to the English language is the verb "dis," which means "to disrespect."[58] To dis someone is worse than to insult them—it is to deny his or her humanity. Hip-hop vocabulary also includes the term "props"—to give props is to afford proper respect. . . . The misogyny and homophobia in some hip-hop makes it difficult to claim a universal value of respect for all persons.[59] Virtually all hip-hop, however, connotes a respect for the dignity of lawbreakers.

In attempting to reconcile hip-hop's impulse for righting wrongs with its respect for dignity—even the dignity of criminals—a criminal law scholar immediately thinks of retribution. This justification of punishment is premised on the idea of "just deserts."[60] When one harms another, justice requires that she be harmed in return. Retributivists believe than punishment communicates respect for the criminal by recognizing him as a moral agent and respect for the victim by avenging his harm.

The Bill of Rights codifies the retributive concern for the criminal's humanity. The Eighth Amendment prohibits the state from punishing criminals in a manner that is inconsistent with their dignity. The Supreme Court has also interpreted the Eighth Amendment as requiring that criminals not be punished disproportionately to their crime, although it has given lawmakers wide latitude in determining what proportionate punishment is.[61]

How would a profound respect for the humanity of criminals change the way we punish them? It might require a more meaningful concept of proportionate punishment than the Supreme Court has currently endorsed. . . . Harsh sentences for drug crimes, for example, are premised on utilitarian, not retributive, justifications. . . . Such penalties have been the subject of much criticism in the hip-hop community. They have been defended by police and lawmakers on the ground that they keep drugs out of low-income and minority communities. If this assertion is true, it would not persuade retributivists, who require proportionality even when disproportionate punishment is socially useful. . . . While I will later suggest that the hip-hop nation probably would not punish drug users, if it did, its embrace of retribution means they would be punished significantly less than they are now.[62]

Hip-hop theory would reject or modify some elements of retribution. Assaultive retribution, for example, is premised on hate of the criminal, which is the opposite of the hip-hop perspective.[63] More significantly, however, some theories of retribution are premised on a world in which benefits and burdens are distributed equally; it is just to punish the criminal, the argument goes, when he upsets the balance.[64]

The hip-hop nation does not share this world view; it sees benefits and burdens as allocated in an uneven and racialist manner. Through this lens, the "choice" of a poor person to sell drugs has a different and less blameworthy social meaning than the choice of a middle class person to engage in, say, insider trading. . . .

Hip-hop culture, like retributive philosophy, emphasizes the importance of moral autonomy and free agency. Both posit that people who freely choose to do wrong should be punished. Where hip-hop theorists and traditional retributivists diverge, however, is on how to determine responsibility for individual acts. Hip-hop culture emphasizes the role of environment in determining conduct, whereas classic retributivist theory focuses on individual choice. In essence, hip-hop culture discounts responsibility when criminal conduct has been shaped by a substandard environment. . . .

The hip-hop analysis does not deny that the poor are moral agents; it is instead a quasiscientific or empirical claim about the nature of free choice. . . .

2. HIP-HOP UTILITY: THIRD PARTY INTERESTS AND THE EFFECTS OF MASS INCARCERATION. . . .

Punishment has had a profound effect on some American communities.[65] There are neighborhoods where so many men are locked up that a male presence seems palpably absent.[66] It approaches gross understatement to note that a community feels it when, as for African Americans, more young men are in prison than in college.

Hip-hop is concerned with the collateral effects of punishment. It acknowledges that even when punishment is deserved, there may be severe and unintended consequences. Dorothy Roberts has described three ways that mass incarceration harms the

African American. It damages social networks, infects social norms, and destroys social citizenship.[67]

Hip-hop has catalogued a number of these harms. Damage to social networks, especially, is a consistent theme. Makaveli, for example, notes that families suffer when incarcerated parents cannot provide for their children. . . .

Should such consequences be considered when an individual offender is punished? . . . Classic retributivists believe that social considerations are immoral. The message from hip-hop, on the other hand, is that such considerations are essential.[68] Hip-hop culture advocates retribution—but not at all costs. If the consequence of making people pay for their crimes is the decimation of a community, then retribution is less important.

Professor Darryl Brown observes that "mitigating third-party interests . . . is necessary to maintain the legitimacy of criminal law, even as conflicting commitments to distributive fairness, retributive justice, and crime prevention necessitate some punishment."[69] Brown notes that when federal prosecutors believe that a corporation has committed a crime, they may decline prosecution upon consideration of "collateral consequences, including disproportionate consequences to shareholders and employees not proven personally culpable."[70] A recent decision by the Supreme Court of Canada applied similar analysis to punishment of native people in Canada.[71]

Hip-hop culture suggests broad support for such an approach in the United States, especially as applied to minority communities. In practice, consideration of collateral consequences might lead to sanctions other than incarceration. When prison is appropriate, sentences might be shorter, or family leave could be allowed. Prisoners might be allowed to work to support their families. The goal would be sentencing targeted not just to the individual offender, but to his entire community.

In practice, a hip-hop construct of punishment would combine retributive and utilitarian justifications but differently than the prevailing mixed-theory model, which assumes that the aim of punishment is utilitarian, but with retributive limits. . . . In the hip-hop construct, the objective of punishment would be retribution—but with utilitarian limits.

B. What to Punish?

1. WHO'S BAD?

Consider the following facts: In the United States, approximately half of the people in prison are African American. A black male born in 1991 has a 29% chance of being imprisoned, compared to a 16% chance for a Hispanic male, and a 4% chance for a white male.

If punishment is being allocated properly, these statistics suggest that half of the most dangerous or immoral Americans are black, even though African Americans make up only about 12% of the population. It means that black men pose such a threat that they must be locked up at a rate more than seven times that of white men, and that Hispanic men must be locked up at four times the rate. The person who has confidence in the American criminal justice system probably has an unfavorable view of blacks and Latinos and a more positive view of whites.

The hip-hop nation rejects this view. It does not see morality or dangerousness as allocated along the race and class lines that the prison population suggests. A frequent theme in hip-hop is that the law does not correctly select the most deserving candidates for punishment. Specifically the law does not properly weigh the immorality posed and danger caused by white elites. On the other hand, it exaggerates the threat posed by the poor and by minorities. From this perspective, blameworthy conduct by privileged white people or the government often goes unpunished.

Thus Ice-T jokes that [the land that we now call America was stolen from the Native Americans].[72]

Hip-hop artists sometimes accuse the state of complicity in crime [such as] [i]n *"Gun Music,"* [by] Talib Kweli[73] . . . [and] another song [by] Kweli . . . .[74]

Of course, complaints that criminal law is selectively enforced against blacks and other minorities are familiar, and not only in hip-hop culture. Hip-hop's indictment of criminal justice goes further; it identifies bias in the way that crime is constructed as well as the way that it is enforced.

Some hip-hop artists have suggested that lawmakers define crime in a way that does not challenge powerful corporate interests—even when corporations cause harm. KRS, in *"Illegal Business,"* explains: [tobacco is legal, weed is illegal.][75] It is legal for a corporation to make a gun. Business people responsible for the sale of defective products are not typically prosecuted—even if the products cause death or severe injuries. Nicotine and alcohol distributors are licensed by the government; in the case of tobacco there are even government subsidies for growers. Sellers of other drugs, including arguably less harmful ones, are punished. Hip-hop suggests that some of the existing distinctions between legal and illegal conduct, and between crimes and torts, are unprincipled.

Hip-hop sometimes presents poor minorities as relatively powerless in the grand scheme. . . . In this view, actual bad actors—including people who profit from widespread alcoholism, tobacco sales, and the demand for guns—are politically powerful. The fact that their injurious conduct is not punished helps explain hip-hop's lack of confidence in American criminal justice.

2. HIP-HOP AND DRUGS: KEEPING IT REAL.

In hip-hop culture, the idea that minorities are selectively prosecuted sometimes seems to border on paranoia. In the case of drug offenses, however, this perception is accurate. According to statistics compiled by the U.S. government, blacks are about 15% of monthly drug users. . . . Yet, they accounted for 33% of drug possession arrests . . . and more than 70% of people incarcerated for drug use. . . . Just because you are paranoid, the old joke goes, doesn't mean they're not out to get you.

The fact that drug offenses are selectively prosecuted in the African American community informs the hip-hop perspective on drug criminalization, but it is only one factor among many. A persistent critique of hip-hop culture is that it glorifies the use of illegal drugs. Upon closer examination, we see that this is partly true.

Hip-hop culture suggests that recreational drugs like marijuana and ecstasy enhance the quality of life and that they are fun.[76] Hip-hop stars Ja Rule, Missy Elliott, and Tweet collaborated on a song called *"X"* which extols the virtues of having sex under the influence of ecstasy.[77]

Marijuana, though, is the hip-hop nation's intoxicant of choice. In a classic song, Snoop Dogg raps about the pleasure of driving through his neighborhood sipping alcohol and smoking weed.[78] The scholar Michael Eric Dyson describes marijuana as "the necessary adjunct to ghetto fabulousness. . . . Getting high is at once pleasurable and political: It heightens the joys to be found in thug life while blowing smoke rings around the constraints of the state."[79]

Indeed there are probably more hip-hop songs critical of the harm posed by alcohol than by other soft drugs. Public Enemy, for example, compared the large cans of malt liquor sold in low-income communities to a [weapon to commit suicide.][80]

Hip-hop offers a more nuanced, and less consistent, perspective on "hard" drugs. Some critics have observed that more respect is accorded sellers than users. 2Pac (a.k.a. Tupac Shukur), for example, criticizes his addict parent. . . .[81] In another song, however, he praises street corner dealers for raising him when his father was not present.[82]

Other hip-hop artists are angrier at drug sellers. Ice Cube raps [that drug dealers are as bad as the police because of the deaths they cause in the community]. . . . He goes on to castigate dealers for [being as exploitative as white society].[83]

Still, there is sympathy for why some people sell drugs. Biggie Small facetiously dedicated his autobiographical song *"Juicy"* to the people who called the police when he was [working to feed his family].[84] Kanye West raps about being [forced to sell drugs] because [there's no other way to get ahead].[85]

Ultimately hip-hop acknowledges the poor consequences that drugs can have on individuals and communities. The culture is not as quick as some scholars to label drug crimes "victimless." Acknowledging these costs, however, does not inevitably lead to a belief that drug offenders should be punished. Because of the environmental factors that contribute to drug use and sales, the government's perceived complicity in the availability of drugs in the ghetto, the fact that the state allows the sale of potentially harmful drugs like tobacco and alcohol, and the selective enforcement of the drug laws in minority communities, the hip-hop consensus seems to be against punishment of drug offenders.[86] In this view, the state may have a legitimate interest in controlling the use and sale of some drugs. First, however, the government bears the burden of proving that it can regulate drugs in a manner free of racial bias and that the benefits of regulation will not be outweighed by the costs. . . .

C. How to Punish?

1. PUNISHMENT FROM INSIDE. . . .

Hip-hop artists frequently express suspicion of discretion exercised by people outside their community, especially white elites. This concern is conveyed most often in critiques of the police. In *"99 Problems,"* Jay-Z wonders if he is stopped by the police because he is young, black, and wearing his hat low on his head.[87] . . .

Many artists also worry about discretion by sentencing authorities. . . . This concern is supported by empirical evidence that blacks and Hispanics receive more severe sentences than whites for the same crime. . . .

Efforts by lawmakers to constrain discretion, however, seem to have exacerbated inequities. The Federal Sentencing Guidelines are one example. Professor Charles Ogletree writes,

[The United States Sentencing Commission's failure] to consider the offender's personal characteristics places too great an emphasis on the harm caused by the offender's act and too little emphasis on circumstances that would serve to mitigate the punishment. The Commission should have realized that it is a person who stands before the bar to accept the punishment imposed by the court.[88]

Mos Def echoes Professor Ogletree's concern about wholesale justice.[89] . . .

One response, from a hip-hop ethos, might be a requirement that punishment be imposed by people within the community. In the context of trials, Professor Sheri Lynn Johnson has observed "the most obvious counterbalance to the bias of white jurors is the mandatory inclusion of black jurors in the decisonmaking process."[90] Professor Johnson's recommendation could be extended to sentencing. Thus, a defendant would have the right to jurors from his community, and these jurors would have sentencing authority.[91]

Advocacy of this kind of reform has been a consistent theme in hip-hop. In *"Escape from Babylon,"* Paris outlined a ten-point plan that included black juries for African American defendants.[92]

"Representation" is an important theme in hip-hop culture. One "represents" by conducting himself or herself in a way that makes the community proud. Representation implies responsibility. In sentencing law-breakers, representation of the hip-hop community would enhance the expressive value of punishment and give it a legitimacy it now lacks.

2. PRISON.

I hold this slow and daily tampering with the mysteries of the brain, to be immeasurably worse than any torture of the body.

—Charles Dickens[93]

Prison is an instrument of punishment that is approximately 200 years old. It was designed in an attempt to punish criminals in a more humane way than killing them or harming their bodies. . . . How successful has the experiment been?

The hip-hop nation is better situated to answer the question than virtually any other community in the world. . . .

Hip-hop became popular during the same period that the prison population experienced its greatest expansion. From 1972 to 1997, the prison population increased by 500%—from 196,000 to 1,159,000 inmates. . . . The rate of violent crime actually decreased during this time, but the number of people locked up for nonviolent offenses rose sharply. . . .

The experiences of the two million people now incarcerated in the United States have been documented more in hip-hop than in any other medium. The portrait is ugly. . . .

The virtually universal view in the hip-hop nation is that punishing people by locking them in cages for years is a miserable public policy. Incarceration is cruel because it is dehumanizing. It is counterproductive because, as discussed in Part III, it has been used so promiscuously in minority communities that it has lost its value as deterrence. The scholar Robin Kelley summarizes the hip-hop perspective as follows: "Prisons are not designed to discipline but to corral bodies labeled menaces to society; policing is not designed to stop or reduce crime in inner-city communities but to manage it."[94]

The artists put it more eloquently. . . .[95]

Hip-hop often depicts incarceration as being driven by profit rather than public safety. Its analysis is that it is socially expedient to warehouse people whose problems are difficult or expensive to treat, especially when there are economic benefits to the (largely white and rural) communities where prisons frequently are situated. This concern is supported in part by the rise in the prison population during an era in which violent crime decreased. The hip-hop perspective is reminiscent of Kant's critique of utilitarianism—that it is immoral to punish people as a means of benefiting society. According to some artists, that is the real meaning of the punishment regime. Mos Def suggests a [prison-industrial complex] that supports [the] . . . economy.[96] . . .

CONCLUSION: WORD IS BORN

Hip-hop culture ascended to national prominence in the post-civil rights era. For the hip-hop nation, one of the enduring lessons of the civil rights movement is that the criminal law was used as an instrument of racial subordination. Images of civil rights activists getting locked up (or brutalized by the police) are common in hip-hop culture, especially music videos.

Hip-hop artists express some of the same concerns as traditional civil rights activists about criminal justice. Both vigorously protest racial profiling by police. Unlike civil rights culture, hip-hop does not practice a politics of respectability. It is less bourgeois. It champions the human rights of criminals as enthusiastically as the rights of the falsely accused. It is as concerned with fairness for drug sellers as for law-abiding middle-class people who are stopped by the police for "driving while black" or "driving while brown." Ultimately, hip-hop culture's reforms focus more on substantive than procedural issues (criminal law more than criminal procedure). Accordingly hip-hop activists may be better equipped to protest the crack cocaine sentencing regime, felony disenfranchisement, or recidivist statutes than organizations like the NAACP. They are also more willing to use nontraditional tactics to change the laws. . . .

Some hip-hop artists seem more optimistic about the potential of the United States to achieve justice than some critical theorists. There is more faith in the potential of the rule of law, even if that potential is not now realized. Some hip-hop artists are less suspicious of capitalism than are many postmodernists. Hip-hop ultimately, however, seems more rooted in critical theory than traditional jurisprudence. It embraces instrumentalist tactics and is deeply suspicious of authority.

One serious deficiency in hip-hop is its endemic sexism and homophobia. Can any credible theory of justice be based on a culture that routinely denigrates more than half the population? The answer must be "no." In order for hip-hop to command the moral authority that, at its best, it deserves, it must address subordination within the hip-hop nation. The problem besmirches hip-hop's extraordinary aesthetic achievement and detracts from its important evaluation of criminal justice. Hip-hop music and videos, especially, contain the kind of depictions of gender and sexuality that we might expect of adolescent boys.

The increasing prominence of women rappers provides limited cause for hope.[97] Hip-hop has a long way to go, however, before its constructive political analysis is not compromised by lyrics, visual images, and attitudes that put down a considerable portion of its own community.

This Article is a beginning. It is an early attempt to fashion a hip-hop jurisprudence. In hip-hop culture there is a tradition of answer raps—of provocative responses to provocative words. I look forward to those responses.

Notes

1. Jay-Z, *Justify My Thug, on* The Black Album (Roc-A-Fella Records 2003) . . .
2. Beanie Sigel, *What Your Life Like, on* The Truth (Def Jam Records 2000) . . .
3. The phrase comes from Chuck D, of the rap group Public Enemy. *See* The History of Hip-Hop, *at* http://www.headbob.com/hiphop/hiphophistory.shtml . . .
4. Other legal scholars have explored relationships between music and law. *See* Christopher A. Bracey, *Adjudication, Antisubordination, and the Jazz Connection,* 54 Ala. L. Rev. 853 (2003) (analogizing between judicial adjudication in civil rights cases and free jazz); John O. Calmore, *Critical Race Theory, Archie Shepp, and Fire Music: Securing an Authentic Intellectual Life in a Multicultural World,* 65 S. Cal L. Rev. 2129 (1992) (discussing the similarity between the artistry of Archie Sheep and critical race theory's intellectual approach and potential).
5. *See* Robert M. Bohm, *Crime, Criminals and Crime Control Policy Myths, in* Justice, Crime and Ethics 327, 343 (Michael C. Braswell, Belinda Rogers McCarthy & Bernard J. McCarthy eds., 1998) . . .
6. For an analysis of the legislative history of the federal crack sentencing laws, see David A. Sklansky, *Cocaine, Race, and Equal Protection,* 47 Stan. L. Rev. 1283, 1290–98 (1995).
7. *Id.* at 1295 & n.59.
8. 132 Cong. Rec. 22,660 (1986) (statement of Rep. Robert H. Michel) (explaining how the "death of basketball star Len Bias shocked us into action").
9. *See* Peter Baker, *Clinton Would Cut Disparity in Some Cocaine Sentences,* Wash. Post, July 23, 1997, at A21.
10. *See Inside Politics* (CNN cable broadcast, Jan. 18, 2001) (transcript available at http://www.cnn.com/TRANSCRIPTS/0101/18/ip.01.html (last visited Mar. 28, 2003)).
11. Ironically, hip-hop culture is credited for influencing social mores other than law. It is said, for example, to encourage marijuana use and to promote gender stereotypes.
12. Austin Sarat, When the State Kills: Capital Punishment and the American Condition 23 (2001).
13. This account is taken from The History of Hip-Hop, *supra* note [3].
14. *See* Baruit N. Kopano, *Rap Music as an Extension of the Black Rhetorical Tradition: 'Keepin It Real',* 26 W. J. Black Stud. 204 (2002) . . . *Keeping Up with Jones: Quincy Jones, Pop Legend, Interview,* Interview Mag., Nov. 1995, at 28 . . .
15. The History of Hip-Hop, *supra* note [3].
16. Teresa Wiltz, *We the Peeps: After Three Decades Chillin' in the Hood, Hip-Hop Is Finding Its Voice Politically,* Wash. Post, June 25, 2002, at C1.
17. *Id.* The author Bakari Kitwana has also described "two sides" to hip-hop. He states:

> Hip-hop has a positive impact, but also has a negative impact in terms of these anti-black images and this misogynistic attitude that comes from rappers who sell multi-platinum records. Like Jay-Z. But at the same time Jay-Z offers a message that the society is screwed up, that it's difficult out here, that the issues of unemployment and education are critical issues. The music is contradictory but the messages that society is sending us are contradictory too. I don't think that it's unusual; I think that's how life is.

Suzy Hansen, *Hip-Hop Nation,* Salon, July 19, 2002, *available at* http://archive.salon .com/books/int/2002/07/10/kitwana/. Many hip-hop artists can not be placed in either category. Eminem, for example, is the best selling rap artist in history, and his music is neither political or gangsta.

18. *See* Cornel West, *Nihilism in the Black Community,* 1991 Dissent 221.

19. Tricia Rose, Black Noise: Rap Music and Black Culture in Contemporary America 100 (1994).

20. *See* Kelefa Sanneh, *Music: The Highs; The Albums and Songs of the Year,* N.Y. Times, Dec. 28, 2003, at § 2, 31 (noting how 50 Cent's "casual jokes about death are his way of reminding us of the price he might have to pay for his success—and for our entertainment").

21. *See* Richard Sandomir, *Founder of TV Network Becomes First Black Owner in Major Sports,* N.Y. Times, Dec. 19, 2002, at A1 (reporting that Robert Johnson sold BET to Viacom in 2000 for three billion dollars).

22. *See* Jeffrey McKinney, *From Rags to Riches: Hip-Hop Moguls Use Groundbreaking Designs and Star Power to Challenge Major Clothing Labels and Become a Force in the $164 Billion Fashion Industry,* Black Enterprise, Sept. 2002, *available at* http://www .blackenterprise.com/printarticle.asp?source-/archive2002/09/0902–41.htm (last visited Jan. 31, 2004).

23. *See* John L. Mitchell, *Baggin' and Saggin': Parents Wary of a Big Fashion Trend,* L.A. Times, Sept. 28, 1992, at B1 (reporting that the "trend toward baggy clothing was started by some of Los Angeles' toughest gangs, emulating the garb of prison inmates whose pants perpetually sag because prisoners are not issued belts"); Guy Trebay, *Maturing Rappers Try a New Uniform: Yo, a Suit!,* N.Y. Times, Feb. 6, 2004, at A1 . . .

24. For a list of the syllabi for these courses, see The Hip-Hop Archive, Course Listings, *at* http://www.hiphoparchive.org/research/course_listings.htm (last visited Feb. 5, 2004).

25. Sara Rimer, *Harvard Scholar Rebuilds African Studies Department,* N.Y. Times, July 16, 2003, at A16.

26. Martin Kilson, *The Pretense of Hip-Hop Black Leadership,* Black Commentator, July 17, 2003, available at http://www.blackcommentator.com/50/50_kilson.html (last visited Feb. 5, 2004).

27. John H. McWhorter, *How Hip-Hop Holds Blacks Back,* City J., Summer 2003, *available at* http://www.city-journal.org/html/13_3_how_hip_hop.html (last visited Mar. 28, 2004).

28. *See* Dasun Allah, *The Swami of Hip-Hop: Russell Simmons Morphs into a Mogul-Activist, Village Voice,* Sept. 4, 2002, *available at* http://villagevoice.com/issues/0236/ allah.php (last visited Jan. 31, 2004).

29. Hip-Hop Summit Action Network, Our Mission, *at* http://www.hiphopsummitactio network.org

30. *See* Ta-Nehisis Coates, *Compa$$ionate Capitali$m: Russell Simmons Wants to Fatten the Hip-Hop Vote—and Maybe His Wallet, Too,* Village Voice, Jan. 7, 2004, *available at* http:// www.villagevoice.com/issues/0401/coates.php (last visited Mar. 28, 2004) (describing the registration of 11,000 new voters at a hip-hop summit in Philadelphia attended by rap stars LL Cool J, Will Smith, and DMX, and a hip-hop summit in Detroit that attracted 17,000 people).

31. Hip-Hop Summit Action Network, What We Want, at http://www.hiphopsummitaction network.org/. . .

32. Press Release, Hip-Hop Summit Action Network, Growing National Momentum Builds for "Countdown to Fairness" Campaign to Repeal Rockefeller Drug Laws in New York (May 12, 2003), *available at* http://www.hiphopsummitactionnetwork.org . . .

33. . . . After HSAN sponsored protests, New York City Mayor Michael Bloomberg restored approximately $ 300 million to the city public schools budget. A HSAN demonstration

on the proposed budget cuts featured hip-hop stars like Sean P. Diddy Combs, Alicia Keys, LL Cool J, and drew between 50,000 and 100,000 people. *See* Hansen, *supra* note [17]; *see also* Wiltz, *supra* note [16].

34. National Hip-Hop Political Convention, *at* http://www.hiphopconvention.org . . .

35. *See, e.g.,* Davey D's Hip Hop Corner, *at* http://www.daveyd.com (last visited Mar. 5, 2004); The Hip-Hop Summit Action Network, *at* http://www.hiphopsummitactionnetwork.org (last visited Mar. 5, 2004); The Temple of Hip Hop, *at* http://www.templeofhiphop.org (last visited Mar. 5, 2004).

36. Juan Pablo, *Rappers' Lament,* Village Voice, Dec. 17, 2003, *available at* http://www .villagevoice.com/issues/0351/pablo.php (last visited Mar. 28, 2004) (reporting "rumors of a 'Hip-Hop Task Force'—a kind of Rap COINTELPRO—within the New York City Police Department").

37. *See* Nicole White & Evelyn McDonnell, *Police Secretly Watching Hip-Hop Artists,* Miami Herald, Mar. 9, 2004, at 1A (describing police secret surveillance of hip-hop artists in Miami and Miami Beach).

38. Source, Mar. 2004 (referencing the article *Operation Lockdown,* Source, Mar. 2004, at 107).

39. *See* Pierre Thomas, *1 in 3 Young Black Men in Justice System,* Wash. Post, Oct. 5, 1995, at A1. . .

40. Marc Mauer, Race to Incarcerate 125 (1999).

41. *See* Fox Butterfield, *Study Finds Big Increase in Black Men as Inmates Since 1980,* N.Y. Times, Aug. 28, 2002, at A14 . . .

42. *See* Tracey L. Meares, *Social Organization and Drug Law Enforcement,* 35 Am. Crim. L. Rev. 191 (1998).

43. *See* Michel Foucault, Discipline and Punishment: The Birth of the Prison 277–78 (Alan Sheridan trans., 1977) (1975).

44. American films like The Godfather (Paramount 1972), Scarface (Universal Studios 1983), and Pulp Fiction (Mirimax Home Entertainment 1994), like gangsta rap, depict criminals as imperfect heroes.

45. *See, e.g.,* G-Unit, *G'up, on* Beg for Mercy (Interscope 2003) . . .

46. Robin D.G. Kelley, *Kickin' Reality, Kickin' Ballistics: Gangsta Rap and Postindustrial Los Angeles, in* Droppin' Science: Critical Essays on Rap Music and Hip Hop Culture 135 (William Eric Pekins ed., 1996) [hereinafter Droppin' Science].

47. Rose, *supra* note [19], at 100–01.

48. Many activists and scholars also address the issue, as do some African American and Latino lawmakers. The phenomenon of mass incarceration is mainly ignored by most white politicians or embraced as a public good.

49. Professor Ernest Allen, Jr. has noted other similarities between gangsta rap and conscious rap (which he describes as "visionary message rap"), including that both reinforce the subjugation of women and that both celebrate the rebel. *See* Ernest Allen, Jr., *Making the Strong Survive: The Contours and Contradictions of Message Rap, in* Droppin' Science, *supra* note 92.

50. Michel Foucault, *Intellectuals and Power, in* Language, Counter-Memory, Practice: Selected Essays and Interviews 205, 209 (Donald F. Bouchard & Sherry Simon trans., Donald F. Bouchard ed., 1977).

51. *See generally* John Rawls, A Theory of Justice (1971).

52. For hip-hop songs expressing sympathy for victims of crime, see Ice Cube, *Dead Homiez, on* Kill at Will (Priority Records 1990) . . . Stop the Violence All-Stars, *Self Destruction, on* Self Destruction 12 (1989) . . . ; The West Coast Rap All-Stars, *We're All in the Same Gang, on* We're All in the Same Gang (Warner Brothers Records 1990) . . .

53. *See* Alan David Freeman, *Legitimizing Racial Discrimination Through Antidiscrimination Law: A Critical Review of Supreme Court Doctrine,* 62 Minn. L. Rev. 1049 (1978) (contrasting the "victim" and "perpetrator" perspectives in antidiscrimination law); Mari J. Matsuda, *Looking to the Bottom: Critical Legal Studies and Reparations,* 22 Harv. C.R.-C.L. L. Rev. 323 (1987) (arguing for the inclusion of the voices of those at the "bottom" in legal scholarship).

54. *See* James Q. Wilson & George L. Kelling, *Broken Windows,* Atlantic Monthly, Mar. 1982, at 29. For a reaction from hip-hop to former New York City mayor Rudolph Guiliani's endorsement of "zero tolerance" policing, see Brand Nubian, *Probable Cause, on* Foundation (Arista Records 1998) . . .

55. This theory is constructed from my reading of the values and concerns expressed in hip-hop culture. It is not intended to be definitive or exhaustive. It is intended to provoke debate.

56. Eve, *Love Is Blind,* on Ruff Ryders' First Lady (Interscope Records 1999).

57. Angie Stone, *Brotha,* on Mahogany Soul (J-Records 2001) . . .

58. A definition can be found at urbandictionary.com . . .

59. *See* Michelle Goodwin, *The Economy of Citzenship,* 76 Temp. L. Rev. 129, 192 (2003) . . .

60. For a famous exposition of retribution, see Immanuel Kant, The Philosophy of Law 194–98 (W. Hastrie trans., 1887) (1797) ("Even if a Civil Society resolved to dissolve itself . . . the last Murderer lying in the prison ought to be executed before the resolution was carried out. . . . This ought to be done in order that every one may realize the desert of his deeds. . .").

61. *See generally* Lockyer v. Andrade, 538 U.S. 63 (2003) (upholding the constitutionality of a defendant's sentence to two consecutive terms of 25 years to life for stealing $ 68.84 worth of videotapes from a K-Mart store); Harmelin v. Michigan, 501 U.S. 957 (1991) (upholding a defendant's sentence of life without parole for possession of cocaine).

62. For an expanded argument that retributive punishment would lower sentences for drug crimes, see Paul Butler, *Retribution, for Liberals,* 46 UCLA L. Rev. 1873, 1884–88 (1999).

63. *See* Joshua Dressler, *Hating Criminals: How Can Something That Feels So Good Be Wrong?,* 88 Mich. L. Rev. 1448, 1451–53 (1990) ("The most famous exponent of assaultive variety [of retributivism] is James Stephen, who claimed that 'it is morally right to hate criminals.' Under Stephen's view, punishment is justified without any consideration of the criminal's rights or best interests . . .").

64. *See* Herbert Morris, *On Guilt and Innocence* 34 (1976) ("It is just to punish those who have violated the rules and caused the unfair distribution of benefits and burdens. A person who violates the rules has something others have—the benefits of the system—but by renouncing what others have assumed, the burdens of self-restraint, he has acquired an unfair advantage. . . . Justice—that is punishing such individuals—restores the equilibrium of benefits and burdens by taking from the individual what he owes, that is, exacting the debt.").

65. *See* Dorothy E. Roberts, *The Social and Moral Cost of Mass Incarceration in African American Communities,* 56 Stan. L. Rev. 1271 (2004) . . .

66. *See* Todd R. Clear, *The Problem with "Addition by Subtraction": The Prison-Crime Relationship in Low-Income Communities, in* Invisible Punishment: The Collateral Consequences of Mass Imprisonment 181, 184 (Marc Mauer & Meda Chesney-Lind eds., 2002) . . .

67. Roberts, *supra* note [65].

68. Kant wrote:

> Juridical Punishment can never be administered merely as a means of pro-
> moting another Good either with regard to the Criminal himself or to Civil
> Society, but must in all cases be imposed only because the individual on
> whom it is inflicted *has committed a Crime*. For one man ought never to be
> dealt with merely as a means subservient to the purpose of another. . . .

Kant, *supra* note [60], at 195 (emphasis in original).

69. *See* Darryl K. Brown, *Third-Party Interests in Criminal Law,* 80 Tex. L. Rev. at
    1384.

70. *Id.* at 1387 (quoting Memorandum from Eric H. Holder, Jr., Assistant Attorney General,
    to all U.S. Attorneys and Heads of Department Components pt. II (June 16, 1999)).

71. *See* R. v. Gladue, [1999] S.C.R. 688 (Can.)

72. Ice-T, *Straight Up Nigga, on* O.G. Original Gangster (Warner Brothers Records 1991) . . .

73. Talib Kweli featuring *Cocoa Brovaz, Gun Music, on* Quality (MCA Records 2002) . . .

74. Talib Kweli, *The Proud, on* Quality, *supra* note [73] . . .

75. Boogie Down Productions, *Illegal Business, on* By All Means Necessary (Jive Records
    1988) . . .

76. For an insightful analysis of hip-hop's treatment of marijuana and crack cocaine, see Ted
    Sampsell-Jones, *Culture and Contempt: The Limitations of Expressive Criminal Law,* 27
    Seattle U. L. Rev. 133, 163–67 (2003).

77. Ja Rule featuring Missy Elliot & Tweet, *X, on* Pain is Love (Sony Records 2001) . . .

78. Snoop Dogg, *Gin and Juice, on* Doggystyle (Death Row Records 1993). . .

79. Michael Eric Dyson, Holler if You Hear Me: Searching for Tupac Shakur 239 (2001).

80. Public Enemy, *1 Million Bottlebags, on* Apocalypse 91 . . . The Enemy Strikes Back (Def
    Jam Records 1991) . . .

81. 2Pac, *Part Time Mutha, on* 2Pacalyspe Now (Jive Records 1992) . . .

82. 2Pac, *Dear Mama, on* Me Against the World (Jive Records 1995) . . .

83. Ice Cube, *Us, on* Death Certificate (Priority Records 1991) . . .

84. Notorious B.I.G., *Juicy, on* Life After Death, [(Bad Boy Records 1997)] . . .

85. Kanye West, *We Don't Care, on* College Dropout (Roc-A-Fella Records 2004) . . .

86. *See* Sampsell-Jones, *supra* note [76].

87. Jay-Z, *99 Problems, on* The Black Album (Def Jam Records 2003) . . .

88. Charles J. Ogletree, Jr., *The Death of Discretion? Reflections on the Federal Sentencing
    Guidelines,* 101 Harv. L. Rev. 1938, 1953 (1988); *see also* Albert W. Alschuler, *The
    Failure of Sentencing Guidelines: A Plea for Less Aggregation,* 58 U. Chi. L. Rev. 901,
    937 (1991) ("Aggregated sentences, whether chosen by a legislature or by a sentencing
    commission, seem likely to be more severe than individualized sentences.").

89. Mos Def, *Mathematics, on* Black on Both Sides (Rawkus Records 1999) . . .

90. Sheri Lynn Johnson, *Black Innocence and the White Jury*, 83 Mich. L. Rev. 1611, 1649
    (1985).

91. *See* Morris B. Hoffman, *The Case for Jury Sentencing,* 52 Duke L. J. 951 (2003)

92. Paris, [*Escape from Babylon, on* The Devil Made Me Do It (Tommy Boy Records 1990)].

93. Lawrence M. Friedman, Crime and Punishment in American History 80 (1993) (quoting
    Charles Dickens, American Notes 146 (Penguin 1972) (1842)).

94. Kelley, *supra* note [46], at 118.

95. Beanie Sigel, *supra* note [2]. Immortal Technique, *Revolutionary, on* Revolutionary
    Volume 1, [(Viper Records 2001)] . . . DMX, *Who We Be, on* The Great Depression
    (Universal Records 2001) . . .

96. Mos Def, *supra* note [89].

97. For an analysis of black women rappers and sexual politics in rap music, see Rose, *supra*
    note [19], at 146–82.

WHEEL OF TORTURE

Robert Johnson

Picture the set of the popular TV show, Wheel of Fortune. Imagine a Vanna White substitute named Veri White, sleek, blonde and fair.

A large wheel is displayed, standing vertically, with numbers representing prison sentences and symbols that represent other sanctions, from probation to house arrest and even corporal punishment. (The death penalty is available on another show, Wheel of Death). The wheel, bright red, has black leather arm and leg straps. Fastened to the wheel is a contestant, whose fate will be decided by the studio audience.

Veri steps forward and says, with growing emphasis,
"Welcome to WHEEL — OF — TORTURE"

Applause, upbeat music

The announcer, Bob Jones,
clean-cut and nondescript,
ordinary and comfortingly familiar,
strides to the center of the stage
in a sensible if unremarkable suit.

"Here's our First Contestant," says Bob.
All eyes are on Veri and the contestant.
That's the way the producers want it.

Victima de Concepcion, strapped in tight, is a single mom,
Black and Hispanic, in her mid-thirties. She looks older.

"People probably call her Vicky," says Bob, "when they call her by name."
Bob talks as if anonymity or undue familiarity were normal for the likes of Victima.
"She holds down two minimum-wage jobs, so money is tight."

"Though not," Bob deadpans, "as tight as Veri's very-tight dress!"

Laughter from the audience

Veri wiggles slightly, a hint of a smile on her lovely face

"Is this a great country, Or what?"

Source: Robert Johnson, *Justice Follies: Parody from Planet Prison.* Reprinted with permission of the publisher, Carolina Academic Press © 2009.

Laughter, applause from the audience

The devil is in the details of Victima's life, but Bob is a big-picture guy,
A kind of walking wide-screen TV kind of man.

He doesn't tell the audience that Victima takes
a long bus ride from the ghetto to the suburbs,
Up and out by five each morning, when it's still dark,
Carries back-to-back shifts, gets off at eleven, home by midnight or so,
Hoping to give her kids a goodnight kiss, tuck them in,
though the sitter usually has them down by ten.

Bob doesn't even know she works under a dress code,
a speech code, submits to drug tests;
Can't stop to pee when nature calls, unless
it's on one of her fifteen-minute breaks,
one every four hours, whether she needs it or not;
Can't miss a day, sick or not,
cause she's got no benefits;
Can't say "No" to overtime,
cause she'll get fired.

"Here's our girl tonight," says Bob, "because . . .
Vicky left her young children home alone and went off to work!"

Audience: Ahh, in a shocked, hushed tone.

"The baby sitter didn't show," adds Bob, knowingly

Audience: Uh huh!

"Vicky just had to go"

Audience: Sure!

"She'd get canned"

Audience: Now, Really!

"Given a one-way ticket"

Audience: Given?

"Heading nowhere but down, she says,
down into unemployment and homelessness"

Audience: Impossible! In America!
Home of the free! How can that be?

"That's what she says!" Bob seems incredulous
"And wait," says Bob, "there's more!"

Audience: Un huh, there's always more!

"Her kids were burned alive that very night!"

Audience: Oh, Good God!, Oh, Good God!

"Burned in a fire set by an itinerant arsonist"

In a soft voice, Bob says:
"probably out on bail; true,
he should've been in jail"

Now more loudly, "while our *little* lady was lazing around . . ."

Bob emphasizes little, and Victima does look small, fixed to the wheel

"*sneaking* breaks . . ."

Audience: Ah!

"and all the while . . .
those *precious* babies . . .
cooked alive!"

Audience: NO!

With fervor, Bob asks
"What kind of woman . . .
"What kind of person . . .
"Would leave her children alone . . .
At the mercy of any passing felon?"

"I ask myself," Bob continues
"and my wife, of course"

Audience: Of course!

"Would we let *our* son
Fall prey to arson?"

Audience: NO, Bob. NEVER.
Not your son. Not our son.
Not arson.

"I ask *you*," shouts Bob,
"Did she *have* to live in a high-crime neighborhood?"

No, Bob. No Way.
This is the richest country on earth!
That's the American Way!
If you want the Good Life
All you have to do is Pay!

"Did all we could, didn't we?" says Bob,
in a low, familiar, we-know-best tone.

"Spared her the indignity of welfare, didn't we?

Audience: Damn right!

"Figured her kids would fare well without her, didn't we?

Audience: Sure did!

"Fare well without pesky government programs getting in the way, right?

The audience chants:
For sure, Bob. For damn sure
Slutty whore, Slutty whore
She chose to be poor
Show her the prison door

Bob raises a hand, taking back the floor.
"Now," says Bob, speaking slowly, as if to a child,
"Some loose-lobed liberal might say,

(Here Bob adopts a nasal, whiney tone)

'Hey, Bob, she's working two jobs to make ends meet
at the longitude and latitude of the third world,
parts of which we want to rebuild, though
not her neighborhood, her life, her family.'"

Bob pauses, to let this sink in. He continues.
"This lousy, lame, lying liberal might even say,

(Again in a whiney tone)

'Bob, We know this is tacky
but wouldn't she be better off
If she were an Iraqi?' "

There is an uncomfortable pause.
Bob, sensing anxiety, jumps in.

"Not true!" says Bob.

Not true! Chimes in the audience
With evident relief.

"Pusillanimous palaver!"
Bob, now in a lather,
"Cause then she wouldn't be free,
like you and me!"

Audience: Right, Right. Of course!
Free, like you and me.

"There you have it," says Bob,
shrugging his shoulders, feeling vindicated.
"Let's get started . . ."

Veri White spins the wheel. It slows down at Life, then edges over onto Fifteen years.

Bob looks at the wheel, then at the audience.
"Folks in the audience, we ask . . .
"Has she suffered enough?"

NO, NO, NO
Fifteen years is a slap on the wrist!
Has it come to this?
She kills, and we sentence her to Penal Bliss?

Bob, moving almost rhythmically with the anger in the air,
"Let's prosecute, Let's persecute
Let's put her in a prison suit."
Bob's on a roll now.
"Won't she look cute—maybe hot to boot!"

Snickers from the audience
"Hot?" Someone mutters.
"Slut," says another.

Bob, loudly:
"Let's send her to the Big House

The American Dream House
A cell in the country!
A toilet with a view
What else are we to do!"

WILD APPLAUSE
Veri is beaming, looking stunning, an American Dream Girl, showing considerable cleavage, her sheer desirability serving as a segway to commercials on The Good Life in Modern America.

The first commercial showcases Pamela's Playthings, a line of lingerie that promises heaven on earth, adorning sultry blonde models with slim waists, large busts and downy wings, each of whom bears an uncanny resemblance to Pamela Anderson. Pamela's Playthings are one of the obvious benefits of a free society.

Our lithesome lingerie-clad ladies are followed by an ad for a new drug, Leviathan, a big seller, sure to vanquish erectile dysfunction, proffered with the implied promise of sex-at-will—as seen in a Freudian sequence in which a man throws a football, over and over again, penetrating a gently swaying, tulip shaped rubber lift, bringing smiles all around, especially to the face of the handsome man himself, the quarterback in every man, with an attractive, approving wife. You won't catch him leaving his family at the mercy of arsonists, muggers, or thieves, though one might wonder if he'd even notice intruders into his home, what with him spending so much time in the sack.

"Welcome back," says Bob. He's been watching Veri, not the commercials, but he is now ready to get back to work. "And here's our next contestant."

Another single, poor mom.
White, but visibly mentally ill.
Her name: Slovena N. Disturbed.
"These things happen," says Bob,
sensing audience discontent . . .
they'd expected a person of color.
"Nobody promised Slovena a Rose Garden."
"Besides," Bob continues, "she'd let it get overrun with weeds!"

Audience: laughter, some relief.

With growing enthusiasm, Bob entones
"Another dead child? This one a suicide?
"Boy hanged himself in a house full of *dirty* laundry?"
Bob emphasizes dirty, then adds,
"Guess you come by your name honestly, Slovena."
Bob's tone is unctuous, soothing to the audience,
Though a few seem to sense Bob's cruel streak.

"Your only son, twisting there," continues Bob,
"like a carcass in a slaughter house,
right there in your closet,
dressed out in dirty old clothes?
Smelling like death warmed over?"

"And where," intones Bob, "was our Slovena
when her boy said his last novena?"

Audience:
Where indeed!
Her Boy in need!
Bitch Abandoned her own seed!

"Oh, audience, we have our work cut out for us!"

Applause, building to a crescendo.

Bob and his audience aren't color blind,
But they are blind to the color of pain
Afflicting lives so different from yours and mine

They might as well unfold on a Martian plain.
"Let it spin!" says Bob
"Let's hear it!"

Audience shouts, "WHEEL — OF — TORTURE"
Veri sways seductively

"Grab her by the leg, Veri, and let it spin
It's time for the game to begin . . ."

*[Note: this play is based on actual cases, though names have been changed to protect
those violated by our justice system.]*

Readings on Criminal *Justice* or *Criminal* Justice

EDITORS' INTRODUCTION

The conclusion of *The Rich Get Richer* asserts that a criminal justice system is a just system only if it protects equally the rights and interests of all members of society. For that, it must punish evenhandedly the rich as well as the poor who violate these rights or endanger these interests. When it does not, the system is criminal; the biased use of the system's coercive power—police, courts, prisons—is force used against some members of society to promote the interests of others. To that extent it does just what crime does and thus is morally equivalent to criminal violence. The conclusion of *The Rich Get Richer* points out several policies that must be put in place if our system is to fulfill the goals of protecting society and promoting justice. The readings in this chapter reinforce some of these policy recommendations and also link back to the issue in Chapter 1 of *The Rich Get Richer* about what works to reduce crime.

The four readings in this chapter come from a special issue of the journal *Criminology and Public Policy* (discussed in Chapter 1 of *The Rich Get Richer*). The idea behind this special issue was to "take stock of the state of affairs of criminology as a social science of policy." The editors asked some leading criminologists "to write brief essays arguing that we now have accumulated enough evidence to recommend a particular policy." The title of each article is meant to convey the nature of the policy recommended, and the article itself reviews the relevant literature to support the recommendation. The editors were clear that the "purpose was not to offer innovative or new policies that should be implemented and evaluated; instead, it was to be a complete issue devoted to noted scholars taking the position that we now have enough knowledge about some aspect of crime and justice that a policy is advised."[1] Just as the authors note that "much more" could be said beyond the twenty-seven essays finally published, we realize that there is much more in this journal issue that is relevant to getting the criminal justice system to truly fulfill the goals of protecting society and promoting justice than the four articles reprinted in this chapter. Thus, in our introductions to those articles, we mention several of the related and supporting articles from this special issue of the journal to give readers a larger view of the range of policy changes that research supports and to encourage readers to look further into these important topics.

The first article in this chapter is "Restore Rationality to Sentencing Policy" by Alfred Blumstein and Alex Piquero. It starts by pointing out that the recent period of continually increasing rates of imprisonment of convicted offenders was preceded by fifty years in which the incarceration rate was stable. The authors contend that this amounts to a change from criminal justice officials and experts determining sentencing policy to one in which sentencing was determined politically, primarily by lawmakers responding to public concerns about crime. Such a political response almost always involves increasing incarceration. And so we saw a period in which laws were made requiring longer sentences, sometimes mandatory and in any event subject to strict limits on judges' discretion, as well as "three-strikes-and-you're-out" laws that require long or even life sentences after a third conviction. "As a result of this succession of 'tough' legislative acts," the authors write, "prison populations in the United States have grown from a level of 110 per 100,000 population that prevailed for over 50 years to a level of almost 500 per 100,000 (or 720 counting local jails), making the U.S. incarceration rate the highest in the world." And much of this happened when crime rates had already been going down for some time! In response to this, the authors call for bringing rationality back into sentencing policy by considering the results of research about the typical length of criminal careers, and in particular, about the "residual criminal career length (RCL)," that is, the expected length of a criminal career after a conviction. Their general point is that keeping offenders in prison beyond the length of time after which their criminal careers would have ended anyway is a waste of prison resources.

A related article from *Criminology and Public Policy* that is not included in this chapter is "End Natural Life Sentences for Juveniles" by Jeffrey Fagin. Another related article from the journal, also not reprinted here, is "Protect Individual Punishment Decisions from Mandatory Penalties" by Franklin Zimring. He notes that in the United States decisions about punishment are less insulated from politics than those of other nations. Other nations have an ideology of professional expertise surrounding legal and penological officials that protects them from political pressure. Zimring contends: "Any mechanism that insulates individual decisions from the mythology of fixed-price justice will help." The conclusion of *The Rich Get Richer* also calls for moving away from politically motivated mandatory sentences toward greater flexibility in sentencing, without returning to uncontrolled judicial discretion. This would require putting in place mechanisms to hold criminal justice officials accountable for how they exercise discretion so that it does not become discrimination.

The second article in this chapter, "Encourage Restorative Justice" by John Braithwaite, discusses a promising approach to dealing with offenders that has shown itself to be both popular and effective in numerous countries. Restorative justice is aimed at bringing offenders and victims together to heal the relationship that crime has disrupted. "It is a process in which all stakeholders have an opportunity to discuss the hurts of a crime, how they might be repaired, how recurrence might be prevented, and how other needs of stakeholders can be met." The author reports on studies that show restorative justice processes to result in greater satisfaction and reduced fears for victims of crimes than normal criminal prosecutions do. Agreements reached between victims and offenders engaged in restorative processes seem more likely to be complied with than court orders issued by judges. Restorative justice places the goal of reconciling criminal and victim above that of harming the criminal and seems to produce greater reductions in reoffending by criminals and more healing of victims than ordinary criminal court processes do. The authors contend that restorative justice should be part of a rational policy for dealing with crime, and readers should consider how far we might replace the current emphasis on punishment with an emphasis on reconciliation.

The third article in this chapter is "Make Rehabilitation Corrections' Guiding Paradigm" by Francis Cullen. Cullen claims that the punishment paradigm that imposes harsh sentences has, after determining correctional policy for more than three decades, "reached the point of exhaustion." He analyzes the move to the punishment paradigm from the emphasis on rehabilitation that started in the 1960s. He contends that this had more to do with loss of faith in criminal justice officials' decisions than with the frequently repeated slogan that, regarding rehabilitation, "nothing works." And he points out that the shift to the punishment or justice model did not do what it was predicted to do. There is little evidence that getting tough actually reduced crime more than a rehabilitation regime (which, after all, would also have incarcerated offenders) would have. Indeed, some research suggests that imprisonment increases recidivism. And other research shows that some rehabilitation programs do work to redirect offenders away from the path of crime. Finally, the author contends that the public wants rehabilitation to be part of the state's response to crime, and that it is, in any event, the morally right thing to do in light of the disproportionate presence in the correctional system of "minorities and the poor—groups socially neglected in our society."

The conclusion of *The Rich Get Richer* argues that correctional programs must promote personal responsibility and offer ex-offenders real preparation and a real opportunity to succeed as law-abiding citizens. Emphasizing rehabilitation is thus an important step, as would be the creation of a "Re-entry Czar" to help state and local governments deal intelligently and humanely with the 700,000 persons released from prison each year.

A related *Criminology and Public Policy* article not included in this chapter is "Abolish Lifetime Bans for Ex-Felons" by Bushway and Sweeten. They note that ex-felons—1 in 19 adults and 1 in 3 black males—are "subject to a wide array of limitations on work, education, family and civic activities." This includes limitations on some 800 occupations, educational loans, public housing, public assistance, child custody, and voting. The research on the lengths of criminal careers cited by Blumstein and Piquero and other research on desistance from crime suggest that lifetime bans are unnecessary. Bushway and Sweeten suggest that "older offenders and individuals who stay arrest-free for 7 years or more simply have very little risk for future crime, and this is similar to that of non-offenders."

Robert Crutchfield adds to this with another article not reprinted here, "Abandon Felon Disenfranchisement Policies." These policies deny the right to vote even after a prison sentence has been served. A related article also not reprinted here is "Ban the Box to Promote Ex-Offender Employment" by Henry and Jacobs. They call for eliminating the requirement that ex-convicts report their criminal records in job applications. Henry and Jacobs note that "the lack of a legitimate job fosters criminality," and they point out that several cities have agreed not to ask about criminal record on initial job applications as part of an effort "not to consider an applicant's prior criminal record unless it is clearly related to the requirements of a particular position."

The fourth article in this chapter is "Save Children from a Life of Crime" by Brandon Welsh and David Farrington. Like the other articles in this chapter, it looks beyond the fixation on punitive strategies for dealing with crime. The authors urge that we take a longer view than that normally taken by correctional officials, arguing that programs of early intervention with at-risk children can effectively reduce crime. Based on the widely accepted view that "the early years of life are most influential in shaping later experiences" and drawing on the highest-quality research and literature reviews, the authors contend that "preschool intellectual enrichment and child skills training programs are effective in preventing delinquency and later offending." They point also to the effectiveness of training programs for new parents as well as to a range of school- and community-based programs that appear to reduce future offending. This article is useful in defending the view that criminal justice problems may sometimes be more effectively and more humanely addressed outside the criminal justice system.

The article by Welsh and Farrington is an important reminder that we have knowledge about how to reduce crime that we are not acting on—a fact that plays a crucial role in *The Rich Get Richer*'s argument that the criminal justice system is failing. One related *Criminology and Public Policy* article not reprinted in this chapter is "Target Juvenile Needs to Reduce Delinquency" by Jones and Wyant. They argue that there is "compelling evidence to support the assertion that we can and do reduce delinquency through an array of successful delinquency intervention strategies. We know a great deal about the types of programs that work, the conditions under which such programs work best, and the types of juveniles with whom their impact is optimal."

Acosta and Chavis also elaborate on effective crime prevention in their article, "Build the Capacities of Communities to Address Crime." They write that "to address crime and promote social justice, the root causes of crime must also be addressed." The policy they recommend, based on accumulated criminological research, is community development, which aims to improve the social, economic, educational, and environmental aspects of communities. Community development includes relationship building, development of community assets, engagement and collective action by citizens, and sustainable and institutional change. Acosta and Chavis propose five directions for future crime policy: (1) form a national community development system, (2) require human and community impact statements to accompany proposed laws, (3) improve communication and collaboration among law enforcement, community development organizations, courts, and supportive agencies, (4) implement systemwide community problem-based policing, and (5) promote community justice emphasizing reparative and reintegrative processes.

Some other evidence-based articles from this special issue of *Criminology and Public Policy* that should be of interest to readers of *The Rich Get Richer* are the following:

"Impose an Immediate Moratorium on Executions" by James Acker (read this in light of the discussion in Chapter 3 of *The Rich Get Richer* about how race and class determine who gets the death penalty)

"Eliminate Race as the Only Reason for Police–Citizen Encounters" by Geoffrey Alpert (compare this with the article in Chapter 3 of this reader on "Why Driving While Black Matters")

"Just Say No to D.A.R.E" by Dennis Rosenbaum (D.A.R.E., which stands for Drug Abuse Resistance Education, "receives over $200 million annually in public funding despite overwhelming evidence of its ineffectiveness")

Note

1. Todd Clear and Natasha Frost, "Informing Public Policy." *Criminology and Public Policy* 6, no. 4 (2007), pp. 633–640.

RESTORE RATIONALITY TO SENTENCING POLICY

Alfred Blumstein
Alex R. Piquero

One of the most striking observations about criminal justice policy since the late 1970s has been the growth of prison populations in the United States (Spelman, 2000). State and federal prison populations have grown at an exponential rate of 6% to 8% per year. This steady growth has occurred during periods of both increases and decreases in crime rates. It is only in the last few years that the growth rates have slowed to about 2% per year, with the bulk of that growth occurring in the federal prison system.

This growth was preceded by a period of at least 50 years of a flat incarceration rate (Blumstein and Cohen, 1973). This transition from a flat rate to a period of rapid growth clearly reflects a regime change from a homeostatic process under control of the criminal justice system to political control, primarily by legislators. The political environment rewards those who could show that they were being "tough on crime" and made those who could be accused of being "soft on crime" very vulnerable politically.

This political arena provides only a limited repertoire of actions they could take to respond to the public's concerns about crime. Because there was little they could do about the "root causes" of crime, especially in the short run, their responses almost always involved an increase in incarceration. Incarceration can be increased by lengthening sentences, by substituting prison for probation by requiring a mandatory-minimum sentence, and by introducing such rhetorically catchy concepts as "three-strikes-and-you're-out" requiring a very long or life sentence after a third conviction.

Source: Criminology and Public Policy, vol. 6, no. 4 (2007). © 2007 American Society of Criminology. Reprinted by permission.

Some of the early uses of mandatory-minimum sentences were targeted at drug crimes as the public was beginning to display concern about kids using drugs (Tonry, 1994). At first, the sentences were fairly modest, 2 years being typical. When that sentence did not do much to change the traffic in drugs (and one would not expect much change because the resilient drug market could readily recruit replacements for those sent away; Blumstein, 1993), then the legislature simply would increase the sentence to 5 years, and then crank it up to 10 years several years later. All this did not do much to solve the drug problem, but it "worked"—at least in terms of gaining public support—because it was responsive and it could be implemented quickly.

This politicization is reflected in the widespread fad in the 1990s of "three strikes and you're out" sentencing bills (Benekos and Merlo, 1995; Turner et al., 1995). Initiated in Washington in 1993, at least 24 states and Congress enacted such laws (Austin et al., 1999). The rhetorical appeal of invoking a baseball rule as a major public policy certainly demonstrates the compulsion to show the public how tough they could be. Such bills were often introduced with a fairly broad scope of offenses that could be classified as "strikes," but broader reason usually prevailed by limiting the offenses only to the most seriously violent. In California, however, the third strike was very broad in scope. In two cases (*Andrade* and *Ewing*) with relatively minor property crimes as the third strikes, sentences of 25 years to life were upheld by the U.S. Supreme Court, to the surprise of people who felt that such a sentence would be "cruel and unusual," but the Supreme Court did not seem to find "excessive" in the Eighth Amendment.

As a result of this succession of "tough" legislative acts, prison populations in the United States have grown from a level of 110 per 100,000 population that prevailed for over 50 years to a level of almost 500 per 100,000 (or 720 counting local jails), making the U.S. incarceration rate the highest in the world. Much of this has occurred at a time when the Part I crime rates have been going down for some time (Blumstein and Wallman, 2006).

BRINGING RATIONALITY INTO SENTENCING POLICY

What, then, can be done to restore rationality to sentencing policy? First and perhaps foremost, it should be clear that the long mandatory-minimum sentences that typically are legislated at a time after some heinous crime has been committed, or when there has been a loud public outcry about some crime of concern, are unwarranted and wasteful. Typically, those mandatory-minimum sentences are made much longer than would be warranted and apply to a much broader class of crimes of which the heinous crime is but one extreme member. Furthermore, once enacted, they stay on the books for a very long time because, even though their obsolescence and inappropriateness may be recognized widely, the fear of appearing "soft on crime" inhibits any action to repeal them.[1]

One solution to this problem would be legislation that repealed all mandatory-minimum sentencing laws. We recognize, however, that there would be considerable difficulty in enacting such legislation. It would be seen as too broad and could too easily be labeled as "soft on crime." A politically more tenable approach would be to pass a law that sunsetted all mandatory-minimum laws, requiring that they be terminated after some reasonable period (say, 3–5 years). As with all such sunset legislation, it would call for a review of the original mandatory law to assess both its positive and its negative features. Certainly, all three-strikes laws should be included in any such legislation.

A second solution is to adopt an approach that has been used in many states and the federal government to provide a rational sentencing-guideline structure via a sentencing commission (von Hirsch et al., 1987). The commissions are created by statute and charged with developing a coherent and proportionate sentencing structure that accounts for the seriousness of the offense and prior record, and in some states, they require that the sentencing structure be compatible with available prison capacity. They should be created as a means of providing a forum outside the political pressures of a legislative body. They can be the vehicle for reviewing and sunsetting mandatory-minimum sentences to maintain coherence within the sentencing structure.

BRINGING KNOWLEDGE ABOUT CRIMINAL CAREERS INTO SENTENCING POLICY

Introduction of rationality will require invoking knowledge about criminal careers (Blumstein et al., 1986). The aspect of criminal careers that is particularly relevant is knowledge about the duration of a criminal career, typically calculated as the time from onset to termination. There has been a rich body of research over the past quarter-century examining this question (Piquero et al., 2003, 2007), and this research has been linked closely to research on the incapacitation effect of incarceration (Piquero and Blumstein, 2007). That research makes clear that most criminal careers are of finite duration, some very short and some few quite long, and recognizes that virtually all offenders desist eventually (Sampson and Laub, 2003). A key feature of that research recognizes that incarceration at the end of an individual's career represents "wastage" from the viewpoint of incapacitation: The prison cell the individual is occupying might better be used for somebody who is in the midst of a career rather than one whose career is over.

This problem is complicated by the difficulty of estimating when a particular individual's criminal career ends. It is difficult to know whether an individual has simply stopped offending for a period and is likely to return (i.e., intermittency) or has indeed terminated his career (Barnett et al., 1987; Bushway et al., 2001; Piquero, 2004). On the other hand, it is reasonably easy to estimate termination rates as a function of individual characteristics such as their prior record, their age, and their family and employment situations. Thus, although one cannot say with certainty that a particular individual has terminated his career, one can make reasonable probability statements about termination that permits judges and parole authorities to make reasoned judgments about individual risks (Gottfredson, 1999). Bringing these perspectives into criminal justice decision making could serve as a constraint on the raw political exploitation that has characterized so much of criminal justice policy over the past quarter-century.

Although information about the duration of an offender's criminal career length is certainly of important criminological interest, the aspect of the career length that is of most policy interest is the "residual criminal career length (RCL)," or the expected amount of time remaining in the career after a conviction, when a sentence is to be chosen (Blumstein et al., 1982). Piquero et al. (2003:479) have outlined the policy implications associated with estimates of RCL. Knowledge of RCL is perhaps one of the most critical areas of research to inform sentencing decisions. For example, if research shows that a median RCL is 5 years, then criminal justice policies requiring multi-decade sentences waste prison resources. Furthermore, as offenders continue to be incarcerated into late adulthood when their residual career lengths have diminished, the costs of their health care will increase, thereby imposing additional strain on an already over-stressed criminal justice system.

One study (Blumstein et al., 1982) of residual criminal careers estimated that, for those who start their adult criminal careers at an early age (say, by 20 years), the residual career length increases through the 20s, reaches a maximum in the 30s, and then decreases in the 40s. This process reflects the fact that offenders in their early 20s include many who will have a short career, whereas those who persist into their 30s are likely to be more committed to offending, whereas those still active in their 40s are likely to "wear out" because of the physically demanding aspects of offending.[2]

This study also estimated an important difference between career lengths of those who committed property crimes compared with those who committed violent crimes. It was found that the total career length for the violent offenders was about 10 years, whereas the property offenders had a career length of 5 years. These results reflect property crimes as more of an issue involving need and opportunity, whereas the violent crimes are more likely to reflect inherent characteristics of the individual offender.

Several other recent studies have addressed career length issues (Ezell, 2007; Piquero et al., 2004), but in the interest of space, we only highlight a few of them here. Spelman (1994) used data from the three-state Rand Inmate Survey and estimated total career length to average about 6 or 7 years. He showed that young and inexperienced offenders, those in the first 5 years of their career, were more likely than older offenders to drop out each year, but after 5 years, the rate of dropout leveled off, rising only after the twentieth year as an active offender.

Farrington (2003) examined the duration of criminal careers in the Cambridge Study using conviction data to age 40 years and found that the average duration of criminal careers for those with two or more convictions was 10.4 years. Kazemian and Farrington (2006) studied issues related to RCL, defined as the number of years remaining in the criminal career up to the last recorded conviction, among the Cambridge males (followed to age 40 years) and their fathers (followed to age 70 years). Although median residual career lengths were not reported, the average residual career length was 8.1 years for the sons and 10.9 years for their fathers.

Blumstein (2005:247) estimated the median adult career lengths for the Glueck delinquent sample (Laub and Sampson, 2003). Measuring career length as the time between their first and their last recorded arrest after age 17 years, he found a median of about 8.5 years for property offenses and 12 years for violent offenses. Francis et al. (2007) estimated career length using six different birth cohorts from England and Wales between 1953 and 1978. Two key findings emerged from their study. Although the highest average career length was 6 years for males in the 1953 birth cohort, 10.8% of them exhibited career lengths of 20 years or more. Second, the rate of desistance remained constant during a period of 20–25 years if the offender did not stop immediately after the first conviction.

Recognizing that each study above was based on a different sample drawn at a different time and followed for a different duration, these various studies show reasonably consistent results. Median career lengths are *well under* 20 years, and RCL's are even shorter. We also recognize that early starters and violent offenders tend to have longer careers. Also, in any population, there are always a small percentage of offenders who continue well past the median of their colleagues.[3]

SUMMARY

Recently, the strong trend toward lengthy incarceration seems to be abating to some degree. States are faced with severe financial constraints, and corrections budgets have been an important part of their expenditure growth. Prison populations in several states have declined in recent years, and much of the recent growth has been in the federal system. All this suggests that we may be seeing for the first time in several decades an opportunity to bring increased rationality into sentencing policy. The nation is not facing a severe crime problem, and the public is not demanding vigorously actions against crime. Crime rates are lower than they have been at any time since the 1960s, and there is a growing recognition of the high cost of incarceration (Nagin et al., 2006). This might well be a good time to bring to the policy arena knowledge of criminal careers that is available widely in criminology, but that has been largely ignored in the political process, and that can inform richly and credibly criminal justice decision making, especially for sentencing.

References

Austin, James, John Clark, Patricia Hardyman, and D. Alan Henry
   1999   The impact of 'Three Strikes and You're Out.' Punishment and Society 1:131–162.
Barnett, Arnold, Alfred Blumstein, and David P. Farrington
   1987   Probabilistic models of youthful criminal careers. Criminology 25:83–107.
Benekos, Peter J. and Alida V. Merlo
   1995   Three strikes and you're out: The political sentencing game. Federal Probation 59:3–9.
Blumstein, Alfred
   1993   Making rationality relevant: 1992 American Society of Criminology Presidential Address. Criminology 31:1–16.
   2005   An overview of the symposium and some next steps. Annals of the American Academy of Political and Social Science 602:242–258.
Blumstein, Alfred and Jacqueline Cohen
   1973   A theory of the stability of punishment. Journal of Criminal Law and Criminology 64:198–207.
Blumstein, Alfred and Joel Wallman (eds.)
   2006   The Crime Drop. New York: Cambridge University Press.
Blumstein, Alfred, Jacqueline Cohen, Jeffrey A. Roth, and Christy A. Visher (eds.)
   1986   Criminal Careers and "Career Criminals." Washington, D.C.: National Academy Press.
Blumstein, Alfred, Jacqueline Cohen, and Paul Hsieh
   1982   The Duration of Adult Criminal Careers. Final report submitted to National Institute of Justice, August 1982 Pittsburgh, Pa.: School of Urban and Public Affairs, Carnegie-Mellon University.

Bushway, Shawn D., Alex R. Piquero, Lisa M. Broidy, Elizabeth Cauffman, and Paul Mazerolle
2001   An empirical framework for studying desistance as a process. Criminology 39:491–515.

Ezell, Michael E.
2007   Examining the overall and offense-specific criminal career lengths of a sample of serious offenders. Crime & Delinquency 53:3–37.

Farrington, David P.
2003   Key Results from the first forty years of the Cambridge study in delinquent development. In Terence P. Thornberry and Marvin D. Krohn (eds.), Taking Stock of Delinquency: An Overview of Findings from Contemporary Longitudinal Studies. Boston, Mass.: Kluwer.

Francis, Brian, Keith Soothill, and Alex R. Piquero
2007   Estimation issues and generational changes in modeling criminal career length. Crime & Delinquency 53:84–105.

Gottfredson, Don M.
1999   Effects of Judges' Sentencing Decisions on Criminal Careers. Research in Brief. Washington, D.C.: National Institute of Justice.

Kazemian, Lila and David P. Farrington
2006   Exploring residual career length and residual number of offenses for two generations of repeat offenders. Journal of Research in Crime and Delinquency 43:89–113.

Laub, John H. and Robert J. Sampson
2003   Shared Beginnings, Divergent Lives. Cambridge, Mass.: Harvard University Press.

Nagin, Daniel S., Alex R. Piquero, Elizabeth Scott, and Laurence Steinberg
2006   Public preferences for rehabilitation versus incarceration of juvenile offenders: Evidence from a contingent valuation survey. Criminology & Public Policy 5:627–652.

Piquero, Alex R.
2004   Somewhere between persistence and desistance: The intermittency of criminal careers? In Shadd Maruna and Russ Immarigeon (eds.), After Crime and Punishment: Pathways to Offender Reintegration. Devon, U.K.: Willan.

Piquero, Alex R. and Alfred Blumstein
2007   Does incapacitation reduce crime? Journal of Quantitative Criminology [2.3: 267–285.]

Piquero, Alex R., Robert Brame, and Donald Lynam
2004   Studying the factors related to career length. Crime and Delinquency 50:412–435.

Piquero, Alex R., David P. Farrington, and Alfred Blumstein
2003   The criminal career paradigm. In Michael Tonry (ed.), Crime and Justice: A Review of Research, vol 30. Chicago, Ill.: University of Chicago Press.
2007   Key Issues in Criminal Career Research: New Analyses of the Cambridge Study in Delinquent Development. New York: Cambridge University Press.

Sampson, Robert J. and John H. Laub
2003   Life-course desisters? Trajectories of crime among delinquent boys followed to age 70. Criminology 41:555–592.

Spelman, William
1994   Criminal Incapacitation. New York: Plenum.
2000   What recent studies do (and don't) tell us about imprisonment and crime. In Michael Tonry (ed.), Crime and Justice: An Annual Review of Research, vol 27. Chicago, Ill.: University of Chicago Press.

Tonry, Michael
1994   Malign Neglect. New York: Oxford University Press.

Turner, Michael G., Jody L. Sundt, Brandon K. Applegate, and Francis T. Cullen
   1995   'Three strikes and you're out' legislation: A national assessment. Federal Probation
          59:16–35.
von Hirsch, Andrew, Kay A. Knapp, and Michael Tonry
   1987   The Sentencing Commission and Its Guidelines. Boston, Mass.: Northeastern
          University Press.

Notes

1. A prime example of this problem is the notorious 100:1 crack/powder difference in the Anti-Drug Abuse Law of 1986 that has stayed on the books for more than 20 years, well after the rationale for the difference in 5-year mandatory minimums between crack (5 grams) and powder cocaine (500 grams) was largely gone. Widespread agreement existed, as reflected in legislation proposed by two Republican senators (Senators Hatch and Sessions), that the difference was excessive and should be reduced or even eliminated, a move that the U.S. Sentencing Commission had tried several times without success.

2. These observations may appear surprising and in contradiction with the age-crime curve, which shows offending declining after a peak in the late teens or early 20s. But the age-crime curve depicts active offenders of a particular age as a fraction of the total population of that age. In contrast, the RCL focuses on offenders who are currently active and estimates how much longer they will continue to be active.

3. Since the duration of criminal careers and especially residual careers is so salient to sentencing policy, and since federal sentencing guidelines have been made "advisory," it becomes incumbent on the National Institute of Justice (NIJ) to undertake a major research program to develop better estimates of RCL (and their functional equivalents, desistance rates) as a function of age, prior crime types, current crime of conviction, work experience, marriage experience, and other risk factors. It would be appropriate to incorporate the results of that research into a format that would be disseminated widely to sentencing judges in both the federal and the state systems and to parole authorities. On this score, there is considerable research in Canada and other countries on the duration of criminal careers and on risk factors for release from corrections. That research should be reviewed, and whatever aspects are appropriate should be provided to sentencing and parole authorities in the United States.

ENCOURAGE RESTORATIVE JUSTICE

John Braithwaite

At the 2000 United Nations (U.N.) Congress on the Prevention of Crime and Treatment of Offenders, many were surprised that a resolution for all nations to encourage restorative justice passed unanimously. Restorative justice comprises the idea that because crime hurts, justice should heal, and especially heal relationships. It is a process in which all stakeholders have an opportunity to discuss the hurts of a crime, how they might be repaired, how recurrence might be prevented, and how other needs

Source: Criminology and Public Policy, vol. 6, no. 4 (2007). © 2007 American Society of Criminology. Reprinted by permission.

of stakeholders can be met. Even the societies with the highest imprisonment rates in the world—the United States, Russia, and South Africa—and most executions—China—have been sites of important innovations in restorative justice. Although most societies have many small programs (perhaps even thousands now in the United States; Bazemore and Schiff (2005) were able to list 773 programs for juveniles alone), and tens of thousands in China (Wong, 1999), mostly the support is rhetorical, not extending to the mainstreaming of restorative justice evident in New Zealand, Norway, and much of the German-speaking world.

A surprisingly universal experience is that restorative justice has not proved politically unpopular. As Frank Cullen points out with rehabilitation (2007), politicians can be punitive in many respects but still support restorative justice because it makes sense to citizens, and because 80% to 99% of people report good experiences with it, whether they are victims, offenders, supporters, or attending police officers (Braithwaite, 2002; Poulson, 2003). Politicians are unafraid to vote for it at the U.N. and at home because when demands for law and order run amok, they can always say they do not mean for restorative justice to be used in "that" kind of case. Since leaders of all religions have tended to be supportive of restorative justice, seeing it as creating spaces where spiritual experience flourishes, the conservative side of politics at least learns to live with restorative justice.

RESTORE A BIT OF DEMOCRACY

One reason restorative justice is popular is that it hands a little piece of power back to the ordinary people. We have become such mass democracies that face-to-face meetings on important questions of governance only include the elite. Not only are New England town meetings a democratic form that is hard to translate to a mass society, but also most citizens do not want to participate in community meetings. Most citizens do want to attend restorative justice conferences, however, when asked by a victim or offender to come along to support them. There is something humbling and ennobling about being asked to help someone in trouble; people tend to be honored to be chosen as a supporter. The personal touch makes it a little opportunity to salvage some democratic participation, and the evidence indicates that most people relish being able to participate (Braithwaite, 2002:45–55,130–134). The procedural justice findings, moreover, show this feature of "process control" by ordinary citizens engenders a sense of fairness (Tyler, 1990).

The Western social science literature on procedural justice, trust building through democratic engagement, and the contribution of restorative justice to all of this has bigger implications in societies recovering from violent conflict than for the West itself. The empirical experience of peace building has been that although democratic elections, national reconciliation, and forgiveness are fundamental ingredients of sustainable peace, they cannot be rushed. The recent mistakes in places like East Timor have been giving postconflict societies an election quickly, and then getting out. We know now that electoral outcomes that do not share power and leave one faction totally in control will exclude ethnic minorities and are not conducive to sustainable peace. Nor do elections work where warlords bribe village heads to get their entire village to vote for their man. Another thing we have learned is that although the time is taken to get electoral institutions to take root, control over most criminal justice can be taken away from hated central police institutions, with their torture chambers and secret dossiers, and returned to villages. There are always survivals of traditional restorative justice practices in villages. These practices have their human rights worries, even if they are less than the abuses of the wartime state. Ali Wardak (2004) has shown how traditional male-dominated village justice might be balanced by an internationally funded female-dominated new central Human Rights Commission to educate village elders about involving women and respecting a new order of human rights. Although warlords blocked Wardak's ideas in his homeland Afghanistan, other postconflict areas such as Bougainville have observed what locals regard as a meaningful form of democratic participation restored through local control over (restorative) criminal justice (Howley, 2002). Restorative justice then becomes much more than a better way of managing crime; it becomes a way to help village societies become more rights-respecting and to learn to become democratic.

RESTORE VICTIMS

When victims have an opportunity to actually participate in restorative justice, they benefit much more consistently (compared to controls) than do offenders (Sherman and Strang, 2007:62–65). Yet victims who want restorative justice are demoralized when it fails to happen or when the offender refuses to attend the meeting (Strang, 2002). Angel (2005) found in an experiment that restorative justice benefits the victim's mental health by reducing post-traumatic stress symptoms. Victims emerge from restorative justice with reduced fear and anger, increased forgiveness, and feel more satisfied. The victim has a stronger sense that his or her rights are respected and that justice was done compared to controls (Strang, 2002; Braithwaite, 2002:45–53).

DELIVER COMMITMENT TO DO WHAT WORKS

Criminology is making progress on what works. But justice systems are not good at motivating people to do what works. Police know that the best predictor of being a victim of burglary is having recently been burglarized (Pease, 1998:v). Getting burglary victims to act preventively on this is the hard part. Routinely, people are imprisoned because this seems politically safer than cheaper, more effective interventions. Restorative circles can invite experts to present the evidence to lay stakeholders. This can overcome the propensity to do the safe punitive thing in favor of effective prevention or rehabilitation. If the victim and other stakeholders in an assault sign an agreement for anger management and compensation (rather than imprisonment), then it can become politically safe for the system to fill fewer prison cells. A small number of restorative programs that steer high-end minority offenders away from prison has shown that restorative justice can motivate a politics of evidence-based, emotionally intelligent justice (Sherman, 2003) to supplant incarcerative justice (Bonta et al., 1998).

A Canadian Ministry of Justice meta-analysis of evaluations of restorative justice with credible control groups was encouraging on many fronts (Latimer et al., 2001). Its biggest effect was that the implementation of agreements was 33% higher in restorative justice cases than in controls. We should not be surprised that a court order is less likely to be complied with than an agreement consensually signed by an offender, his mother, his girlfriend, and his victim even if the court order can be legally enforced by another court order! Family and close friends are more powerful regulators of behavior than are the police and the courts.

So the largest promise of restorative justice is not that it is more directly effective than alternatives such as court or plea bargains. It is that evidence-based restorative justice is a superior delivery vehicle for interventions that work when compared with traditional criminal justice. As criminology discovers more ways of reducing crime at lower cost in dollars and injustice, restorative justice can deliver the bottom-up commitment to realize implementation.

REDUCE CRIME DIRECTLY

That said, the evidence has progressively become stronger that restorative justice in itself is directly effective in reducing criminal reoffense. Moreover, restorative justice is a learning tradition. In an update and tightening of the methodological criteria of the Latimer et al. (2001) meta-analysis, Bonta et al. (2006) found the recidivism effect was notably higher for second generation post-1997 restorative justice programs. All meta-analyses suggest significant but only modest direct effects in reducing reoffending. This result is what most restorative justice theorists predicted. Why would you expect the direct effects of interventions of an hour or two to be large? Actually, the most recent review by Sherman and Strang (2007) suggests that we were wrong in that the modest positive result overall combines some very large positive effects, especially with violence, zero effects, and occasional negative effects when compared with controls. We do not yet understand the drivers of these big variations in success and failure.

It is also with violence that we get some surprisingly huge healing effects. In the Canberra RISE experiments, 45% of court case victims wanted to harm their offenders, compared with 9% for victims who went to a restorative justice conference (Sherman and Strang, 2007:63). For property offenses, this difference more than halved. Restorative justice delivers more apologies to victims, and apologies they view as sincere, than do court cases. This difference is also particularly strong with violence cases. Again, because it is with violence that we find the biggest effects, I suspect evidence-based criminology has a major contribution to make to how we can be more effective in peace building after war.

INCREASE JUSTICE

Criminology was born with too myopic a concern with preventing crime. Some healthy developments have balanced that in recent decades. The rise of victimology has helped us prioritize better recovery for victims. Most nations have moral equivalents to Rodney King, O. J. Simpson, Klan killing and cover-up, the Japanese internment camps of World War II, and the contemporary diaspora of internment camps for Muslims alleged to be terrorists. Therefore, all nations' justice systems should be evaluated in terms of how successful they are in affecting reconciliation within and between communities after cases that question discrimination and respect for rights. The restoration of a sense of justice and reintegration of communities thus stands beside reintegration of victims and offenders as outcomes that should concern criminologists. The social psychology of procedural justice is another recent tradition that adds a set of facets—consistency, decision accuracy, correctability, process control, impartiality, and ethicality (Lind and Tyler, 1988)—in terms of which the "justice" in "justice systems" is evaluated.

The criminological community working on restorative justice, community justice, and cognate innovations deserves credit for being theoretically serious, non-dogmatic, and plural. This effort has led them to be evidence-based and remarkably assiduous in a short space of years in generating a large body of outcome evaluation that explores the entire range of dimensions mentioned above. Moreover, so far restorative justice has fared well against these tests (for a now out-of-date survey, see Braithwaite, 2002). The restorative justice research tradition has advanced criminology's normative conversation on how justice should be defined, and its explanatory conversation on what responses to crime do best in promoting justice for victims, offenders, families of offenders, and other stakeholders.

Justice can be conceived in a republican way (Braithwaite and Pettit, 1990). The evidence suggests what is good for republican justice is good for crime control and for democracy (when democracy is conceived in a civic republican way as contestatory and deliberative democracy, as opposed to the rule of opinion polls (Pettit, 1997)). This combination of normative and empirical conclusions runs against the intuitions of many who view justice, rights, and democracy as obstacles to crime control. Yet the restorative justice literature is increasingly compelling that we can get less crime through more justice and more democracy.

One of the shocking things about law school debate on justice is the assumption that justice ordered is justice delivered. Criminologists from many jurisdictions have always known that one half or one third of all fines that are imposed are never collected (Sherman and Strang, 2007). Here is where the superior implementation certainty of restorative justice increases the consistency of justice as delivered. In addition, the Sherman and Strang (2007:4) review concludes that diverting cases to restorative justice at least doubles (and can quadruple) the proportion of offenses that actually go to justice. Just-deserts advocates of formal prosecution rather than of restorative justice ignore the realities of absconding, loss of files, and no shows of witnesses, which means surprisingly often the prosecution never happens. Attrition can even be a primary reality of prosecutorial justice in experiments (Sherman and Strang, 2007:82). Perhaps this is because some are allowed to abscond because they are innocent. Yet randomization should deliver equal numbers of innocents in control and experimental groups. Another important finding in this respect is Daly et al. (2005): that there is more "charging down" of sexual assaults that are prosecuted than sexual assaults that go to restorative justice conferences. The latter has particularly important implications for justice as victim vindication (see also McAlinden, 2007).

NO PANACEA

The evidence suggests that all justice interventions, including restorative justice, frequently fail with terrible consequences. If it is right that restorative justice is the best delivery vehicle for other interventions that work, then it can be applied to interventions that can repair the harm done by bad restorative justice itself. Moreover, responsive regulatory theory (Braithwaite, 2002) argues that restorative justice should be a presumptively preferred option at the base of a regulatory pyramid. Such responsive justice pyramids cover the weaknesses of one strategy with the strengths of other strategies higher up the pyramid, including more deterrent and incapacitative options.

References

Angel, Caroline
   2005   Crime victims meet their offenders: Testing the impact of restorative justice conferences on victims' post-traumatic stress symptoms. Doctoral Dissertation. University of Pennsylvania.
Bazemore, Gordon and Mara Schiff
   2005   Juvenile Justice Reform and Restorative Justice. Portland, Ore.: Willan Publishing.
Bonta, James, Jennifer Rooney, and Suzanne Wallace-Capretta
   1998   Restorative Justice: An Evaluation of the Restorative Resolutions Project. Ottawa, Canada: Solicitor General Canada.
Bonta, James, Rebecca Jesseman, Tanya Rugge, and Robert Cormier
   2006   Restorative justice and recidivism: Promises made, promises kept? In D. Sullivan and L. Tifft (eds.), Handbook of Restorative Justice: A Global Perspective. London: Routledge.
Braithwaite, John
   2002   Restorative Justice and Responsive Regulation. New York: Oxford University Press.
Braithwaite, John and Philip Pettit
   1990   Not Just Deserts: A Republican Theory of Criminal Justice. Oxford, U.K.: Oxford University Press.
Cullen, Francis T.
   2007   Make rehabilitation corrections' guiding paradigm. Criminology & Public Policy [6:717–728].
Daly, Kathleen, Brigitte Bouhours, Sarah Curtis-Fawley, Leanne Weber, and Rita Scholl
   2005   South Australia Juvenile Justice and Criminal Justice (SAJJ-CJ) Technical Report No. 3: Sexual Assault Archival Study (SASS), An Archival Study of Sexual Offence Cases Disposed of in Youth Court and by Conference and Formal Caution, 2d edition, revised and expanded. Brisbane, Queensland, Australia: School of Criminology and Criminal Justice, Griffith University. Available online: http://www.griffith.edu.au/school/ccj/ kdaly.html.
Howley, Patrick
   2002   Breaking Spears and Mending Hearts. Sydney, Australia: Federation Press.
Latimer, Jeff, Craig Dowden, and Danielle Muise
   2001   The Effectiveness of Restorative Justice Practices: A Meta-Analysis. Ottawa, Canada: Department of Justice, Canada.
Lind, E. Allan and Tom R. Tyler
   1988   The Social Psychology of Procedural Justice. New York: Plenum Press.
McAlinden, Anne-Marie
   2007   The Shaming of Sexual Offenders: Risk, Retribution and Reintegration. Portland, Ore.: Hart Publishing.
Pease, Ken
   1998   Repeat Victimisation: Taking Stock. Police Research Group Crime Detection and Prevention Series Paper 90. London: Home Office.

Pettit, Philip
  1997   Republicanism. Oxford, U.K.: Clarendon Press.
Poulson, Barton
  2003   A third voice: A review of empirical research on the psychological outcomes of
          restorative justice. Utah Law Review 1:167–204.
Sherman, Lawrence
  2003   Reason for emotion: Reinventing justice with theories, innovations, and research. The
          American Society of Criminology, 2002 Presidential Address. Criminology 41:1–38.
Sherman, Lawrence and Heather Strang
  2007   Restorative Justice: The Evidence. London: The Smith Institute.
Strang, Heather
  2002   Repair or Revenge: Victims and Restorative Justice. Oxford, U.K.: Oxford University
          Press.
Tyler, Tom
  1990   Why People Obey the Law. New Haven, Conn.: Yale University Press.
Wardak, Ali
  2004   Building a post-war justice system in Afghanistan. Crime, Law and Social Change
          41:319–341.
Wong, Dennis
  1999   Delinquency control and juvenile justice in China. Australian and New Zealand
          Journal of Criminology 32:27–41.

MAKING REHABILITATION CORRECTIONS' GUIDING PARADIGM

Francis T. Cullen

The punishment paradigm has reached the point of exhaustion. After three decades of mean-spirited rhetoric, efforts to mandate harsh sanctions, and prison populations surpassing record highs annually, this approach has achieved all it is going to achieve. It would be naïve, of course, to suggest that the punishment crowd is going to forfeit easily its control over the correctional system. But calls for more of the same will increasingly ring hollow. In a parallel eerily similar to Iraq, their plan for yet another surge in the war on crime will bankrupt the public treasury further and make us no safer. It is time to withdraw from this fruitless war.

But beyond being naysayers, what strategy—what fresh vision—for American corrections will criminologists propose? For good reason, we have spent three decades seeking to expose the limits of the punishment paradigm. We have become experts at showing that one foolish idea after another inspired by the punishment paradigm—whether boot camps, scared straight programs, or intensive supervision—has no hope of reducing recidivism (Cullen, Pratt, et al., 2002; MacKenzie, 2006). In so doing, we have stood face to face with the punitive tsunami sweeping across the nation and

Source: Criminology and Public Policy, vol. 6, no. 4 (2007). © 2007 American Society of Criminology. Reprinted by permission.

should be credited with preventing at least some of the wreckage. More lasting, I suspect that we are the prime contributors to the idea that we cannot imprison and punish our way out of the crime problem.

But now what? The challenge is to make the transition from those who deconstruct stupid crime-control proposals to those who construct a credible agenda for correctional policy and practice. Meeting this challenge, however, means articulating a clear vision for what should be done in corrections. This task is daunting precisely because corrections is a social domain characterized by hard cases (changing high-risk offenders for the better) and by critics waiting to capitalize on inevitable failures (released offenders who commit heinous crimes). These stubborn realities mean that any positive agenda that is put forward will be imperfect—its flaws known not only by its opponents but also by its advocates. Even so, we must take a stand and give strong advice on what principles should guide the correctional enterprise. It is no longer enough to say what not to do; we must say what to do.

In this context, criminologists should take a stand to reaffirm rehabilitation as the guiding paradigm of correctional policy and practice. I offer five reasons for this assertion.

REASON #1: REJECTING REHABILITATION WAS A MISTAKE

Beginning in the late 1960s, criminologists joined with others on the political left to reject forcefully the rehabilitative ideal. Contemporary observers believe that this forsaking of treatment was a rational response to the revelation by Martinson (1974) that "nothing works" to reform offenders, but this was not the case. Rather, this attack on rehabilitation was initiated several years earlier and had far more to do with a declining trust in the state to exercise its discretionary powers, especially in the courts and in prisons, in a humane and equitable way (Cullen and Gendreau, 2000; Cullen and Gilbert, 1982; Rotman, 1990). The individualized treatment model was based on the questionable assumption that state officials—judges, wardens, and parole boards—would use discretion not to discriminate or control but to deliver finely calibrated treatment to offenders. Critics believed that this ostensibly benevolent model had the bad consequences of masking state officials' abuse and repression of mostly minority offenders. As an alternative, they favored a "justice model" that would purge corrections of discretion through due process rights and determinate sentencing (Cullen and Gilbert, 1982).

The difficulty, however, was that criminologists and fellow progressive critics ignored the unanticipated consequences of this policy choice, three of which are most salient. First, their faith in the law to restrict state power made sense in the progressive 1960s but ultimately was a "bad bet" when the courts and legislatures turned conservative. In particular, those attacking rehabilitation did not appreciate the dangers of determinate sentences. By eliminating parole release, these sentences transferred discretionary power from corrections officials and parole boards to legislators and prosecutors. Critics did not anticipate that, as America lurched to the right, these elected officials would engage in symbolic politics and use their newfound power to pass increasingly long, harsh, and mandatory determinate sentences that squeezed any hope of mercy from the system (Cullen and Gilbert, 1982; see also Beckett, 1997).

Second, the critics' embrace of a justice model undermined the social welfare purpose of corrections, saying, in essence, that the state should not be in the business of providing services to offenders. In so doing, they robbed corrections of any persuasive rationale for why offenders, especially those imprisoned, should be treated decently. It is no coincidence that the attack on rehabilitation was accompanied by the elimination of Pell grants and college programs for inmates and by efforts to make prisons more painful (e.g., restrict access to air conditioning, television, and similar amenities). "[P]rograms for inmate education, training, and drug treatment have been made scarce," observes De Parle (2007:34). "If policymakers were once too credulous about rehabilitation, they are now too dismissive."

Third, even more consequential, the justice model rejected the idea that corrections had a utilitarian purpose—that this system should be used to prevent crime. As a result, criminologists offered no blueprint for how to reduce recidivism; justice, not crime control, was their concern. They simply did not count on conservative commentators stepping into this policy void with clear prescriptions for enhancing public safety and for defending crime victims that criminologists ostensibly ignored. Their proposal was simple and compelling: Reduce crime and prevent victimization through the greater use of prisons, which can be counted on to deter some predators and to incapacitate the rest (see, e.g., Wilson, 1975). Although the punishment movement over the past three decades had diverse sources (see, e.g., Garland, 2001; Gottschalk, 2006; Lynch, 2007; Tonry, 2004; Whitman, 2003), a contributing factor was the removal, by well-meaning criminologists, of the rehabilitative ideal as the one powerful ideological bulwark capable of combating and deconstructing "get tough" policy and rhetoric.

REASON #2: PUNISHMENT DOES NOT WORK

Locking up over 2 million offenders is bound to prevent some crime (Spelman, 2000; but see Currie, 1998; Lynch, 2007). But this is not a prima facie case for the punishment paradigm. First, under rehabilitation, incapacitation effects also would occur (as well as general deterrent effects because offenders would receive a state sanction). It is just that through offender assessment, the goal would be to limit the use of incarceration to high-risk offenders and not to sweep offenders indiscriminately into the nation's prisons. Second, beyond incapacitation, the punishment paradigm has no empirical case that its "get tough" strategies specifically deter offenders. Ironically, despite its "we-are-for-the-victims-and-you-are-not" rhetoric, this approach poses a threat to public safety.

Indeed, the empirical literature is damning of punishment-oriented interventions. There is growing evidence that imprisonment is related to higher levels of recidivism (Chen and Shapiro, 2007; Gendreau et al., 2000; Nieuwbeerta et al., 2006; Petersilia et al., 1986; Sampson and Laub, 1993; Smith, 2006; Spohn and Holleran, 2002; see also Doob and Webster, 2003). Even clearer, a relatively voluminous, often experimental, set of studies demonstrates that control-oriented intensive supervision, scared straight, and boot camp programs have no overall impact on recidivism (Cullen et al., 2005; Cullen et al., 1996; Howell, 2003; Lipsey, 1999a; MacKenzie, 2006; MacKenzie et al., 2001; Petersilia and Turner, 1993; Petrosino et al., 2003). Of course, there is a reason why these interventions fail: They are based on a limited theory of crime (rational choice) and do not target the known proximate risk factors for re-offending (Andrews and Bonta, 2006).

REASON #3: REHABILITATION DOES WORK

If punishment is not the answer, then what should be done within corrections to reduce the likelihood of offenders recidivating? For the most part, it is here that criminologists have been bereft of any good answers (Cullen and Gendreau, 2001). By embracing a general professional ideology that "nothing works" to change offenders, the best advice they offer is "don't send offenders to prison." But this answer has two obvious flaws. First, if "nothing works" to change offenders, then it seems to make sense to place these intractable criminals behind bars. And second, once offenders are in prison, why shouldn't we simply warehouse them? After all, why give them services or try to help them to change if such efforts are fruitless? The point, of course, is that we must be able to provide a coherent, defensible answer specifying what we should do with offenders who are under the supervision of the correctional system. Saying that "nothing works" is simply a rationale for more, rather than less, incarceration and neglect.

The good news is that a small but growing group of scholars has been working to document that rehabilitation programs can be effective (Cullen, 2005). Through the use of meta-analyses that survey the studies in the area, they show that rehabilitation programs achieve meaningful reductions in recidivism (Lipsey, 1999a; Lipsey and Cullen, 2007; MacKenzie, 2006; McGuire, 2002; Palmer, 1992; Petrosino, 2005; cf. Petrosino and Soydan, 2005). Most promising, an evolving theory of rehabilitation details the "principles of effective correctional treatment" (Andrews and Bonta, 2006; Gendreau, 1996). Programs based on these principles have been shown to achieve high reductions in reoffending (Andrews and Bonta, 2006; Andrews et al., 1990; Cullen and Gendreau, 2000; Gendreau et al., 2006).

This is not an occasion for heady optimism. The challenge still exists to transfer the "technology" of effective offender change to correctional agencies and to sustain such programs in organizational contexts that may lack human and economic capital (Cullen and Gendreau, 2000; Petrosino and Soydan, 2005; Latessa et al., 2002; Lin, 2000). Even so, there is increasing knowledge about how to change offenders and numerous demonstrations in real-world settings that treatment programs can be effective (Lipsey, 1999b; Lowenkamp et al., 2006). Although mentioned only in passing here, there is also increasing evidence of the effectiveness of early intervention programs (Farrington and Welsh, 2007; Greenwood, 2006; Howell, 2003). This finding suggests the possibility of building a coherent system of intervention that offers a continuum of care that extends from the prenatal period into adulthood.

In short, it simply is not accurate criminologically that "nothing works" to change offenders. Life-course research reveals that offenders have the potential to redirect their behavior along a prosocial pathway (Giordano et al., 2002; Laub and Sampson, 2003; Maruna, 2001). The extant rehabilitation scholarship shows that such change not only occurs fortuitously in natural settings but also can be achieved through carefully planned, criminologically informed interventions. We know as well that in bringing about offender reformation, rehabilitation is our "best bet"; indeed, the alternatives—doing nothing or punishing offenders—are certain failures.

REASON #4: THE PUBLIC LIKES REHABILITATION . . . EVEN IF IT IS A LIBERAL IDEA

Despite the attack on the treatment ideal and the near-hegemony of the punishment paradigm in shaping correctional policy, research over the past three decades has shown consistently that the public supports rehabilitation (Cullen and Moon, 2002; Cullen et al., 2000). More recent polls confirm that this support remains firm (Cullen et al., 2007; Cullen, Pealer, et al., 2002; Nagin et al., 2006). In effect, Americans favor a balanced approach, one that exacts a measure of justice, protects the public against serious offenders, and makes every effort to change offenders while they are within the grasp of the state. Rehabilitation often is characterized as a "liberal idea" because it endorses "going easy" on offenders. But the public recognizes a canard when it sees one. Here is one liberal idea that citizens embrace because it is eminently rational: Why would we return any offender to the community without making a good faith effort to "save" the person and, in so doing, reduce the collateral threat to public safety? The failure to do so, Americans recognize, makes little sense and, in fact, borders on outright irresponsibility.

REASON #5: REHABILITATION IS THE MORAL THING TO DO

As part of a broader challenge to therapeutic thinking in modern society, rehabilitation is criticized for sending a corrosive message that offenders are not responsible for their actions. Punishment, it is claimed, reinforces moral boundaries and communicates that offenders are moral agents who deserve to be held accountable for their bad choices. This reasoning has surface appeal, but it also borders on the ridiculous—for three reasons.

First, it conveniently ignores the criminological fact that the choice of crime is not "free" but bounded—often quite tightly—by the circumstances into which offenders are born. Advocates of the punishment model feel free to acquit society—us—of any complicity in the conditions that breed crime. They feel free to ignore the disquieting reality that the correctional system disproportionately supervises minorities and the poor—groups socially neglected in our society. This blindness might prove comforting, but it hardly comprises the moral high ground.

Second, rehabilitation does not excuse victimization but rather demands that offenders work to change those parts of themselves that lead them into crime—whether that is how they think or how they design their lives. However, in embarking on this reformation, offenders are not simply placed in a cell and told to make better decisions in the future—"or else." Rather, a recognition exists that change is challenging and that corrections should be a partner in enabling offenders to lead lives that do less harm and contribute more to the commonweal. Supporting others to live a better life hardly is morally bankrupt; indeed, it seems more akin to the Golden Rule.

Third, rehabilitation does not demean human dignity but emphasizes its value. It is the punishment crowd that depicts offenders as predators (if not "scum"), embraces chain gangs and oppressive prison conditions, and wishes to turn prisons into warehouses. By contrast, advocates of treatment do not reduce offenders to a philosophical myth (rational actors fully free to make choices) or to the nature of the crime they committed (which might be minor or might be heinous). Rather, they confront offenders in the fullness of their humanity, not afraid to assess their level of pathology but also not afraid to recognize offenders' humanity and to inspire their personal growth.

In the end, the punishment and treatment paradigms offer different visions of offenders, intervention strategies of different scientific merit, and distinctly different moral choices. No correctional approach is a panacea, but neither are all approaches equal. And when we compare, as we must, these two correctional visions, their relative merits seem clear. What the punishment paradigm has wrought "in the real world" over the past decades is disquieting; doing more of the same would be an unpardonable mistake. It is time to take a new pathway—one that draws on Americans' long-standing cultural belief in offender reformation and on the emergent "what works" scientific literature. We should reaffirm rehabilitation as corrections' guiding paradigm.

References

Andrews, D. A. and James Bonta
  2006   The Psychology of Criminal Conduct, 4th ed. Cincinnati, Ohio: Anderson/ LexisNexis.
Andrews, D. A., Ivan Zinger, Robert D. Hoge, James Bonta, Paul Gendreau, and Francis T. Cullen
  1990   Does correctional treatment work? A clinically relevant and psychologically informed meta-analysis. Criminology 28:369–404.
Beckett, Katherine
  1997   Making Crime Pay: Law and Order in Contemporary American Politics. New York: Oxford University Press.
Chen, M. Keith and Jesse M. Shapiro
  2007   Do harsher prison conditions reduce recidivism: Does prison harden inmates? A discontinuity-based approach. American Law and Economic Review [9:1–29.]
Cullen, Francis T.
  2005   The twelve people who saved rehabilitation: How the science of criminology made a difference—The American Society of Criminology, 2004 Presidential Address. Criminology 43:1–42.
Cullen, Francis T. and Paul Gendreau
  2000   Assessing correctional rehabilitation: Policy, practice, and prospects. In Julie Horney (ed.), Criminal Justice 2000: Volume 3—Policies, Processes, and Decisions of the Criminal Justice System. Washington, D.C.: U.S. Department of Justice, National Institute of Justice.
  2001   From nothing works to what works: Changing professional ideology in the 21st century. Prison Journal 81:313–338.
Cullen, Francis T. and Karen E. Gilbert
  1982   Reaffirming Rehabilitation. Cincinnati, Ohio: Anderson.
Cullen, Francis T. and Melissa M. Moon
  2002   Reaffirming rehabilitation: Public support for correctional treatment. In Harry E. Allen (ed.), What Works—Risk Reduction: Interventions for Special Needs Offenders. Lanham, Md.: American Correctional Association.

Cullen, Francis T., Kristie R. Blevins, and Paul Gendreau
  2005   The rise and fall of boot camps: A case study in common-sense corrections. Journal of Offender Rehabilitation 40:53–70.

Cullen, Francis T., Bonnie S. Fisher, and Brandon K. Applegate
  2000   Public opinion about punishment and corrections. In Michael Tonry (ed.), Crime and Justice: A Review of Research, vol 27. Chicago, Ill.: University of Chicago Press.

Cullen, Francis T., John Paul Wright, and Brandon K. Applegate
  1996   Control in the community: The limits of reform? In Alan T. Harland (ed.), Choosing Correctional Interventions That Work: Defining the Demand and Evaluating the Supply. Newbury Park, Calif.: Sage.

Cullen, Francis T., Travis C. Pratt, Sharon Levrant Miceli, and Melissa M. Moon
  2002   Dangerous liaison? Rational choice theory as the basis for correctional intervention. In Alex R. Piquero and Stephen G. Tibbetts (eds.), Rational Choice and Criminal Behavior: Recent Research and Future Challenges. New York: Taylor and Francis.

Cullen, Francis T., Brenda A. Vose, Cheryl Lero Jonson, and James D. Unnever
  2007   Public support for early intervention: Is child saving a "habit of the heart"? Victims and Offenders 2:109–124.

Cullen, Francis T., Jennifer A. Pealer, Bonnie S. Fisher, Brandon K. Applegate, and Shannon A. Santana
  2002   Public support for correctional rehabilitation in America: Change or consistency? In Julian V. Roberts and Mike Hough (eds.), Changing Attitudes to Punishment: Public Opinion, Crime and Justice. Cullompton, U.K.: Willan.

Currie, Elliott
  1998   Crime and Punishment in America. New York: Metropolitan Books.

De Parle, James
  2007   The American prison nightmare. The New York Review of Books (April 12):33–36.

Doob, Anthony N. and Cheryl M. Webster
  2003   Sentence severity and crime: Accepting the null hypothesis. In Michael Tonry (ed.), Crime and Justice: A Review of Research, vol 30. Chicago, Ill.: University of Chicago Press.

Farrington, David P. and Brandon C. Welsh
  2007   Saving Children from a Life of Crime: Early Risk Factors and Effective Interventions. New York: Oxford University Press.

Garland, David
  2001   The Culture of Control: Crime and Social Order in Contemporary Society. Chicago, Ill.: University of Chicago Press.

Gendreau, Paul
  1996   The principles of effective correctional intervention with offenders. In Alan T. Harland (ed.), Choosing Correctional Interventions That Work: Defining the Demand and Evaluating the Supply. Newbury Park, Calif.: Sage.

Gendreau, Paul, Paula Smith, and Susan A. French
  2006   The theory of effective correctional intervention: Empirical status and future directions. In Francis T. Cullen, John Paul Wright, and Kristie R. Blevins (eds.), Taking Stock: The Status of Criminological Theory, Vol 15 of Advances in Criminological Theory. New Brunswick, N.J.: Transaction Press.

Gendreau, Paul, Claire Goggin, Francis T. Cullen, and Donald A. Andrews
  2000   The effects of community sanctions and incarceration on recidivism. Forum on Corrections Research 12 (May):10–13.

Giordano, Peggy C., Stephen A. Cernkovich, and Jennifer L. Rudolph
  2002   Gender, crime, and desistance: Toward a theory of cognitive transformation. American Journal of Sociology 107:990–1064.
Gottschalk, Marie
  2006   The Prison and the Gallows: The Politics of Mass Incarceration in America. New York: Cambridge University Press.
Greenwood, Peter W.
  2006   Changing Lives: Delinquency Prevention as Crime-Control Policy. Chicago, Ill.: University of Chicago Press.
Howell, James C.
  2003   Preventing and Reducing Delinquency: A Comprehensive Framework. Thousand Oaks, Calif.: Sage.
Latessa, Edward J., Francis T. Cullen, and Paul Gendreau
  2002   Beyond correctional quackery: Professionalism and the possibility of effective treatment. Federal Probation 66 (September):43–49.
Laub, John H. and Robert J. Sampson
  2003   Shared Beginnings, Divergent Lives: Delinquent Boys to Age 70. Cambridge, Mass.: Harvard University Press.
Lin, Ann Chih
  2000   Reform in the Making: The Implementation of Social Policy in Prison. Princeton, N.J.: Princeton University Press.
Lipsey, Mark W.
  1999a   Can intervention rehabilitate serious delinquents? Annals of the American Association of Political and Social Science 564:142–166.
  1999b   Can rehabilitation programs reduce the recidivism of juvenile offenders? An inquiry into the effectiveness of practical programs. Virginia Journal of Social Policy and Law 6:611–641.
Lipsey, Mark W. and Francis T. Cullen
  2007   The effectiveness of correctional rehabilitation: A review of systematic reviews. Annual Review of Law and Social Science [3:161–187.]
Lowenkamp, Christopher T., Edward J. Latessa, and Paula Smith
  2006   Does correctional program quality really matter? The impact of adhering to the principles of effective intervention 2006. Criminology & Public Policy 5:201–220.
Lynch, Michael J.
  2007   Big Prisons, Big Dreams: Crime and the Failure of America's Penal System. New Brunswick, N.J.: Rutgers University Press.
MacKenzie, Doris Layton
  2006   What Works in Corrections: Reducing the Criminal Activities of Offenders and Delinquents. New York: Cambridge University Press.
MacKenzie, Doris Layton, David B. Wilson, and Suzanne B. Kider
  2001   Effects of correctional boot camps on offending. Annals of the American Academy of Political and Social Science 578:126–143.
McGuire, James
  2002   Integrating findings from research reviews. In James Maguire (ed.), Offender Rehabilitation and Treatment: Effective Programmes and Policies to Reduce Re-Offending. West Sussex, U.K.: John Wiley and Sons.
Martinson, Robert
  1974   What works? Questions and answers about prison reform. The Public Interest 35 (Spring):22–54.

Maruna, Shadd
  2001   Making Good: How Ex-Convicts Reform and Rebuild Their Lives. Washington,
          D.C.: American Psychological Association.
Nagin, Daniel S., Alex R. Piquero, Elizabeth S. Scott, and Laurence Steinberg
  2006   Public preferences for rehabilitation versus incarceration in juvenile offenders:
          Evidence from a contingent valuation survey. Criminology & Public Policy
          5:627–652.
Nieuwbeerta, Paul, Daniel S. Nagin, and Arjan A. Blokland
  2006   The relationship between first imprisonment and criminal career development:
          A matched samples comparison. Paper presented at the 2nd Annual Workshop on
          Criminology and Economics, Queenstown, Md, June 6.
Palmer, Ted
  1992   The Re-Emergence of Correctional Intervention. Newbury Park, Calif.: Sage.
Petersilia, Joan and Susan Turner
  1993   Intensive probation and parole. In Michael Tonry (ed.), Crime and Justice: A Review
          of Research, vol 17. Chicago, Ill.: University of Chicago Press.
Petersilia, Joan and Susan Turner, with the assistance of Joyce Peterson
  1986   Prison Versus Probation in California: Implications for Crime and Offender
          Recidivism. Santa Monica, Calif.: RAND.
Petrosino, Anthony
  2005   From Martinson to meta-analysis: Research reviews and the U.S. offender treatment
          debate. Evaluation and Policy 1:149–171.
Petrosino, Anthony and Haluk Soydan
  2005   The impact of program developers as evaluators on criminal recidivism: Results from
          meta-analyses of experimental and quasi-experimental research. Journal of
          Experimental Criminology 1:435–450.
Petrosino, Anthony, Carolyn Turpin-Petrosino, and John Buehler
  2003   Scared straight and other juvenile awareness programs for preventing juvenile delin-
          quency: A systematic review of the randomized experimental evidence. Annals of the
          American Academy of Political and Social Science 589:41–62.
Rotman, Edgardo
  1990   Beyond Punishment: A New View on the Rehabilitation of Criminal Offenders. New
          York: Greenwood Press.
Sampson, Robert J. and John H. Laub
  1993   Crime in the Making: Pathways and Turning Points Through Life. Cambridge, Mass.:
          Harvard University Press.
Smith, Paula
  2006   The effects of incarceration on recidivism: A longitudinal examination of program
          participation and institutional adjustment in federally sentenced adult male offenders.
          Unpublished Ph.D. dissertation. University of New Brunswick, Canada.
Spelman, William
  2000   What recent studies do (and don't) tell us about imprisonment and crime. In Michael
          Tonry (ed.), Crime and Justice: A Review of Research, vol 27. Chicago, Ill.: University
          of Chicago Press.
Spohn, Cassie and David Holleran
  2002   The effect of imprisonment on recidivism rates of felony offenders: A focus on drug
          offenders. Criminology 40:329–57.
Tonry, Michael
  2004   Thinking About Crime: Sense and Sensibility in American Penal Culture. New York:
          Oxford University Press.

Whitman, James Q.
  2003   Harsh Justice: Criminal Punishment and the Widening Divide between America and
          Europe. New York: Oxford University Press.
Wilson, James Q.
  1975   Thinking About Crime. New York: Vintage Books.

SAVE CHILDREN FROM A LIFE OF CRIME

Brandon C. Welsh
David P. Farrington

Convincing research evidence exists to support a policy of saving children from a life of crime by intervening early in childhood to tackle key risk factors. Two separate but interrelated research developments are at the heart of this policy position. First, after decades of rigorous research in the United States and across the Western world—using prospective longitudinal studies—a great deal is known about early risk factors for delinquency and later criminal offending. (Disappointingly, less is known about protective factors against offending, but recent empirical research provides some important insights.) Early risk factors that are associated strongly with delinquency and later criminal offending can be found at the individual, family, and environmental levels.

The second development is the growing body of high-quality scientific evidence on the effectiveness of early prevention programs designed to tackle these risk factors from which evidence-based conclusions can be drawn. Many early prevention trials have followed up with children long enough to measure delinquency. Systematic literature reviews and meta-analyses of early prevention programs provide scientific evidence that a wide range of programs in different domains (individual, family, school, and community) can be effective and others are promising in preventing delinquency and later offending.

Support for a policy of saving children from a life of crime can also be found on other research fronts. Recent U.S. national scientific commissions on early childhood development and juvenile offending that have examined some of this evidence also have identified the many benefits of early prevention programs and have called for concrete action to make early prevention a top government priority (McCord et al., 2001; Shonkoff and Phillips, 2000; U.S. Department of Health and Human Services, 2001). Widespread public support exists in this country for early prevention programs compared with more punitive measures (Cullen et al., 2007; Nagin et al., 2006). A growing number of cost–benefit and cost-effectiveness analyses show that early prevention programs provide value for money and can be a worthwhile investment of government resources compared with prison and other criminal justice responses (Aos et al., 2004; Greenwood, 2006; Welsh, 2001, 2003).

Source: Criminology and Public Policy, vol. 6, no. 4 (2007). © 2007 American Society of Criminology. Reprinted by permission.

In our book *Saving Children from a Life of Crime: Early Risk Factors and Effective Interventions* (Farrington and Welsh, 2007), we assess the highest quality scientific evidence on early risk factors for offending and effective interventions targeting these risk factors and outline a policy strategy—early prevention—that uses this current research knowledge to bring into sharper focus what should be the national crime-fighting priorities in America. This essay draws on our book. It summarizes findings on the effectiveness of early prevention programs and ends with policy recommendations.

EARLY PREVENTION

The field of early prevention centers on measures implemented in the early years of the life course, from (or sometimes before) birth to early adolescence. It focuses on intervening in the lives of children and youths before they engage in delinquency in the first place. In this respect, early prevention includes interventions applied to the whole community to prevent the onset of delinquency and interventions targeted toward children and youths who are at risk for becoming offenders because of the presence of one or more risk factors. Early prevention measures are largely developmental or social and aim to prevent the development of criminal potential in individuals or to improve the social conditions and institutions (e.g., families, peers, or social norms) that influence offending.

Developmental theory postulates that the early years of life are most influential in shaping later experiences. As Duncan and Magnuson (2004:101) note: "Principles of developmental science suggest that although beneficial changes are possible at any point in life, interventions early on may be more effective at promoting well being and competencies compared with interventions undertaken later in life." They also state that (2004:102–103):

> [E]arly childhood may provide an unusual window of opportunity for interventions because young children are uniquely receptive to enriching and supportive environments. . . . As individuals age, they gain the independence and ability to shape their environments, rendering intervention efforts more complicated and costly.

SCIENTIFIC SUPPORT FOR EARLY PREVENTION

This section summarizes the key conclusions of our reviews of the effectiveness of early prevention programs, as organized around three main categories of risk factors.[1] Our reviews draw on the highest quality research studies (i.e., experiments and quasi-experiments), as well as on the most rigorous literature reviews (i.e., systematic and meta-analytic reviews) that include only high-quality projects. This approach ensures that conclusions are based on the best available evidence.

INDIVIDUAL PREVENTION

At the individual-level, preschool intellectual enrichment and child skills training programs are effective in preventing delinquency and later offending. Results are also highly favorable and robust for impacts on other important life-course outcomes, such as education, government assistance (e.g., welfare), employment, income, substance abuse, and family stability. Some evidence suggests that these programs not only pay back their costs but also produce substantial monetary benefits for the government and taxpayers.

Preschool intellectual enrichment programs are generally targeted at children with the risk factors of low intelligence and attainment. Improved cognitive skills, school readiness, and social and emotional development are the main goals of these programs. We identified four high-quality preschool programs that measured delinquency. Combining the effect sizes[2] of these programs yielded a mean effect size of 0.242, which corresponds to a 12% reduction in offending in the experimental group compared with the control group.

Social skills training or social competence programs for children generally target the risk factors of impulsivity, low empathy, and self-centeredness. As noted by Webster-Stratton and Taylor (2001:178), this type of individual-based program is designed to "directly teach children social, emotional, and cognitive competence by addressing appropriate social skills, effective problem-solving, anger management, and emotion language."

Lösel and Beelmann (2006) carried out a systematic review of the effects of child social skills training on antisocial behavior (including delinquency). The review included 55 randomized experiments with 89 separate experimental–control group comparisons. A meta-analysis found that at immediate outcome or postintervention (defined as within 2 months after treatment), the mean effect sizes for all outcomes favored the treatment condition, although the smallest effect size was for delinquency. At later follow-up (defined as 3 months or more after treatment), delinquency was the only outcome that was significantly improved by skills training.

FAMILY PREVENTION

At the family level, general parent education in the context of home visiting and day care, as well as parent management training programs, are effective in preventing delinquency and later offending. Both types of programs also produce a wide range of other important benefits for families: improved school readiness and school performance on the part of children, greater employment and educational opportunities for parents, and greater family stability in general. Some evidence suggests that home visiting programs can pay back program costs and produce substantial monetary benefits for the government and taxpayers. Little is known about the economic efficiency of day care and parent management training programs.

Home visiting with new parents, especially mothers, is a popular method of delivering the family-based intervention known as general parent education. The main goals of home visiting programs center around educating parents to improve the life chances of children from a very young age, often beginning at birth and sometimes in the final trimester of pregnancy. In our meta-analysis that included four home visitation programs, the mean effect size was 0.235, which corresponds to a significant 12% reduction in antisocial behavior/delinquency in the experimental group compared with the control group.

Parent management training refers to "treatment procedures in which parents are trained to alter their child's behavior at home" (Kazdin, 1997:1349). Patterson (1982) developed behavioral parent management training. He attempted to train parents in effective child-rearing methods, namely noticing what a child is doing, monitoring behavior over long periods, clearly stating house rules, making rewards and punishments contingent on behavior, and negotiating disagreements so that conflicts and crises do not escalate.

In our meta-analysis that included ten parent management training programs, the mean effect size was 0.395, which corresponds to a significant 20% reduction in antisocial behavior/delinquency in the experimental group compared with the control group. Each of the ten parent management training programs included in the meta-analysis aimed to teach parents to use rewards and punishments consistently and contingently in child rearing.

SCHOOL AND COMMUNITY PREVENTION

At the environmental-level, several school-based programs are effective in preventing delinquency and later offending, and two community-based programs (after-school and mentoring) hold promise as efficacious approaches, but more evaluation research is needed on them.[3]

Schools are a critical social context for crime-prevention efforts, from the early to later grades. Wilson et al. (2001) conducted a meta-analysis that included 165 randomized and quasi-experimental studies with 216 experimental–control group comparisons. They found that four types of school-based programs are effective in preventing delinquency: school and discipline management, classroom or instructional management, reorganization of grades or classes, and increasing self-control or social competency using cognitive behavioral or behavioral instructional methods. Three of these four effective types of school-based programs (other than school and discipline management) also produced benefits in other areas, such as alcohol and drug use and other problem behavior in general. Two other meta-analyses (Mytton et al., 2002; Wilson and Lipsey, 2007) provide additional support for the effectiveness of school-based prevention programs in general, especially those that target the children at highest risk.

After-school programs are premised on the belief that providing prosocial opportunities for young people in the after-school hours can reduce their involvement in delinquent behavior in the community. After-school programs target a range of risk factors for delinquency, including alienation and association with delinquent peers. As part of an effort to update Sherman's review (1997), Welsh and Hoshi (2002) identified three high-quality after-school programs with an evaluated impact on delinquency. Each program produced desirable effects on delinquency, and one program also reported lower rates of drug activity for program participants compared with controls. The authors concurred with Sherman's assessment that community-based after-school programs represent a promising approach to preventing juvenile offending.

Community-based mentoring programs usually involve nonprofessional adult volunteers spending time with young people at risk for delinquency, dropping out of school, school failure, and other social problems. Mentors behave in a "supportive, nonjudgmental manner while acting as role models" (Howell, 1995:90). In many cases, mentors work one-on-one with young people, often forming strong bonds. Care is taken in matching the mentor with the young person.

Welsh and Hoshi (2002) identified seven community-based mentoring programs (of which six were high quality) that evaluated their impact on delinquency and other problem behaviors. Two programs had a direct measure of delinquency and showed mixed results: One found desirable effects on delinquency for youths with prior offenses but undesirable effects on delinquency for youths with no prior offenses, and the other found desirable effects on delinquency. On the basis of these two programs and the evidence provided by the four programs that measured outcomes related to offending (e.g., disruptive and aggressive behavior), which mostly found favorable results, the authors concluded that community-based mentoring represents a promising approach to preventing delinquency.

FUTURE DIRECTIONS

The stakes are high. In the United States, crime rates are lower than they have been in more than a generation. An opportunity exists to keep crime rates in check or perhaps to lower them even more. Early prevention is by no means a panacea. But it does represent an integral part of any plan to reduce the nation's crime rate. We believe that the time is right to move beyond rhetoric and to implement a risk-focused, evidence-based national strategy for early prevention.

The federal government should establish a council to support a national early crime-prevention strategy in the United States. This council should be permanent and have similar characteristics to its counterparts in other Western industrialized countries. It should provide technical assistance, skills, and knowledge to state and local agencies in implementing prevention programs, should provide funding for such programs, and should ensure continuity, coordination, and monitoring of local programs. It also should provide training in prevention science for people in local agencies and should maintain high standards for evaluation research. Additionally, this council should act as a center for the discussion of how policy initiatives of different government agencies influence crime and associated social problems. It should set a national and local agenda for research and practice in the early prevention of crime, as well as drug and alcohol abuse, mental health problems, and associated social problems. Furthermore, the national council should provide support for systematic reviews of the evaluation literature on the effectiveness of early interventions that may impact delinquency and later offending. Following Greenwood (2006), we suggest that this national council should be located in the Department of Health and Human Services, which should be the lead department for early prevention.

These proposals are just some of the key proposals (see Farrington and Welsh, 2007) that would help to translate the convincing research evidence on early prevention into effective action at the local level, which would lead to enormous benefits in saving children from a life of crime and in contributing to a safer, more sustainable society for all.

References

Aos, Steve, Roxanne Lieb, Jim Mayfield, Marna Miller, and Annie Pennucci
  2004   Benefits and Costs of Prevention and Early Intervention Programs for Youth. Olympia, Wash.: Washington State Institute for Public Policy.

Cullen, Francis T., Brenda A. Vose, Cheryl N. Lero, and James D. Unnever
  2007   Public support for early intervention: Is child saving a 'habit of the heart'? Victims and Offenders 2:108–124.

Duncan, Greg J. and Katherine Magnuson
  2004   Individual and parent-based intervention strategies for promoting human capital and positive behavior. In P. Lindsay Chase-Lansdale, Kathleen Kiernan, and Ruth J. Friedman (eds.), Human Development Across Lives and Generations: The Potential for Change. New York: Cambridge University Press.

Farrington, David P. and Brandon C. Welsh
  2007   Saving Children from a Life of Crime: Early Risk Factors and Effective Interventions. New York: Oxford University Press.

Greenwood, Peter W.
  2006   Changing Lives: Delinquency Prevention as Crime-Control Policy. Chicago, Ill.: University of Chicago Press.

Howell, James C. (ed.)
  1995   Guide for Implementing the Comprehensive Strategy for Serious, Violent, and Chronic Juvenile Offenders. Washington, D.C.: Office of Juvenile Justice and Delinquency Prevention, U.S. Department of Justice.

Kazdin, Alan E.
  1997   Parent management training: Evidence, outcomes, and issues. Journal of the American Academy of Child and Adolescent Psychiatry 36:1349–1356.

Lipsey, Mark W. and David B. Wilson
  2001   Practical Meta-Analysis. Thousand Oaks, Calif.: Sage.

Lösel, Friedrich and Andreas Beelmann
  2006   Child social skills training. In Brandon C. Welsh and David P. Farrington (eds.), Preventing Crime: What Works for Children, Offenders, Victims, and Places. New York: Springer.

McCord, Joan, Cathy Spatz Widom, and Nancy A. Crowell (eds.)
  2001   Juvenile Crime, Juvenile Justice. Panel on Juvenile Crime: Prevention, Treatment, and Control. Committee on Law and Justice and Board on Children, Youth, and Families, National Research Council and Institute of Medicine. Washington, D.C.: National Academy Press.

Mytton, Julie A., Carolyn DiGuiseppi, David A. Gough, Rod S. Taylor, and Stuart Logan
  2002   School-based violence prevention programs: Systematic review of secondary prevention trials. Archives of Pediatric and Adolescent Medicine 156:752–762.

Nagin, Daniel S., Alex R. Piquero, Elizabeth S. Scott, and Laurence Steinberg
  2006   Public preferences for rehabilitation versus incarceration of juvenile offenders: Evidence from a contingent valuation survey. Criminology & Public Policy 5:627–652.

Patterson, Gerald
  1982   Coercive Family Process. Eugene, Ore.: Castalia.

Sherman, Lawrence W.
  1997   Communities and crime prevention. In Lawrence W. Sherman, Denise C. Gottfredson, Doris L. MacKenzie, John E. Eck, Peter Reuter, and Shawn D. Bushway (eds.), Preventing Crime: What Works, What Doesn't, What's Promising. Washington, D.C.: National Institute of Justice, U.S. Department of Justice.

Shonkoff, Jack P. and Deborah A. Phillips (eds.)
2000   From Neurons to Neighborhoods: The Science of Early Childhood Development. Committee on Integrating the Science of Early Childhood Development, National Research Council and Institute of Medicine. Washington, D.C.: National Academy Press.

U.S. Department of Health and Human Services
2001   Youth Violence: A Report of the Surgeon General. Rockville, Md.: U.S. Department of Health and Human Services.

Webster-Stratton, Carolyn and Ted Taylor
2001   Nipping early risk factors in the bud: Preventing substance abuse, delinquency, and violence in adolescence through interventions targeted at young children (0–8 years). Prevention Science 2:165–192.

Welsh, Brandon C.
2001   Economic costs and benefits of early developmental prevention. In Rolf Loeber and David P. Farrington (eds.), Child Delinquents: Development, Intervention, and Service Needs. Thousand Oaks, Calif.: Sage.

2003   Economic costs and benefits of primary prevention of delinquency and later offending: A review of the research. In David P. Farrington and Jeremy W. Coid (eds.), Early Prevention of Adult Antisocial Behaviour. Cambridge, U.K.: Cambridge University Press.

Welsh, Brandon C. and Akemi Hoshi
2002   Communities and crime prevention. In Lawrence W. Sherman, David P. Farrington, Brandon C. Welsh, and Doris L. MacKenzie (eds.), Evidence-Based Crime Prevention. New York: Routledge.

Wilson, David B., Denise C. Gottfredson, and Stacy S. Najaka
2001   School-based prevention of problem behaviors: A meta-analysis. Journal of Quantitative Criminology 17:247–272.

Wilson, Sandra Jo and Mark W. Lipsey
2007   School-based interventions for aggressive and disruptive behavior: Update of a meta-analysis. American Journal of Preventive Medicine 33(2S):130–143.

Notes

1. For more details and full references, see Farrington and Welsh (2007).
2. The main measure of effect size was the standardized mean difference d, which summarizes the difference between the control and the experimental groups in standard deviation units. Because these are mean offending scores, a positive value of d (control greater than experimental) indicates a desirable effect of the intervention. Confidence intervals indicate the range within which the population mean (the mean of the included studies) is likely to fall, based on the observed data (Lipsey and Wilson, 2001:114). As is standard practice in meta-analysis, we used a 95% confidence interval.
3. In our book we also reviewed peer risk factors and peer-based prevention programs. We found that a peer-based approach is currently of unknown effectiveness in preventing delinquency or later offending because few evaluations of peer-based programs and few evidence-based reviews exist on this topic (see Farrington and Welsh, 2007:138–139).